Prima's Official Guide to

Compilation

David Ladyman
Beth Loubet
Melissa Tyler

Design

Jennifer Spohrer

Art

Guy Baruch, Idan Nizan, Yaniv Goldmark, Sharon Amit Rosental, Oren Nahum, Michael Grosberg, Danny Hecht, Hili Mohr, Gilat Lerer, Michael Applebaum, Keren Gilboa, Elada Menasherov, Yarden Tadmor, Shira Derman, Gonen Lifshitz, and Bozell Worldwide, Inc.

Special Thanks to

Ilia Brouk, Bryan Brown, Roy Gatchalian and Robert Walker for even more tips

The United States Air Force *www.af.mil & www.usaf.com*
Jane's World Air Forces ©1999, 1997
Note: The Air Force is constantly changing its allocation of assets, and no list of those assets can hope to stay current. All information here reflects the most recently available published material.

TABLE OF CONTENTS

Air Force Commendation

(VN) The DMZ Deception
[2500 BP]

Air Force Cross

(VN) The Khe Sahn Siege
[3000 BP]

(DS) Warthog to the Rescue
[2500 BP]

(SG) Finders Keepers
[400 BP]

Air Medal

(VN) First Airfield Attack
[2500 BP]

(VN) Operation Bolo
[2500 BP]

(VN) You're Never Alone
[2500 BP]

(VN) Linebacker At Sea
[2500 BP]

(VN) Busting the Bridge
[3000 BP]

(DS) Showdown
[2500 BP])

(DS) Where It Hurts Most
[2500 BP]

(DS) Heavy Metal
[2500 BP]

(RA) Umbilical Cord
[2500 BP]

(SG) The Battle of Salzburg
[2500 BP]

(SM) Osiraq Take 2
[2500 BP]

Distinguished Flying Cross

(VN) You're Never Alone
[2500 BP]

(DS) Putting Out Fire
[3000 BP]

(RA) Scramble
[2000 BP]

(RA) The Leading Force
[2000 BP]

(RA) Eagle Eyes
[3000 BP]

(SG) Red Alert
[2000 BP]

(SG) Special Delivery
[2000 BP]

(SM) Fasten Seat Belts
[2500 BP]

US Vietnam Service Medal

Win all Vietnam Service Missions

Red Arrow Medal

Win all Red Arrow Missions

Sleeping Giant Medal

Win all Sleeping Giant Missions

US Emirate of Kuwait Liberation

Win all Desert Storm Missions

Silver Star

(DS) First Kill
[2500 BP]

(DS) Runaways
[2500 BP}

(RA) Blue Block
[2000 BP]

(RA) Take Aim
[4000 BP]

(SG) Open a Corridor
[2000 BP]

(SG) Lock and Load
[2500 BP]

(SG) Watership Down
[3000 BP]

(SG) Watch Your Assets
[3000 BP]

(SM) A Day at the Beach
[2500 BP]

(SM) Bring the Boys Home
[2500 BP]

(SM) Barrier
[2500 BP]

Medal of Honor

(SM) Air Force One
[2500 BP]

BASIC TRAINING

TAKEOFF

In this introductory mission you will meet your instructor, and learn how to taxi and takeoff.

Date 15 MAY 2002

Time 1200 HRS

Training Stage

Basic

Instructor

Lt. Col. Pat 'Scooter' Davis

Subject

Takeoff and basic aircraft operation

Weather

10000' scattered, visibility 20 miles

Mission Description

This is your first flight lesson. My name is Pat 'Scooter' Davis and I'm going to be your IP (Instructor Pilot) for the rest of this course. We're going to start in the hangar. I will be in the back seat and explain the basic avionics and operations necessary to start your engines and take off. You will then taxi to the active runway and perform the takeoff.

Typical Errors

1. Forgetting to retract the landing gear.

2. Taxiing too fast, which could result in aircraft damage.

Mission Objectives

1. Take off safely and retract the landing gear.

Safety

1. Failing to retract the landing gear before accelerating to 300 knots will result in aircraft damage.

Commander's Summary

Every path, even the longest one, begins with a first step. Listen to your IPs (Instructor Pilots). They are the best.

Flyable Aircraft

A-10, F-4E, F-15C, F-15E, F-16C, F-22, F-105, F-117

LANDING

In this mission you will learn how to safely land your aircraft on the ground.

Date   16 MAY 2002

Time   1200 HRS

Training Stage

Basic

Instructor

Lt. Col. Pat 'Scooter' Davis

Subject

Landing practice

Weather

10000' scattered, visibility 20 miles

Mission Description

In your second flight lesson, you will learn the all-important skill of landing your jet. We will begin in a long final leg approach. I will be in the back seat and explain the procedures for safe landing. You will control the plane throughout the mission.

For a successful long final approach, the first thing you should do is slow down to about 250 knots. Close your throttle to 70% power, and extend the Speed Brakes by pressing ⓢ. Next, lower your landing gear by pressing ⓖ, and extend flaps by pressing ⒡.

After your gear is down, the HUD ILS indicators will be displayed. Point the velocity vector at the intersection of the vertical line (Localizer) and the horizontal line (Glide Slope).

The correct approach is achieved when the ILS localizer is lined up with the center of the runway and the glide slope is 4° below the horizon. Keep the ILS indicators centered like a cross.

When crossing the runway threshold, set the throttle to idle and bring the velocity vector slowly to the horizon.

After touching down on the runway, don't forget to apply brakes (by pressing ⒝) until the plane comes to a stop.

Typical Errors

1. Inaccurate flight performance (airspeed and altitude).
2. Forgetting to extend the flaps. The flaps reduce the chance of stalling and allow you to make a safe and slow approach.

Mission Objectives

1. Land safely on your own.

Safety

1. Limit your airspeed to a maximum 300 knots while the gear is down, to avoid damage.
2. Minimum airspeed should be around 130 knots to avoid stalling the plane.
3. Make sure your gear is down and locked before landing (3 green lights).

Commander's Summary

The key to a successful landing is executing all the procedures in the correct order and as accurately as possible.

Flyable Aircraft

A-10, F-4E, F15C, F-15E, F-16C, F-22, F-105, F-117

STEP DOWN TRAINING

This mission will teach you the basics of low-level flight and navigation.

Date   17 MAY 2002

Time   1200 HRS

Training Stage

Basic

Instructor

Lt. Col. Pat 'Scooter' Davis

Subject

Low level flight & navigation practice

Weather

Clear, with unlimited visibility

Mission Description

In this mission you will learn the basics of low-level flight, navigation, and how to use the INS (Inertial Navigation System). These skills will allow you to avoid enemy radar and reach your target accurately.

Take a look at the Tactical Display and study your flight plan. Your flight plan consists of waypoints. Waypoints are landmarks that you should pass, in order to reach your destination safely. Waypoints are displayed as circles on the map, and are connected by lines to show your route. The waypoints are fed to your navigation computer before the flight.

Begin your flight by checking that you're in NAV mode. In this mode, the altitude displayed on your

Colorado River

HUD is AGL (Above Ground Level). This means you will see the exact altitude above the ground surface. You can press [N] to enter NAV Mode.

The inverted 'V' on the top of the HUD is called the waypoint caret. It shows the direction to the next waypoint. The caret on the speed scale shows the correct speed you should maintain to get to the next waypoint on time.

As you get closer to a waypoint, you will see the range to waypoint decreasing. As soon as you pass a waypoint, the waypoint caret will automatically change to the next waypoint.

At first you will be allowed to activate the Autopilot which will fly the aircraft for you. (Press [A] twice to activate Autopilot NAV).

Then, when the instructor asks you to fly 300 feet AGL, take control of the aircraft (just start using the joystick) and dive gently towards the terrain. Lower your aircraft gently to 300 feet AGL. After that he will instruct you through the entire flight.

When you reach the hilly area, don't forget to aim the velocity vector above the highest point of terrain. This will assure you won't run into the ground.

There are SAMs scattered around the training area, and they will locate and fire on you if you don't fly low.

Keep your velocity around 450 knots. This is a convenient velocity for low-level flight. Use the full-screen HUD view (F1) for a better view from your cockpit.

Typical Errors

1. Not looking far enough ahead and crashing into the terrain.

2. Ignoring the automatic change of the waypoints, and continuing to fly in the same direction (Keep your eyes on the waypoint range in your HUD).

3. Chasing the heading caret at close range to the waypoint, resulting in missing the flight path.

4. Not paying attention to velocity.

Mission Objectives

1. Pass over all waypoints within 300 feet of each.

2. Survive the mission.

Safety

1. Always be on the lookout for unexpected obstacles.

2. Beware of CFIT (Controlled Flight Into Terrain).

Commander's Summary

This mission will take you into enemy territory. Be alert at all times. Use the terrain to avoid detection. Fly between the hills and gorges whenever possible.

Flyable Aircraft

A-10, F-4E, F-15C, F-15E, F-16C, F-22, F-105, F-117

IN-FLIGHT REFUELING

In this mission you will learn how to connect to a KC-135 tanker and refuel.

Date 18 MAY 2002

Time 1220 HRS

Training Stage

Basic

Instructor

Lt. Col. Pat 'Scooter' Davis

Subject

Perform mid-air refueling from a KC-135

Weather

10000' scattered, visibility unlimited.

Mission Description

In this mission you will learn all you need to know about mid-air refueling. The necessary skills are locating the tanker, approaching and communicating with the tanker, and performing the refueling. Your instructor will help you through your first attempt, then you will perform a second attempt on your own.

Typical Errors

1. Approaching the tanker too fast.

2. Making course corrections at the tanker area.

3. "Accidental" fire at the tanker.

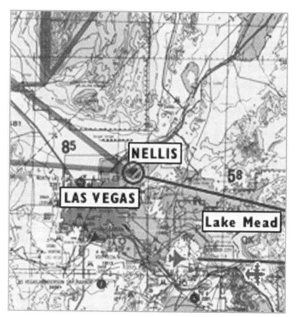

Mission Objectives

1. Perform two successful connections to the tanker. You may try the second attempt in manual mode or use the automatic mode.

2. The tanker and your plane should suffer no damage.

Commander's Summary

Using your air-to-air radar can help you on your approach. Use it to monitor your range and closing velocity.

Many missions are long range flights. Knowing how to refuel is essential to your career.

Flyable Aircraft

A-10, F-4E, F-15C, F-15E, F-16C, F-22, F-105, F-117

All have guns, chaff, flares and AIM-9 missiles (F-117 has no missiles.)

WEAPON SCHOOL TRAINING

BASIC A/A MODES

In this mission you will learn the basics of air-to-air radar and the corresponding HUD modes. You will also be instructed on how to launch various types of air-to-air missiles, and how to use your gun.

Date 19 MAY 2002
Time 1200 HRS

Training Stage

Weapon School

Instructor

Lt. Col. Pat 'Scooter' Davis

Subject

Learn the fundamentals of air-to-air combat: intercepts, radar operation, and weapon handling

Weather

10000' scattered, visibility unlimited

Mission Description

In this mission you will learn how to seek and lock onto targets, use the air-to-air radar modes, and launch air-to-air weapons at these targets. You will also learn about the IFF system and how to use it to avoid firing at friendly planes. We have set several target drones in the firing range for you to practice against. The nice thing about drones is that they do not shoot back. This is a luxury you will not have in actual combat, but for today's goals they will be sufficient. Follow the navigation route and listen to what your instructor says.

Typical Errors

1. Using the wrong radar mode for your situation.
2. Launching a missile beyond weapon envelope.

Mission Objectives

1. Shoot down all the target drones.

2. Do not shoot any friendly aircraft.

Safety

1. There will be several friendly aircraft on your way to the range and back. Do not confuse these planes with the target drones.

Flyable Aircraft

F-15E	PGU-28 (250), Chaff (60), Flare (30), AIM-120 (2), AIM-9M (2)
F-16C	PGU-28 (250), Chaff (60), Flare (30), AIM-120 (2), AIM-9M (2)
F-22	PGU-28 (250), Chaff (60), Flare (30), AIM-120 (2), AIM-9X (2)
F-15C	PGU-28 (250), Chaff (60), Flare (30), AIM-120 (4), AIM-9M (4)

BASIC A/G MODES

In this mission you will learn the basics of air-to-ground radar and the corresponding HUD modes. You will also be instructed on the use of the CCIP bombsight and your A/G guns.

Date   20 MAY 2002

Time   1200 HRS

Training Stage

Weapon School

Instructor

Lt. Col. Pat 'Scooter' Davis

Subject

Learn the basics of air-to-ground attack and radar operation

Weather

10000' scattered, visibility unlimited

Mission Description

In this mission you will learn to identify and destroy ground targets using radar. You will also learn how to deliver GP (general purpose) bombs using CCIP mode, and to use your gun on ground targets using STRF mode. You'll be leading this mission, with me flying next to you.

First, taxi your plane towards Nellis runway 22, and take off with me. Fly to waypoint 1, and then to waypoint 2 at 16,000 feet. Your first target is at waypoint 2, and will be marked on the HUD as 'T.' The target consists of two fuel dumps in a fenced operational area. Lock onto them using the A/G radar in Map mode, and bomb them using the CCIP sight and Mk 82 bombs. You will probably have to make two bombing runs in order to take them both out.

When finished, fly to waypoint 3 at 8,000 feet, where you will find a moving convoy of three tanks. Lock onto them using the A/G radar in GMT mode, and destroy them using your guns in STRF sight.

After destroying the convoy you may head back home.

Fuel Dumps

Tanks

Typical Errors

1. Using the wrong radar mode for your situation.

2. Acquiring targets too late.

3. Using the wrong aiming method.

4. Beginning the maneuver too low, resulting in limited aiming time.

Mission Objectives

1. Destroy the two fuel dumps.

2. Eliminate three convoy tanks.

Safety

1. Do not release GP bombs at less than 2,000 feet AGL (Above Ground Level) or your plane may be damaged from the bombs' explosion.

2. Watch your altitude when using CCIP and STRF. Pilots have been known to crash into the ground while concentrating on aiming at their target.

Commander's Summary

Once you've mastered the techniques of ground assault, you will be able to crush the enemy and help our forces.

Bombs that miss their target are a waste of resources. Accurate aiming is the key to success.

Concentration on the target is a fighter pilot's most powerful weapon. We do not leave until our mission is accomplished.

Flyable Aircraft

A-10	PGU-14B (250), Chaff (60), Flare (30), Mk 82 (4)
F-4E	M61 Vulcan (200), Chaff (60), Flare (30), Mk 82 (6)
F-15E	PGU-28 (250), Chaff (60), Flare (30), Mk 82 (12)
F-16C	PGU-28 (250), Chaff (60), Flare (30), Mk 82 (6)
F-105	M61 Vulcan (250), Chaff (60), Flare (30), Mk 82 (4)
F-117	M61 Vulcan (250), Chaff (60), Flare (30), Mk 82 (2)

SEAD PRACTICE

SEAD (Suppression of Enemy Air Defense) is a major USAF task. In this mission you will practice a SEAD mission and learn how to effectively use your HARM missiles.

Date 21 MAY 2002

Time 1700 HRS

Training Stage

Weapons School.

Instructor

Lt. Col. Pat 'Scooter' Davis

Subject

Learn how to attack SAM sites and effectively avoid incoming missiles.

Weather

Clear, with unlimited visibility

Mission Description

SEAD (Suppression of Enemy Air Defense) missions are carried out when there is a need to destroy hostile SAM units limiting our air operation in target areas. Most SAM sites are mobile and can be difficult to locate.

The most effective weapon against SAM sites is the AGM–88 HARM missile. In this mission you will use this weapon to destroy a dummy SA-3 site near waypoint 2. You will then practice flying within the lethal range of the SAM sites and avoiding incoming missiles. The missiles fired at you are called "Smoky SAMs," used by the Air Force to train airmen against SAM missiles. The "Smoky SAM" will not damage your jet. To succeed in this mission you must pass waypoints 3 and 4.

Typical Errors

1. Getting within range of the SAM without speed and at high altitude.
2. Breaking too early from the missile and losing energy.
3. Not using chaff and flares.

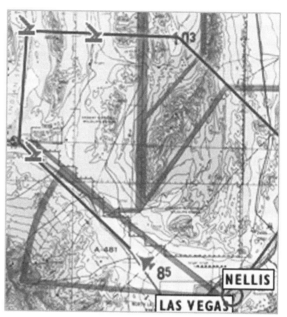

Mission Objectives

1. Destroy the SA-3 at waypoint 2.
2. Pass through waypoints 3 and 4.
3. Avoid incoming missiles. You are allowed to be hit by three missiles in this mission. More than that and you will fail.

Safety

1. One of your worst enemies in this mission is the ground. Do not fly too low. The limit in our training missions is 100 feet.
2. You are not allowed to fire at anything but the SA-3 site at waypoint 2.

Commander's Summary

This is a very tough mission, one that will help you later in actual combat. Good luck.

Flyable Aircraft

F-4E PGU-28 (200), Chaff (60), Flare (30), AGM-45 (2), ALQ-119

F-15E or F-16C PGU-28 (250), Chaff (60), Flare (30), AGM-88 (2)

F-105D PGU-28 (250), Chaff (60), Flare (30), AGM-45 (2)

GUIDED WEAPON DELIVERIES

In today's battlefield you must be skilled in the use of precision-guided weapons. In this mission you will practice the use of guided munitions such as laser-guided bombs (LGBs) and TV-guided missiles.

Date   22 MAY 2002

Time   1200 HRS

Training Stage

Weapons School

Instructor

Lt. Col. Pat 'Scooter' Davis

Subject

Destroy targets using JDAM bombs, Maverick missiles, and TV-guided missiles

Weather

Clear, with unlimited visibility

Mission Description

In this sortie you will use JDAM bombs, Mavericks and TV missiles. You will start the mission in a firing range west of Nellis AFB. Begin the mission by dropping JDAM bombs on a weapon bunker located at waypoint 2. Use your AGM-65 Maverick missiles against some moving vehicles at waypoint 3. Finally, you will take out a Scud missile launcher using the AGM-130 TV missile. More objects are scattered around the firing range area. Make sure you hit the ones assigned to you. Your instructor, Scooter, will be giving you some useful tips along the way, so you better listen up.

Typical Errors

1. Detecting the target too late.

2. Delivering the weapon when too close to the target.

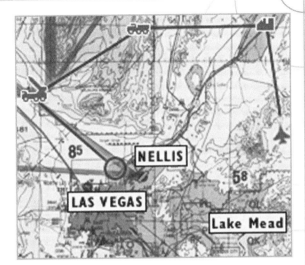

3. Not using autopilot and the full screen MFD ([Z]) when guiding the weapon.

Mission Objectives

1. Destroy weapon bunker.

2. Destroy two out of three vehicles.

3. Destroy Scud launcher.

4. Do not hit the wrong targets (the other buildings must survive).

Safety

1. Do not forget to control the plane while guiding your weapon.

2. Do not fire too close to the targets. Avoid the explosions from your own bombs.

Commander's Summary

Guided weapons are used for accurate, standoff attacks, and can be difficult to operate. Make the most out of this training mission by learning all you can about these weapons before the flight. If you are unfamiliar with guided weapons delivery theory, refer to the flight manual.

Flyable Aircraft

F-15E or F-16C PGU-28 (250), Chaff (60), Flare (30), AGM-130 (1), AGM-65D (3), GBU-30 (2)

NIGHT PRACTICE

In order to become a USAF pilot you must learn how to fly by night. This evening you will perform some basic night maneuvers, such as LANTIRN bomb deliveries and a night landing.

Date   23 MAY 2002

Time   2000 HRS

Training Stage

Weapon School

Instructor

Lt. Col. Pat 'Scooter' Davis

Subject

Learn how to operate your aircraft at night

Weather

Clear night, full moon

Mission Description

In this sortie you will learn how to fly your airplane in night missions. You will use night vision systems to navigate and locate targets, and use the LANTIRN infrared pod to designate and attack targets using laser-guided bombs. You begin the mission at Nellis AFB. After taking off you will practice low-level navigation using the NVG system. A Special Forces unit will laser-designate a T-62 target for you near waypoint 2. Wait for their clearance to fire at the target and make sure you fire only at the designated target. Next you will continue on to waypoint 3, where you will locate and attack an SA-2 radar using laser-guided bombs. This time you will need to designate the target by yourself. After the two targets are destroyed head back and land at Nellis AFB.

Typical Errors

1. Detecting the target too late.

2. Delivering the weapon when too close to the target.

3. Not using autopilot and full screen MFD ($\boxed{Z}$) when guiding the weapon.

Mission Objectives

1. Destroy the target assigned by the ground force.

2. Locate and destroy the SA-2 radar near way-point 3.

3. Land at Nellis AFB.

Safety

1. It is very easy to become disoriented at night (vertigo). Pay attention to your cockpit instruments.

2. The Special Forces unit is located two miles west of the first target. Make sure you do not bomb in their area.

3. Watch your landing. Altitude perception at night can be confusing.

Commander's Summary

The night can be used to great advantage, so make the best out of this training mission.

Listen to what 'Scooter' has to tell you. You will seldom get the chance to have a pilot like him in real combat.

Communicating with friendly ground units and laser co-op missions are top secret! Never discuss these missions outside of this room.

Flyable Aircraft

A-10	PGU-14B (250), Chaff (60), Flare (30), GBU-12 (4), LANTIRN Pod
F-117	Chaff (60), Flare (30), GBU-12D (4)
F-15E	PGU-28 (250), Chaff (60), Flare (30), GBU-12 (6)
F-16C	PGU-28 (250), Chaff (60), Flare (30), GBU-12 (4)
F-4E	PGU-28 (200), Chaff (60), Flare (30), GBU-12 (4), LANTIRN Pod

STEALTH TACTICS

In this mission you will be instructed in the fundamentals of flying a stealth aircraft and how to effectively keep out of radar coverage.

Date   24 MAY 2002

Time   2000 HRS

Training Stage

Weapon School

Instructor

Lt. Col. Pat 'Scooter' Davis

Subject

Practice stealth flight in the F-117 aircraft

Weather

Clear, with unlimited visibility

Mission Description

In this sortie you will learn about stealth tactics of the USAF. You will fly a typical F-117 combat flight, where you must locate and attack targets in a SAM-protected area. Most of the F-117 flights are carried out at night. This makes the plane even harder to spot. Your target for this mission is a Scud launcher that will be located in one of four available hangars. We are unable to determine in which of the four hangars the Scud will be located, so use your LANTIRN system to locate the correct hangar.

The simulated "Red Force" opposition for this drill will include several ground units that will visually try to locate you and fire AAA and heat missiles at you. There will also be several simulated SAM sites armed with "Smokey SAMs." You must clear the target area to finish this mission.

'Scooter' will follow you, flying another F-117, and will give you tips during this sortie.

Typical Errors

1. Leaving your external light on.

2. Loitering too long at the target area.

3. Dropping your bombs at the wrong target.

Mission Objectives

1. Do not get spotted by the ground forces before destroying the Scud.

2. Locate and destroy the Scud launcher in one of the hangars.

3. Avoid all SAM sites and get to waypoint 5 without being hit by Smokey SAMs.

In Addition

✈ All houses must survive.

Safety

1. It is very easy to become disoriented at night. Pay attention to your cockpit instruments.

2. You are not allowed to fire on anything but the four hangars. Remember that there are innocent people over there.

3. The F-117 is a very expensive piece of equipment. Bring it back in one piece.

Commander's Summary

Don't forget all you have learned from your first night training mission. The NVG system is a great help in this sort of mission.

Flyable Aircraft

F-117   Chaff (80), Flare (60), GBU-27 (2)

TWO-SHIP ACM

ACM (Air Combat Maneuvering) is a major Weapon School subject. In this ACM mission you will be flying as flight lead for the first time, and you'll learn how to utilize your wingmen by the use of wingman commands.

Date   25 MAY 2002

Time   1200 HRS

Training Stage

Weapon School

Instructor

Lt. Col. Pat 'Scooter' Davis

Subject

Practice the use of wingman commands in a two-ship flight

Weather

10000' scattered, with unlimited visibility

Mission Description

In this mission, you will have the chance to lead a two-ship flight for the first time. I'll be flying next to you, as your wingman. You will also practice the use of wingman commands.

Wingman commands allow you to direct your wingman to engage targets, change formation, and more.

We will begin by flying a short low-level navigation route, until we enter enemy territory, where we'll have to destroy two SA-3 radars located at the same SAM site. You will destroy one and I'll get the other.

Our next target will be a group of five Mi-8 choppers. You'll have to tell me what to do in order to help you destroy them as quick as possible.

Then, right before the end of the mission, we'll have to shoot down two MiG-29s and two Su-35s intercepting our territory.

Your last mission will be to BUZZ the tower. You'll have to fly as close as you can to the tower, less than 200m. If you don't do it, you won't pass the mission.

Typical Errors

1. Not utilizing your wingman efficiently by the use of wingman commands.

2. The wingman commands for target engagement depends on your radar lock. Pay attention to what you say, according to the target you are locked onto.

Mission Objectives

1. Destroy two SA-3 radars.

2. Shoot down all five choppers.

3. Shoot down two MiG-29s and two Su-35s.

4. Buzz the tower within 200 meters.

Safety

1. We are in enemy territory, so watch out for the SAMs and the interceptors.

2. You are flying close to the terrain, and using the wingman commands may distract you. If it becomes a safety issue, climb a bit.

Commander's Summary

Efficient use of the wingman commands is the key to success. I'm here as your wingman to help you.

Assets & Opposition

Assets

2 X F-15C (Austin 1, 2) PGU-28 (600), Chaff (60), Flare (60), AIM-120 (4), AIM-9M (4), Mk 83 (2); Austin 2 has 2 more Mk 83

Opposition Aircraft

2 X MiG-29   GSh-301 (301), Chaff (60), Flare (60), AA-11 (4); one has AA-10 (2)

2 X Su-35 30mm (600), Chaff (60), Flare (60), AA-10 (2), AA-11 (2), AA-8 (2)

5 X Mi-8

TACTICAL INTERCEPT PHASE

In this mission you will be introduced to multi-formation flying and the JTIDS (Joint Tactical Information Distribution System) display. You will now be leading a four-ship flight.

Date 26 MAY 2002

Time 1200 HRS

Training Stage

Weapon School

Instructor

Lt. Col. Pat 'Scooter' Davis

Subject

Multi-flight missions

Four-ship flight control

Introduction to JTIDS

Weather

20000' scattered, with unlimited visibility

About Multi-Flight Missions

In *USAF*, all large operations consist of multiple flights. Each flight has its own task. For example: in a typical Strike mission the first flight is usually an SEAD (Suppression of Enemy Air Defense) flight and takes out the SAMs. Then comes a CAP (Combat Air Patrol) flight that takes out enemy aircraft. Finally, a Strike flight will ingress and destroy the primary target.

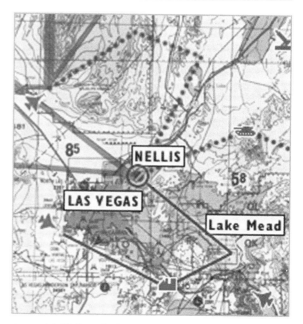

In multi-flight missions, you have the chance to fly all these flights during the same mission. You will start the mission flying Austin flight. After completing Austin's objectives you should switch to Buick flight. You will be taken to the cockpit of Buick lead, and from now on you will be controlling this flight. Austin flight will continue flying on its own. Repeat this process for Corvette and Dodge flights.

Switching flights is accomplished by pressing (Shift)+ 1 / 2 / 3 / 4 for Austin / Buick / Corvette / Dodge flights, respectively. You may also switch flights by going to the Tactical Display Screen ((Esc)), clicking the required flight button, and pressing Fly.

Mission Description

This is the first mission in which you will be a part of a multi-flight operation. You will need to fly each flight in order to pass the mission. You'll also have the chance to lead a four-ship flight for the first time. Throughout the mission I'll introduce you to the JTIDS, which will improve your situational awareness.

Today, Austin will be an F-16C flight. Its mission is

to destroy two buildings named Target 1 and Target 2, and shoot down two Su-35 fighters. You'll have to send Austin 3 and 4 to get the bandits, since they don't have the right ammo to destroy the buildings. In order to do so, you'll have to lock onto the Su-35 and press [Alt][E] (wingman commands).

After that, switch to A/G radar, lock onto your building (make sure it's the right building) and destroy it. Your No. 2 will destroy the other building, since it's his primary target.

Next, you should switch to Buick formation using [Shift][2]. You will enter Buick F-15E flight. You should now shoot down a couple of MiG-29s and a couple of Su-22s. Use your wingmen wisely.

Afterwards, switch formation to Corvette F-4E flight using [Shift][3], and destroy two SA-2 sites and two Rolands at waypoint 3, using AGM-45.

Your final mission will be inside an A-10 flight called Dodge ([Shift][4]). Your target is a tank convoy (T-72s) at waypoint 3, heading southwest.

It seems complicated, but it's really pretty simple. Don't worry, I'll let you know when to switch flights.

Typical Errors

1. Not switching flights in time.

2. Forgetting to check the situation of the other flights using the Tactical Display.

Mission Objectives

Austin

1. Destroy the two buildings.

2. Shoot down two Su-35s.

Buick

3. Shoot down two MiG-29s.

4. Shoot down two Su-35s.

Corvette

5. Destroy two SA-2 sites.

6. Destroy two Roland launchers.

Dodge

7. Eliminate all the convoy tanks.

Safety

1. Do not forget that you are in enemy territory.

2. Look out for AAA and enemy SAMs in the area.

Commander's Summary

This is a complicated and important mission. Plan your flight and formation control over the Tactical Display. Utilize all your resources, and don't forget where the other formations are.

Assets & Opposition

Assets

F-16C (Austin 1-2) PGU-28 (600), Chaff (90), Flare (90), AIM-120 (2), AIM-9M (2), Mk 83 (6), Small Fuel Tank

F-16C (Austin 3-4) PGU-28 (600), Chaff (90), Flare (90), AIM-120 (3), AIM-9M (2), Small Fuel Tank

F-15E (Buick 1-4) PGU-28 (250), Chaff (120), Flare (60), AIM-120 (4), AIM-9M (3)

F-4E (Corvette 1-4) 30mm (600), Chaff (60), Flare (60), AGM-45 (4), AIM-7B (2), Fuel Tank

A-10 (Dodge 1-4) PGU-14B (270), Chaff (100), Flare (80), AGM-65B (6), AIM-9M (4), Rocket (38)

Opposition Aircraft

2 X MiG-29 GSh-301 (300), Chaff (60), Flare (60), AA-10 (2), AA-8 (4)

2 X Su-35 30mm (300), Chaff (60), Flare (60), AA-11 (4)

2 X Su-27

TRAINING: RED FLAG

AIRFIELD STRIKE

In this mission, Blue aircraft have been tasked with striking the Red airfield located south of Lake Mead.

Date 20 MAY 2002

Time 1200 HRS

Mission Type

Strike

Mission Description

Destroy Red Force Airfield

Situation

Welcome to the 414th Combat Training Squadron (CTS) at Nellis AFB, hosting the Red Flag Exercise.

We are at day one of the war. All Red Force defensive systems are up, and Red aircraft are on alert. Blue forces should achieve air supremacy by destroying the airfield's defensive systems, the runways, and as many aircraft as possible.

Weather

Clear, with unlimited visibility

Intel

Targets

Your targets are the runway intersection, control tower, and two flightlines. These must all be destroyed to successfully accomplish the mission!

Red Airfield

Threats

Possible SA-2, SA-3, SA-6. Probable ZSU-23X4 AAA sites. The air threat will consist of F-16 Aggressors. These are F-16s painted in enemy colors, which simulate MiG-25s and MiG-29s.

Primary Flights

Austin

Airframe   4 x F-16C
Task   SEAD + Strike
Target   SA-6, SA-2, SA-3, Runway Intersection
Loadout   AGM-88, AIM-9M, AIM-120, Mk 84

Buick

Airframe   4 x F-15E
Task   Sweep, Strike
Target   Control Tower
Loadout   AIM 120, AIM-9M, GBU-24.

Corvette

Airframe   4 x A-10A
Task   Strike
Target   Flight Line A, Flight Line B
Loadout   AGM-65B, Mk 82, CBU-87, AIM-9M

Supporting Flights

Big Bird

Airframe   E-3C AWACS
Task   AWACS
Target   N/A
Loadout   N/A

Shell

Airframe   KC-135R
Task   Tanker
Target   N/A
Loadout   N/A

Tasking

Austin

Take out the SAM sites and AAA defending the airfield, using HARM (radar homing anti-radiation missiles launched from 8-10 miles), then pull up and bomb the runway intersection. After hitting the target, egress to waypoint 3. Buick will then ingress to the target area.

Buick

Perform a MiG Sweep, and bomb the control tower using GBU-24 laser-guided bombs. Remain on CAP over the airfield.

Corvette

Strike all parked aircraft in flight line A and flight line B using AGM-65 Mavericks, CBU-87s, and Mk 82 bombs.

Mission Objectives

Austin

1. Destroy runway intersection.

Buick

2. Destroy control tower.

Corvette

3. Destroy all aircraft in flight line A.

4. Destroy all aircraft in flight line B.

Mission Tips

+ If laser guided bombs are too difficult for you, change Buick's loadout to Mk 84 GP bombs.

+ To launch an AGM-88 (HARM) anti-radar missile, toggle your AG armament using [;] until 'AGM-88' is displayed.

+ When the right MFD shows 'In Range,' at about 10 miles from target, you may launch the radar-homing missile. To toggle targets in the HARM display, press [Ctrl][Enter].

+ AGM-65B, or Maverick, locks onto the target that the radar, in Map mode, is locked onto (view the target by pressing [F4]). If it's the target you want, just press pickle! You can view the missile flight with [F11].

+ You may also lock optically onto the target with the AGM-65. To do this, press [Z] to bring the MFD to full screen. Using the stick with [Ctrl] pressed, you can point at the desired target with the crosshairs, till the optical eye locks onto the contrast.

+ This mission will require you to use all your flights. Don't give up!

+ **Austin.** Come low and pop over the mountains to get the SAMs.

+ **Buick.** Attack with AMRAAMs to clear the area of MiGs.

+ **Corvette.** Watch out for incoming MiGs.

Commander's Summary

A large number of aircraft are going to attack the airfield today and the spacing is tight. Keep your eyes open, check 6, check 12, and check each other. Good luck.

Assets & Opposition

Assets

F-16C (Austin 1-2) PGU-28 (510), Chaff (120), Flare (90), AGM-88 (2), AIM-120 (2), AIM-9M (2), Mk 84 (2), Small Fuel Tank

F-16C (Austin 3-4) PGU-28 (510), Chaff (90), Flare (90), AGM-88 (2), AIM-120 (2), AIM-9M (2), Mk 84 (2), Small Fuel Tank

F-15E (Buick 1-2) PGU-28 (510), Chaff (90), Flare (60), AIM-120 (4), AIM-9M (2), Fuel Tank, GBU-24 (2)

F-15E (Buick 3-4) PGU-28 (600), Chaff (60), Flare (60), AIM-120 (2), AIM-9M (2), CBU-93 (6), Fuel Tank

A-10 (Corvette 1-2) 30mm (510), Chaff (90), Flare (60), AGM-65B (8), AIM-9M (4), CBU-87 (2), Mk 82 (2)

A-10 (Corvette 3-4) PGU-14B (600), Chaff (100), Flare (80), AGM-65B (6), AIM-9M (4), CBU-87 (2), Mk 82 (2), Mk 83 (2)

E-3C (Big Bird)

KC-135 (Shell)

Opposition Aircraft

2 X F-16 PGU-28 (600), Chaff (90), Flare (60)

F-16 PGU-28 (510), Chaff (90), Flare (90), AIM-120 (2), AIM-9M (2)

3 X F-16 PGU-28 (510), Chaff (90), Flare (90), AIM-9M (2)

2 X F-16 PGU-28 (600), Chaff (60), Flare (60), AIM-9M (2)

2 X F-16 PGU-28 (600), Chaff (60), Flare (60), AIM-9P (2)

F-16 PGU-28 (510), Chaff (90), Flare (60), AIM-9M (1), AIM-120 (1)

F-16 PGU-28 (510), Chaff (90), Flare (60), AIM-9M (2)

2 X AH-64 30mm (100)

RAH-66 30mm (100)

COUNTER ATTACK

In this mission, Blue forces launch a nuclear attack on Red strategic facilities while simultaneously preventing a Red nuke strike on Blue assets.

Date   21 MAY 2002

Time   0530 HRS

Mission Type

Strike, BARCAP (Barrier Combat Air Patrol)

Mission Description

Escort a package of Blue B-2s performing a nuclear strike on Red strategic facilities, while preventing retaliatory Red strikes.

Situation

The general assessment is that when reverting to nuclear measures by one side, the other side will retaliate similarly. So far, both sides' cruise missiles and ballistic attacks have been taken out. This Red Flag training mission exercises formation control and target prioritization, as well as multiple flight switching.

We are sending two strike packages this morning into the Red area, targeting the Red ammunition factory and the Red power plant. B-2A bombers will do the bombing, with fighters to escort them and clear the way of Red interceptors.

Over our two main assets, the arms factory and power plant, we are assigning fighters to perform CAP and intercept any incoming Red strike packages, all throughout the operation.

Austin and Buick are to the east of the operation, Corvette and Dodge are to the west.

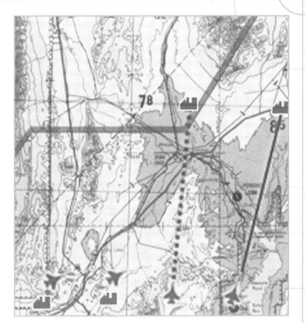

Weather

20000' scattered, visibility 20 miles

Intel

Targets

Power Plant, Factory

Power Plant

Factory

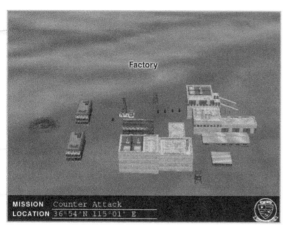

MISSION Counter Attack
LOCATION 36°54'N 115°01' E

Threats

F-16C aggressors will simulate Russian MiG-29s and Su-27 fighters.

Primary Flights

Austin

Airframe	4 x F-22A
Task	Escort Olds
Target	N/A
Loadout	AIM-120, AIM-9X

Buick

Airframe	4 x F-15C
Task	Escort Ford
Target	N/A
Loadout	AIM-120, AIM-9M

Corvette

Airframe	4 x F-22A
Task	CAP at Blue factory
Target	N/A
Loadout	AIM-120, AIM-9X

Dodge

Airframe	4 x F-16C
Task	CAP at Blue Power Plant
Target	N/A
Loadout	AIM-120, AIM-9M

Supporting Flights

Olds

Airframe	2 x B-2A
Task	Strike
Target	Red Factory
Loadout	Mk 84, simulates B-61 'nuclear bombs'

Ford

Airframe	2 x B-2A
Task	Strike
Target	Red Power Plant
Loadout	Mk 84, simulates B-61 'nuclear bombs'

Big Bird

Airframe	E-3C AWACS
Task	AWACS
Target	N/A
Loadout	N/A

Shell

Airframe	KC-135R
Task	Tanker
Target	N/A
Loadout	N/A

Tasking

Austin

Escort Olds, the first Blue B-2 strike package.

Clear the way of Red interceptors, making sure the B-2s bomb their target, which is the Red factory.

Buick

Escort Ford, the second Blue B-2 strike package.

Clear the way of Red interceptors, making sure the B-2s bomb their target, which is the Red power plant.

Corvette

Fly CAP over our armament factory.

Dodge

Fly CAP over our power plant center.

Mission Objectives

Austin and Buick

1. B-2s should safely reach the Red power plant and bomb it.

2. B-2s should safely reach the Red factory and destroy it.

Corvette and Dodge

3. The Blue power plant must not be destroyed.

4. The Blue factory must not be destroyed.

In Addition

✦ All B-2s must survive until the completion of the mission

Mission Tips

✦ This mission exercises wingmen and multi-flight control. Prioritize your targets, deploy your wingmen accordingly, and switch flights when you hear the threats on the radio.

✦ Keep the 'big picture' of the entire operation in mind. Use your JTIDS and the tactical display!

✦ This is a difficult air-to-air mission and will require you to use all your flights. Engage the enemy early. Use your wingmen for dogfighting while you go after the bombers.

Commander's Summary

We have to stop the nukes. I don't care if all our aircraft wind up chasing a single Buff, think of the holocaust if they manage to drop one nuke. Top priority is that Red bombers cannot reach their destination. If you don't stop them, you will be making a silk landing!

Assets & Opposition

Assets

F-22 (Austin 1-4) PGU-28 (600), Chaff (90), Flare (60), AIM-120 (3), AIM-9X (3)

F-15C (Buick 1-2) PGU-28 (600), Chaff (90), Flare (60), AIM-120 (4), AIM-9M (4), Fuel Tank

F-15C (Buick 3-4) PGU-28 (600), Chaff (120), Flare (90), AIM-120 (4), AIM-9M (4)

F-22 (Corvette 1-2) PGU-28 (600), Chaff (60), Flare (60), AIM-120 (3), AIM-9X (3)

F-22 (Corvette 3-4) PGU-28 (600), Chaff (120), Flare (90), AIM-120 (3), AIM-9X (3)

F-16C (Dodge 1-4) PGU-28 (510), Chaff (90), Flare (60), AIM-120 (4), AIM-9M (2)

B-2 (Ford) 30mm (100), Chaff (60), Flare (30), Mk 84 (8)

B-2 (Olds) 30mm (100), Chaff (60), Flare (30), Mk 84 (8)

E-3C (Big Bird)

KC-135 (Shell)

Opposition Aircraft

4 X F-16 PGU-28 (600), Chaff (90), Flare (90), AIM-120 (4), AIM-9M (4)

14 X F-16 PGU-28 (510), Chaff (60), Flare (60), AIM-120 (2), AIM-9M (2)

2 X F-16 PGU-28 (510), Chaff (90), Flare (90), AIM-120 (4), AIM-9M (2)

2 X F-16 PGU-28 (600), Chaff (90), Flare (90), AIM-9P (2)

4 X B-52 30mm (100), Chaff (60), Flare (30), Mk 84 (8)

HOSTAGE SITUATION

This mission is a combined Special Forces Operation. You are tasked with the successful rescue of 20 hostages being held in an enemy camp.

Date   21 MAY 2002

Time   1730 HRS

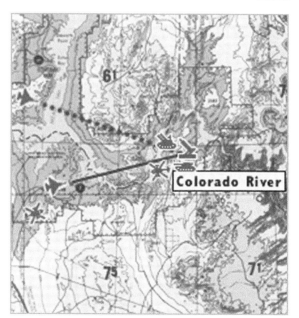

Mission Type

Special Forces Operation

Mission Description

Rescue hostages from an enemy camp.

Situation

This Red Flag mission implements a Special Forces rescue operation, in coordination with and with assistance from USAF SOCOM forces. Twenty hostages are being kept in a bunker in an enemy camp, under close guard and an umbrella of SAM and fighter defense.

A successful rescue operation requires "peeling" off the threats to the SAR helicopters, which include SAMs, tanks guarding the periphery of the camp, attack helicopters, and enemy fighters which might be scrambled during the operation. The two SAR helicopters will airlift a Special Force called 'Fox Team' who will take over key positions in the camp and guide the hostages to the helicopters, under cover of the night.

The timing and tasking intervals are crucial in this operation, as each element depends on the others. Mission start time is planned in such a manner that the Black Hawks will land in the camp at dusk, giving the Special Forces cover while they use NVGs to see the enemy.

Weather

20000' scattered, visibility 20 miles, full moon

Intel

Targets

The target consists of an SA-10 site, SA-2 site and the camp.

Target Area

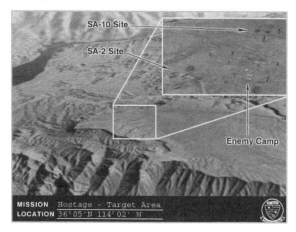

SA-10 Site

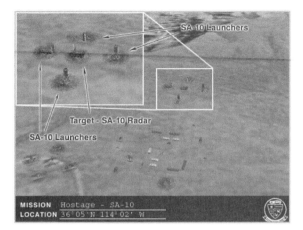

SA-2 Site

Threats

One SA-10 and one SA-2 battery are located in camp vicinity.

M1A1 tanks are on 24-hour patrol in the camp periphery. They may threaten our Special Ops force.

Red AH-64 'Apache' attack helicopters are on alert status.

One ZSU-23X4 AAA vehicle.

Red F-16C aggressors, on alert.

Any ground threats that may arise against the Special Operations Task Force.

Camp

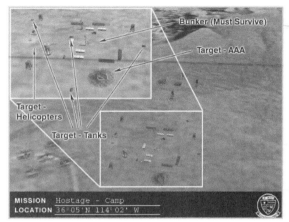

Primary Flights

Austin

Airframe	2 x F-15E
Task	SEAD + CAP
Target	SA-10 site
Loadout	GBU-15, AIM-9M, AIM-120

Buick

Airframe	2 x A-10A
Task	CAS
Target	Camp: four tanks and two Mi-24 helicopters, SA-2 site
Loadout	AGM-65B, AIM-9M

Supporting Flights

Saratoga

Airframe	2 x UH-60 'Black Hawk'
Task	SAR
Loadout	'Fox' team

Big Bird

Airframe	E-3C AWACS
Task	AWACS

Shell

Airframe	KC-135R
Task	Tanker

Tasking

Austin

Take out the SA-10 radar. The mission starts by climbing to 22,000 feet to waypoint 2, then turning east to waypoint 3, the target area. At 20 miles from target, Austin 1 will launch a TV bomb, GBU-15, and turn back to waypoint 4, so as not to enter the SA-10 hit radius. Launching at a distance less than 20 miles might cause the SA-10 to launch at us.

Austin will then remain over target area and provide CAP against possible incoming enemy fighters or helicopters.

Buick

You will already be in range of the camp. Take out the four tanks and two helicopters in the camp, using AGM-65B Mavericks. Buick may also take out the SA-2 radar and the AAA using one of the Mavericks.

Saratoga

The two UH-60 helicopters will fly in a Special Operation team, callsign 'Fox,' and land in the camp after receiving the all-clear signal from mission control. This will be given after Austin and Buick report their targets destroyed and area clear.

'Fox' team will take control of the camp, take the hostages from the bunker, and egress back to the Jollies. Any ground threats which might arise during the mission will be dealt with by Buick flight, while aerial threats will be tasked to Austin. Fighters will egress back to Nellis AFB once the SAR helicopter declares they are in friendly territory.

Mission Objectives

Austin

1. Destroy the SA-10 site.

2. Keep all Red air threats away from the SAR helicopters — Saratoga must survive.

Buick

3. Destroy the four tanks guarding the camp.

4. Destroy the two attack helicopters guarding the camp.

5. Destroy all incoming ground threats that might arise during the operation.

In Addition

✦ The hostage bunker must survive.

Mission Tips

✦ The GBU-15 is a TV bomb. Launch it at 20,000 feet, 18-20 miles from target. Pressing Z will give you the full screen MFD, with the TV image transmitted from the bomb camera.

✦ After launching, fly your plane to waypoint 4, away from the SAMs' killing range. Press A to get AP level. Now, press Z for full screen MFD, and toggle W until you see the 'T' indicator. This is the target! To steer the bomb, use Ctrl + ↑, ↓, ←, →.

✦ The target in any SAM site is the SAM radar, usually located in the middle of the site.

✦ AGM-65B Maverick is a TV A/G missile, which will home on any target that the radar is locked on in Map mode (press F4 to view target).

♣ You may also lock optically onto the target using the AGM-65. To do this, press [Z] to bring the MFD to full screen. Using the stick, you can point at the desired target with the crosshairs, till the optical eye locks on the contrast.

♣ **Austin.** Race to the camp at full AB (afterburners) to get there ahead of the choppers. Change your loadout to HARMs to perform SEAD quicker.

♣ **Buick.** Do not hit the bunker!

Commander's Summary

OK, twenty people are counting on us to save their butts. You are in a tightly coordinated operation, which requires precise mission execution. Everyone has to depend on each other doing their jobs to have a successful mission. Let's do this job right and get those people out of there.

Assets & Opposition

Assets

F-15E (Austin 1-2) PGU-28 (510), Chaff (120), Flare (90), AIM-120 (6), AIM-9M (2), GBU-15 (2)

A-10A (Buick 1-2) PGU-14B (500), Chaff (90), Flare (60), AGM-65B (8), AIM-9M (4), Fuel Tank

2 X UH-60 (Saratoga 1-2)

E-3C (Big Bird)

KC-135 (Shell)

Opposition Aircraft

F-16   PGU-28 (510), Chaff (60), Flare (60), AIM-9M (2)

F-16   PGU-28 (600), Chaff (90), Flare (90), AIM-9M (2)

F-16   PGU-28 (600), Chaff (90), Flare (90), AIM-120 (2), AIM-9M (2)

3 X F-16   PGU-28 (510), Chaff (60), Flare (60), AIM-120 (2)

2 X AH-64 Rocket (20)

2 X AH-64 30mm (300), Chaff (60), Flare (60), Rocket (20)

SINGLE MISSIONS

NO TO DRUGS

In this mission you will intercept a package of cargo helicopters over the US, simulating a drug-smuggling scenario. It is your job to stop them.

Date   27 MAR 2001

Time   1200 HRS

Mission Type

CAP (Combat Air Patrol)

Mission Description

A training model, in which USAF aircraft prevent drug-smuggling aircraft from getting to Las Vegas.

Situation

In this mission the Red force will simulate Colombian drug traffickers, using smuggling routes below US radar coverage. They will be using Russian air transports, including Mi-8 Hip helicopters and large Ilyushin transports. They are escorted by fighters flown by mercenaries. The USAF is trying to stop these smuggler flights as part of the United States' overall fight against drugs.

Your mission is to locate the smugglers' aircraft and shoot them down before they land.

Weather

10000' scattered, visibility unlimited

Intel

Targets

The drug transports are the primary target. They include Il-76 transport aircraft and Mi-8 Hip. Some ZIL-157 trucks are also in the area.

Threats

MiG-29s and Su-35s are expected to be escorting the transports.

Primary Flights

Austin

Airframe 4 x F-15C
Task CAP
Target N/A
Loadout AIM-9M, AIM-120

Tasking

Austin

Provide CAP around waypoint 4 and search for choppers and transports.

Mission Objectives

Austin

1. Destroy all six enemy choppers before they land.

2. Destroy the two cargo aircraft before they land.

Mission Tips

✈ Press ⌈↑⌉ to switch to the AIM-120 AMRAAM.

The display on the lower-left side should be 'AIM-120.'

The AIM-120 is a fire-and-forget missile. You can launch it and lock onto the next target.

When launching, make sure that the small dot on your HUD is inside the circle.

If this condition is met, and the target is within the missile's range, a small triangle will appear under the target box. This means your missile will likely hit the target.

Commander's Summary

I have nothing to add. Good luck.

Assets & Opposition

Assets

4 X F-15C (Austin 1-4) PGU-28 (600), Chaff (60), Flare (60), AIM-120 (4), AIM-9M (4)

Opposition Aircraft

2 X MiG-29 PGU-28 (600), Chaff (60), Flare (60), AA-10 (2), AA-8 (2)

2 X Su-35 PGU-28 (600), 2100lb (2), AA-11 (2), AA-8 (2), Mk 82 (2)

2 X Il-76

6 X Mi-8

FASTEN SEAT BELTS

USAF aircraft rescue a hijacked French airliner over Iraq.

Date   2 JAN 2001

Time   1700 HRS

Mission Type

Special Operation — Rescue

Mission Description

Rescue a hijacked civilian aircraft.

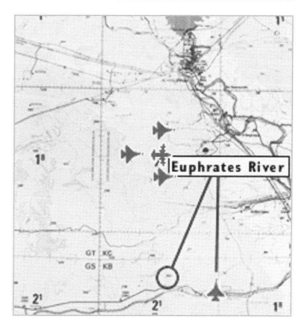

Situation

In an effort to stop the coalitions' bombing of chemical warfare plants in Iraq, the Iraqis have come up with a plan to hijack one of the western airlines' commercial flights, and hold it hostage.

We have just been informed that a French airliner, a 707, callsign Pacific Sun, flying in a commercial route to the west of Iraq, has been intercepted by three Iraqi fighters: two Mirage F-1s and a MiG-29. The Boeing is being forced to land in Baghdad, or be shot down. Naturally, the pilot has complied with their instructions, and is flying east, escorted by the three fighters. One is on his tail, and two are flanking him.

We have received directions from the Pentagon to do whatever it takes to foil the Iraqi plan. We're going to send a single F-22A so as not to draw attention to ourselves, on a low-altitude mission to intercept the three fighters and rescue the Boeing before landing in Baghdad.

In order get in close to the Iraqi fighters without them seeing you, you will have to come in very low and pull up to launch at about three miles. Remember that ID'ing is critical. It would be a

tragedy to shoot down the friendly airliner so a VID (Visual Identification) is required before you can shoot.

The first target is the rear MiG. We recommend shooting it down at about three miles or whenever you can VID with heaters or guns. Once the rear MiG is down, switch to the other two and take them out quickly before they can achieve firing positions on the Boeing.

Once the three fighters are shot down, Austin 1 will guide the Boeing to a safe landing in Saudi Arabia.

An MH-53J Pave Low helicopter is on alert status to the south, just in case developments call for its intervention.

Weather

Clear, with visibility unlimited

Intel

Targets
N/A

Threats
MiG-29, F-1 fighters.

Primary Flights

Austin
Airframe F-22A
Task OCA (Offensive Counter-Air)
Target Iraqi Aircraft
Loadout AIM-9X, AIM-120

Supporting Flights

Chicago
Airframe MH-53J
Task SAR
Target N/A
Loadout N/A

Big Bird
Airframe E-3C AWACS
Task AWACS
Target N/A
Loadout N/A

Shell
Airframe KC-135R
Task Tanker
Target N/A
Loadout N/A

Tasking

Austin
Fly to waypoint 2, low altitude, acquire a lock on the rear MiG (MiG 2), pull up at five miles, and launch at three miles, using two AIM-120 missiles.

After the rear MiG is down, engage and splash the two remaining F-1s.

After all three fighters are splashed, escort the Boeing to Saudi Arabia (waypoint 3).

Mission Objectives

Austin
1. Protect the 707.

In Addition
✦ Chicago must survive.

Commander's Summary

This is it. We can't let that madman take an airliner hostage. There are 360 people on that plane and they are depending on us to save them. There's no time, so scramble and knock out those three terrorists before they know what hit them.

Assets & Opposition

Assets
F-22A (Austin 1) PGU-28 (600), Chaff (120),
　　　　　　　　Flare (60), AIM-120 (3), AIM-9X (3)

Opposition Aircraft
2 X F-1 GSh-301 (300), Chaff (30), Flare (60),
　　　　AA-8 (2)
MiG-29 PGU-14B (300), Chaff (60),
　　　　Flare (30), AA-11 (4)
Mi-24 30mm (300), Rocket (20)
Mi-24 Rocket (20)

Commercial Flight
Boeing 707 (Pacific Sun 101)

OSIRAQ TAKE 2

The nuclear facility in Osiraq was bombed by the Israeli Air Force 15 years ago. USAF aircraft are now on their way to strike the facility once again, with the cooperation of the IAF.

Date 21 JUN 2001

Time 1630 HRS

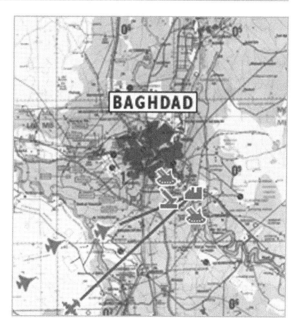

Mission Type

Strike

Mission Description

Destroy the Osiraq nuclear facility near Baghdad.

Situation

In 1981 the Israeli Air Force executed a brilliant long-range strike on the Iraqi nuclear center at Osiraq, thus robbing Saddam of potential nuclear arms for nearly two decades. However, Intelligence informs and warns us that the Iraqi leader has not given up hope in trying to produce the deadly weapons, and that the Osiraq facility is operational, and in its final stage of weapon development and construction. The President of the US has declared this situation to be intolerable, and has directed an attack to be carried out on this facility, ASAP, in collaboration with the Israeli Air Force.

We are arming our aircraft with various weapons, in order to destroy as many of the facility's components as possible, and to be ready for surprises. We must make an effort not to go there again.

Weather

20,000' scattered, visibility unlimited

Intel

Targets

The main targets in the Osiraq facility are the reactor buildings and the weapon storage dumps. Direct hits on these targets will reduce the Iraqis' nuclear ability to zero.

Osiraq Target

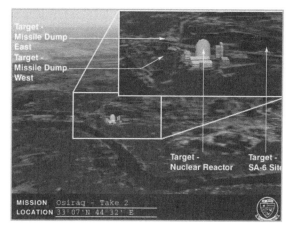

Threats

Probable SA-6, Roland SAMs and ZSU-23X4 AAA defense.

Probable MiG-29s, Mirage F-1s on alert in the vicinity.

Primary Flights

Austin

Airframe	4 x F-15E
Task	SEAD, CAP
Target	SA-6 site, ZSU-23X4 AAA
Loadout	AGM-88, CBU-93, AIM-9M, AIM-120

Buick

Airframe	4 x F-16C
Task	Strike
Target	Reactor dome, west missile dump, east missile dump
Loadout	Mk 84, Mk 83, AIM-9M, AIM-120

Supporting Flights

Nesher

Airframe	2 x F-15E
Task	Strike
Target	Labs
Loadout	AIM-7M, AIM-9M, Mk 82

Keshet

Airframe	2 x F-15E
Task	SEAD
Target	AAA
Loadout	AIM-7M, AIM-9M, Mk 82

Selek

Airframe	2 x F-16D
Task	SEAD
Target	AAA
Loadout	AIM-7M, AIM-9M, Mk 82

Shell

Airframe	KC-135R
Task	Tanker
Target	N/A
Loadout	N/A

Big Bird

Airframe	E-3C AWACS
Task	AWACS
Target	N/A
Loadout	N/A

Tasking

Austin

Destroy the 2 SA-6 radar centers and Gundish AAA sites using HARMs, and then provide CAP for the mission. The second SA-6 site is 20 miles to the east of the facility!

Buick

Ingress to target area at low altitude, pop up to 12,000 feet, and then dive bomb, targeting the main nuclear reactor.

After the nuclear reactor and the west missile dump are destroyed, make another bombing run and destroy missile dump east. Buick 2 will strike missile dump west.

IAF formations Nesher, Selek and Keshet are tasked to strike AAA and chemical laboratories in the periphery, and will ingress target area with Austin flight.

Mission Objectives

Buick

1. Destroy the nuclear reactor.

2. Destroy the east missile dump.

In Addition

✈ The BMP-1 must be destroyed.

Mission Tips

✦ To launch an AGM-88 (HARM) anti-radar missile, toggle your A/G armament using [↑].

When the right MFD shows 'In Range' (at about 10 miles from target), you may launch the radar-homing missile. To toggle targets in the HARM display, press [Ctrl][Enter]. You can also use the mouse.

✦ If Buick 2 fails to destroy the west missile dump, Buick 1 has enough bombs to make another pass on the target, and bomb them.

✦ Listen carefully to the radio for surprise, unplanned developments.

Commander's Summary

We can't afford this madman to have nukes. No way, José. We're going to hit him again and again if required. Remember that the main target is the reactor. Buick has enough bombs to destroy all 3 targets. Watch out for the Israeli jets and keep down the B.S. on the radio. Make sure you make smart use of your ordnance — we need all the help we can get.

Assets & Opposition

Assets

F-15E (Austin 1) PGU-28 (600), Chaff (120), Flare (60), AGM-88 (4), AIM-120 (4), AIM-9M (2), CBU-93 (1)

F-15E (Austin 2) PGU-28 (510), Chaff (90), Flare (60), AGM-88 (4), AIM-120 (4), AIM-9M (2), CBU-93 (1)

F-15E (Austin 3) PGU-28 (600), Chaff (120), Flare (60), AGM-88 (2), AIM-120 (5), AIM-9M (2)

F-15E (Austin 4) PGU-28 (600), Chaff (120), Flare (60), AGM-88 (2), AIM-120 (6), AIM-9M (1)

2 X F-16C (Buick 1-2) PGU-28 (600), Chaff (90), Flare (90), AIM-120 (2), AIM-9M (2), Mk 83 (6), Mk 84 (3)

2 X F-16C (Buick 3-4) PGU-28 (510), Chaff (90), Flare (90), AIM-120 (2), AIM-9M (2), CBU-87 (6), Mk 84 (3)

2 X F-15E (Keshet 1-2) PGU-28 (600), Chaff (60), Flare (60), AIM-7M (4), AIM-9M (4), Mk 82 (8)

2 X F-15E (Nesher 1-2) PGU-28 (600), Chaff (60), Flare (60), AIM-7M (4), AIM-9M (4), Mk 82 (8)

2 X F-16D (Selek 1-2) PGU-28 (510), Chaff (90), Flare (90), AIM-7M (4), AIM-9M (2), Mk 82 (6)

Opposition Aircraft

F-1 30mm (600), Chaff (60), Flare (60), AA-10 (2), AA-8 (2)

F-1 30mm (600), Chaff (60), Flare (60), AA-8 (2)

MiG-23 GSh-301 (100), Chaff (40), Flare (20), AA-6 (2), AA-8 (2)

6 X MiG-29 GSh-301 (300), Chaff (60), Flare (60), AA-10 (4), AA-8 (4)

A DAY AT THE BEACH

USAF aircraft are sent to stop Chinese Marines from quietly taking over a strategic island on the eve of a coming conflict.

Date   15 MAY 2003

Time   0600 HRS

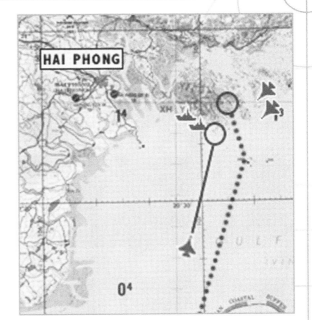

Mission Type

Strike

Mission Description

Prevent the landing of Chinese Marines on Gua -Loc Island.

Situation

China is taking advantage of Vietnam's focus on internal affairs and is trying to capture the island of Gua-Loc, which offers strategic advantages in radar coverage of the area and an ideal position for forward command posts.

USAF Intel has acquired this last-minute information, and a package of fighters is sent to stop the ongoing invasion to the island.

Weather

12000' scattered, visibility unlimited

Intel

On the island there is a friendly radar post. The enemy forces landing on the island are likely to go for this target first.

Targets

N/A

Threats

The strike is likely to include Chinese Su-27s. OSA missile ships are expected as well. These ships may include anti-aircraft artillery. T-72 tanks will perform the landing.

Primary Flights

Austin

Airframe	4 x F-16C
Task	CAP
Target	Su-27
Loadout	AIM-9M, AIM-120

Buick

Airframe	4 x A-10A
Task	CAS
Target	As assigned in the air
Loadout	Mk 82, AIM-9M, AGM-65B

Tasking

Austin

Pull up to intercept the enemy Su-27 CAP flight above the island. After achieving air superiority, provide CAP to secure Buick.

Buick

Follow Austin and ingress to the island after the Chinese CAP is destroyed. You will deal with the Chinese vessels and Marine forces on the island.

Mission Objectives

Austin

1. Destroy all Su-27s.

Buick

2. Hit all ground and naval forces on and around the island. (Seven SAMs and five T-72s must be destroyed.)

Commander's Summary

The Chinese move was expected but yet surprised us. We can still stop the invasion if we move fast and with determination. Go get 'em!

Assets & Opposition

Assets

4 X F-16C (Austin 1-4) PGU-28 (600), Chaff (90), Flare (90), AIM-120 (4), AIM-9M (2), Small Fuel Tank

3 X A-10A (Buick 1-3) PGU-14B (270), Chaff (100), Flare (80), AGM-65B (12), AIM-9M (4), Fuel Tank, Mk 82 (4)

A-10A (Buick 4) PGU-28 (300), Chaff (60), Flare (60), AGM-65B (12), AIM-9M (4), Fuel Tank, Mk 82 (4)

Opposition Aircraft

4 X Su-27 GSh-301 (600), Chaff (90), Flare (90), AA-11 (6)

3 X Su-27 30mm (600), Chaff (90), Flare (90), AA-10 (5), AA-11 (8)

3 X Su-27 AA-10 (2), AA-11 (4)

Su-27 30mm (600), Chaff (90), Flare (90), AA-10 (5), AA-11 (7), AA-8 (1)

Su-27 GSh-301 (600), Chaff (90), Flare (90), AA-10 (2), AA-11 (6)

Su-27 AA-11 (6)

BRING THE BOYS BACK HOME

USAF aircraft rescue civilian prisoners from a terrorist camp in Vietnam.

Date   DEC 2002

Time   0540 HRS

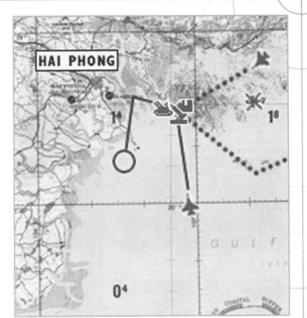

Mission Type

Special Ops

Mission Description

Rescue prisoners from a terrorist drug camp.

Situation

A group of 25 backpackers who disappeared last month is being held in a terrorist camp in South Vietnam. The camp is well defended, so a combined Strike and Special Ops force will perform this rescue mission. It is needless to mention that the most sensitive part of the mission is to avoid hitting the hostages.

This SAR operation will consist of three stages: Austin flight will ingress to target area from the south and destroy the SA-6 site in the camp perimeter. It will also destroy the OSA boats, and then provide CAP for the remainder of the operation. The SA-6 and OSA boats must be destroyed prior to the arrival of the SAR helicopter, to keep it from being shot down.

Buick flight, consisting of two A-10s, will ingress after Austin from the north, and take out the four AAA Gundish vehicles in the camp. Do not attack tents A and B, where the prisoners are kept. The SAR helicopter, callsign 'Olds,' will land near the camp, take the prisoners on board, and egress quickly out.

Weather

18000' scattered, visibility 20 miles

Intel

Targets

The Terrorist Camp (photos on next page).

Threats

SA-6, ZSU-23X4 (Gundish), AAA from the OSA boats.

The Vietnam or Chinese Air Force could scramble against us.

SA-6 Site

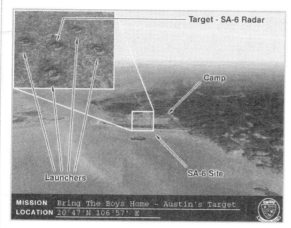

Gundish AAA

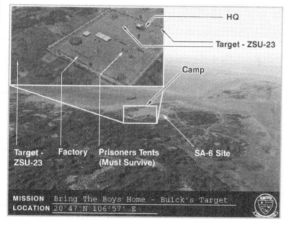

Primary Flights

Austin

Airframe 2 x F-16C
Task   SEAD + CAP
Target   SA-6
Loadout   CBU-87, AIM-9M, AIM-120

Buick

Airframe 2 x A-10A
Task   Strike
Target   4 x Gundish
Loadout   AGM-65B, CBU-87, AIM-9M

Supporting Flights

Olds

Airframe UH-60
Task   SAR
Target   N/A
Loadout   N/A

Tasking

Austin

Ingress from the south toward the camp area, at low altitude. Locate the SA-6 radar using the radar in Map mode. At 5-6 miles from the target pull up to 12,000 feet and perform a bomb run on the SA-6 radar.

After the radar is destroyed, locate the two OSA boats guarding the camp, and dive-bomb them until eliminated. Finally, remain on CAP. Enemy fighters may be scrambled to that area, so remain alert.

Buick

Ingress from the north, choose AGM-65B missiles, and switch your radar to Map mode. Locate the ZSU-23x4 guns (use object ID in the Preferences or view with F4). Once you are locked onto the targets, launch the missiles. Destroy all four Gundish guns. After they are destroyed, destroy all you can in the camp. Pay special attention to the fact that the two prisoner tents are also located in the camp! Do not hit these tents!

Mission Objectives

Austin

1. Destroy the SA-6 radar.

2. Destroy the two OSA patrol boats.

3. Protect the SAR helicopter from all air threats.

Buick

4. Destroy the four Gundish AAA guns.

Mission Tips

✈ In this mission you will have to switch between formations.

✈ Choose 'Display Object ID' in the Preferences option.

Commander's Summary

Those good-for-nothing terrorists! Not only are they pushing drugs into the western world and poisoning us, and not only are they using the money they make from it to buy arms against us, now they're kidnapping innocent civvies to do their God-awful work for them! Uncle Sam says no way! It's a mission with the highest moral purpose attached to it, and every one of us is geared up to get those boys out of that rat hole. Under no circumstances are those two tents to be hit where the prisoners are being held. Let's bring 'em back for Christmas. After our boys are safe, be sure to burn the place to the ground! Let's go!

Assets & Opposition

Assets

2 X F-16C (Austin 1-2) PGU-28 (510), Chaff (90), Flare (60), AIM-120 (4), AIM-9M (2), CBU-87 (6), Small Fuel Tank

A-10A (Buick 1) PGU-14B (500), Chaff (100), Flare (80), AGM-65B (12), AIM-9M (6), CBU-87 (2)

A-10A (Buick 2) PGU-14B (370), Chaff (100), Flare (80), AGM-65B (12), AIM-9M (6), CBU-87 (2)

UH-60 (Olds)

Opposition Aircraft

4 X Su-27 30mm (300), Chaff (60), Flare (60), AA-10 (2), AA-8 (4)

4 X Su-27 30mm (500), Chaff (90), Flare (90)

BARRIER

USAF jets defend a highly valuable Early Warning Radar station in Germany against multiple waves of Russian attackers.

Date   20 SEP 2005

Time   0600 HRS

Mission Type

BARCAP (Barrier Combat Air Patrol)

Mission Description

Defend an EWR site south of Munich from a surprise air raid.

Situation

Relationships with the Russian neighbor have been tense ever since the previous battles of Operation "Sleeping Giant." Germany has established a new EWR (Early Warning Radar) site on the southern Alp slopes to prevent a second upheaval in this area. There has been much Russian objection to the construction of this site. This morning we have received an intelligence update, stating that an Su-35 flight has penetrated through Austrian airspace and is now making its way to a surprise attack on the radar complex. USAF aircraft on alert at Landsberg are being scrambled to the area.

Weather

10000' scattered, visibility 30 miles

Intel

Targets

USAF aircraft are to defend the radar complex, consisting of three main domes and an administration area.

Threats

The attack waves may consist of all possible fighters and bombers, such as Su-35 fighter/bombers, Su-22 and Su-24 bombers, and Tu-22 heavy bombers. Escort may include MiG-29 and Su-27 'Flanker' fighters.

The resident Patriot site is active, and will participate in the effort to stop the attack.

Primary Flights

Austin

Airframe	2 x F-22A
Task	BARCAP
Target	N/A
Loadout	AIM-120, AIM-9X

Buick

Airframe	2 x F-15E
Task	BARCAP
Target	N/A
Loadout	AIM-120, AIM-9M

Supporting Flights

Big Bird

Airframe E-3C AWACS
Task AWACS
Target N/A
Loadout N/A

Tasking

Austin

You are on your way to the radar complex, located at waypoint 2. You should clear the area of bandits, and pay attention to AWACS messages regarding any other attack waves. At any time you may enter Buick F-15C flight ([Shift][2]) and take off from Landsberg.

Buick

You are on alert at Landsberg AFB. You should scramble at AWACS request and assist Austin.

The mission will be over as soon as the last attack wave is destroyed and AWACS clears the friendly forces to return to base.

Mission Objectives

Austin and Buick

1. No building in the radar complex may be hit.

Mission Tips

✈ Select the AIM-120 long-range missile by pressing [↑]. Look for 'AIM-120' on the left side of the HUD.

✈ In closer ranges you can press [↑] again to switch to AIM-9 heat missiles and follow the same procedure.

✈ Assign targets to your wingman by using wingman commands — "Engage My Target" ([Alt][E]), "Engage the Other One" ([Alt][W]) or "Sort Targets" ([Alt][S]).

✈ Press [Z] to view the JTIDS in full-screen and get a better situational awareness. You can also switch to your Tactical Display by pressing [Esc].

Commander's Summary

Guys, there's not much time for talk right now. Get those G-suits on and start your engines.

Assets & Opposition

Assets

2 X F-22A (Austin 1-2) PGU-28 (200), Chaff (90), Flare (90), AIM-120 (3), AIM-9X (3)

2 X F-15E (Buick 1-2) PGU-28 (250), Chaff (120), Flare (60), AIM-120 (4), AIM-9M (4), Fuel Tank

E-3C (Big Bird)

Opposition Aircraft

4 X Mi-24 Flare (60), Rocket (1)

4 X Su-35 30mm (500), Chaff (90), Flare (90), AA-8 (2), Mk 82 (4)

2 X Su-27 GSh-301 (600), Chaff (90), Flare (90), AA-10 (4), AA-11 (4)

Tu-22 30mm (500), Chaff (60), Flare (60), Mk 83 (2)

2 X MiG-29 30mm (600), Chaff (90), Flare (90), AA-10 (4), AA-8 (4)

Su-24 30mm (500), Chaff (90), Flare (90), AA-6 (2), Mk 83 (4)

Su-24 AA-6 (2), Mk 83 (4)

AIR FORCE 1

You are leading a four-ship formation of F-15Es on a training mission in Germany.

Date 4 AUG 2001

Time 1715 HRS

Mission Type

Training

Situation

The president of the US has finished the Munich summit talks, and has taken off from Erding AFB, headed back home. We're going back to our routine training program.

Weather

20000' scattered, visibility unlimited

Intel

Targets

N/A

Threats

N/A

Primary Flights

Austin

Airframe 4 x F-15E
Task Refuel Training
Target N/A
Loadout AIM-9M, AIM-120

Supporting Flights

Shell

Airframe KC-135R
Task Refuel
Target N/A
Loadout N/A

Tasking

Austin

Lead a four-ship formation to the Innsbruck patrol area, and perform a refueling exercise with Shell.

Mission Objectives

Austin

1. All four planes must perform a refueling process.

In Addition

+ Air Force 1 must survive.

+ All eight MiG-29s must be destroyed.

Mission Tips

+ In order to refuel, press Ctrl R.

+ To refuel automatically, press A.

+ To let your wingmen refuel, press Shift Alt F for wingman 2, and Ctrl Alt F for wingmen 3 and 4.

Commander's Summary

OK, you guys, regular refueling drill. Just be careful not to hit that tanker!

Assets & Opposition

Assets

4 X F-15E (Austin 1-4) PGU-28 (600), Chaff (120), Flare (120), AIM-120 (6), AIM-9M (2), Fuel Tank (3)

Air Force 1 Chaff (120), Flare (120)

KC-135R (Shell)

Opposition Aircraft

2 X MiG-29 30mm (600), Chaff (90), Flare (90)

MiG-29 GSh-301 (300), Chaff (10), Flare (10), AA-10 (4), AA-8 (4)

MiG-29 GSh-301 (300), Chaff (60), Flare (60)

MiG-29 GSh-301 (300), Chaff (60), Flare (60), AA-10 (4), AA-8 (4)

3 X MiG-29 GSh-301 (300), Chaff (60), Flare (60)

2 X MiG-29 GSh-301 (300), Chaff (60), Flare (60), AA-8 (4)

2 X MiG-29 GSh-301 (300), Chaff (60), Flare (60), AA-8 (2)

MULTIPLAYER MISSIONS

FUEL LOW (BLUE)

Each side has two formations, both low on fuel, one tanker, one target to destroy and one to protect — what will you do first?

Time   1200 HRS

Mission Type

Strike, CAP (Combat Air Patrol), Refuel

Mission Description

Air-refuel your jets, then attack the enemy's central base. Be careful! The enemy is trying to attack your base at the same time.

Situation

Two Blue formations are low on fuel and approaching the Blue tanker. At the same time two Red formations, also low on fuel, are approaching the Red tanker. Both sides' missions are to attack the enemy's communications center. The first one to destroy the opponent's center or all the opponent's planes wins.

Weather

Clear

BAGHDAD

Intel

Targets

One communications center building, located in the Red central control base.

Threats

Red F-16Cs and F-15Es are protecting the Red base and trying to attack the Blue base.

Primary Flights

Austin

Airframe 4 x F-15E
Task Refuel, Strike
Target Red Communications Center
Loadout AIM-9M, Mk 84

Buick

Airframe 4 x F-16C
Task Refuel, CAP (Combat Air Patrol)
Target N/A
Loadout AIM-9M

Tasking

Austin

You are very low on fuel. Your first priority is to refuel. Next, attack the Red communications center located in the Red base.

Buick

Protect the Blue tanker while Austin is refueling. Then refuel yourself and fly to protect the Blue base from a possible Red aerial attack.

Mission Objectives

Austin

1. Destroy the Red communications center.

Buick

2. Protect the Blue communications center.

Mission Tips

✈ Coordinate you flights. First, one plane refuels while the others protect. Then, one formation attacks while the other protects.

✈ You are low on fuel, but have enough to either protect your tanker, or to attack the enemy's tanker.

✈ No plane (Red or Blue) has enough fuel to reach the enemy's base without refueling.

✈ One undetected plane getting to the enemy's tanker or base may win the mission for everyone.

Commander's Summary

This mission demands fast and accurate analysis of the situation, as well as outstanding flight skills and perfect coordination with the other pilots. You'll have to assess your situation at all times and decide whether to refuel, intercept enemy planes, attack the enemy base, or protect the home base. Make the right decision, and you'll be successful.

Blue Assets

4 X F-15E (Austin 1-4) PGU-28 (250), Chaff (120), Flare (60), AIM-9M (4), Mk 84 (4)

4 X F-16C (Buick 1-4) PGU-28 (510), Chaff (90), Flare (90), AIM-9M (4)

KC-135R

Red Assets

4 X F-15E (Corvette 1-4) PGU-28 (250), Chaff (120), Flare (60), AIM-9M (4), Mk 84 (4)

4 X F-16C (Dodge 1-4) PGU-28 (510), Chaff (90), Flare (90), AIM-9M (4)

KC-135R

FUEL LOW (RED)

Each side has two formations, both low on fuel, one tanker, one target to destroy and one to protect — what will you do first?

Time 1200 HRS

Mission Type

Strike, CAP (combat air patrol), Refuel

Mission Description

Air-refuel your jets, then attack the enemy's central base. Be careful! The enemy is trying to attack your base at the same time.

Situation

Two Red formations are low on fuel and approaching the Red tanker. At the same time two Blue formations, also low on fuel, are approaching the Blue tanker. Both sides' missions are to attack the enemy's communications center. The first one to destroy the opponent's center or all the opponent's planes wins.

Weather

Clear

Intel

Targets

One communications center building, located in the Blue central control base.

Threats

Blue F-16Cs and F-15Es are protecting the Blue base and trying to attack the Red base.

Primary Flights

Corvette

Airframe 4 x F-15E
Task Refuel, Strike
Target Blue Communications Center
Loadout AIM-9M, Mk 84

Dodge

Airframe 4 x F-16C
Task Refuel, CAP (Combat Air Patrol)
Target N/A
Loadout AIM-9M

Tasking

Corvette

You are very low on fuel. Your first priority is to refuel. Next, attack the Blue communications center located in the Blue base.

Dodge

Protect the Red tanker while Austin is refueling. Then refuel yourself, and fly to protect the Red base from a possible Blue aerial attack.

Mission Objectives

Corvette

1. Destroy the Blue communications center.

Dodge

2. Protect the Red communications center.

Mission Tips

✦ Coordinate you flights. First, one plane refuels while the others protect. Then, one formation attacks while the other protects.

✦ You are low on fuel, but have enough to either protect you tanker, or to attack the enemy's tanker.

✦ No plane (Red or Blue) has enough fuel to reach the enemy's base without refueling.

✦ One undetected plane getting to the enemy's tanker or base may win the mission for everyone.

Commander's Summary

This mission demands fast and accurate analysis of the situation, as well as outstanding flight skills and perfect coordination with the other pilots. You'll have to assess your situation at all times and decide whether to refuel, intercept enemy planes, attack the enemy base, or protect the home base. Make the right decision, and you'll be successful.

Red Assets

4 X F-15E (Corvette 1-4) PGU-28 (250), Chaff (120), Flare (60), AIM-9M (4), Mk 84 (4)

4 X F-16C (Dodge 1-4) PGU-28 (510), Chaff (90), Flare (90), AIM-9M (4)

KC-135R

Blue Assets

4 X F-15E (Austin 1-4) PGU-28 (250), Chaff (120), Flare (60), AIM-9M (4), Mk 84 (4)

4 X F-16C (Buick 1-4) PGU-28 (510), Chaff (90), Flare (90), AIM-9M (4)

KC-135R

CONVOY RUN (BLUE)

An enforcement convoy of five tanks is making its way to a small Red army base. The Blue side's mission is to destroy all of the tanks, the Red side's mission is to protect them.

Time 1200 HRS

Mission Type

Strike

Mission Description

Destroy a Red enforcement convoy of five tanks before it reaches its destination.

Situation

In an attempt to control one of the main roads in the area, the Red side is enforcing a small army base, guarding it with tanks. The tank convoy is now four miles from the Red base, and entering a SAM-protected area. Once the tanks reach the base the Red side will control the road and may prevent the Blue side from using it, cutting off supplies for important areas.

Weather

Clear

Intel

Targets

Five T-72 tanks are currently located at waypoint 1, making their way along the trail (waypoint 2) to the Red army base at waypoint 3.

Threats

An unknown number of SA-8 vehicles are protecting the convoy on the road (exact location unknown).

Two SAM sites, an SA-6 in the north and an SA-3 site in the south, protect the base area.

Red fighters were scrambled to protect against possible air strikes.

Primary Flights

Austin

Airframe 2 x F-15E

Task SEAD (suppression of enemy air defense) & Strike

Target Red Convoy

Loadout AIM-9M, AGM-88

Buick

Airframe 2 x F-16C

Task CAP (Combat Air Patrol)

Target N/A

Loadout AIM-9M

Tasking

Austin

Your mission is to locate and destroy the SAM sites protecting the convoy and then destroy the convoy itself.

Buick

Your mission is to protect Austin formation against Red interceptors, enabling Austin to eliminate the convoy.

Mission Objectives

Austin

1. Destroy all five red tanks before they reach the red army base.

Mission Tips

✈ Remember your primary task — attack the convoy, and do not be tempted by easy AA kills.

✈ Try to divide your forces — one formation for air-to-air protection, and the other for destroying the convoy.

Commander's Summary

Time is limited and the area is protected both from the ground and air. Divide the tasks between the formations and remember what the real objective is — eliminating the convoy before it reaches its base.

Blue Assets

2 X F-15E (Austin 1-2) PGU-28 (250), Chaff (120), Flare (60), AGM-88 (2), AIM-9M (4)

2 X F-16C (Buick 1-2) PGU-28 (510), Chaff (90), Flare (90), AIM-9M (4)

Red Assets

2 X F-16C (Corvette 1-2) PGU-28 (510), Chaff (90), Flare (90), AIM-9M (4)

2 X F-22A (Dodge 1-2) PGU-28 (200), Chaff (120), Flare (60), AIM-9X (2)

CONVOY RUN (RED)

An enforcement convoy of five tanks is making its way to a small red army base. The Blue side's mission is to destroy all of the tanks, the Red side's mission is to protect them.

Time   1200 HRS

Mission Type

CAP (Combat Air Patrol)

Mission Description

Protect a supply convoy of five tanks from Blue strike planes.

Situation

A convoy of five tanks is on its way to supply a small Red army base located on the main road in the area. In an act of aggression, trying to control the road, the Blue side is attempting to prevent the supply convoy from reaching its destination. At least one of tanks must reach the base to enable its continuous operation and win the mission.

Weather

Clear

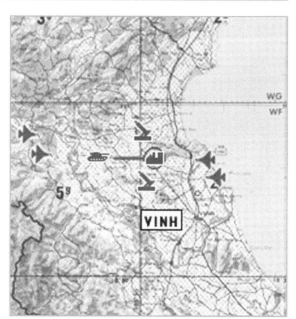

Intel

Targets

Two Blue F-15E fighters

Two Blue F-16C fighters

Threats

N/A

Primary Flights

Corvette

Airframe 2 x F-16C
Task CAP
Target N/A
Loadout AIM-9M

Dodge

Airframe 2 x F-22A
Task CAP
Target N/A
Loadout AIM-9X

Tasking

Corvette and Dodge

Prevent Blue fighters from attacking the Red convoy and secure its way to the base.

Mission Objectives

Corvette and Dodge

1. Ensure that at least one tank reaches the base.

Mission Tips

✦ Keep close to the convoy — do not engage in unnecessary dogfights.

✦ Remember your primary task — intercept planes attacking the convoy even if there are easier targets around.

Commander's Summary

The Blue enemy is disturbing the status quo in the area by trying to control the main road. Our mission is clear and we must perform it boldly. Destroy any Blue airplanes endangering our convoy.

Red Assets

2 X F-16C (Corvette 1-2) PGU-28 (510), Chaff (90), Flare (90), AIM-9M (4)

2 X F-22A (Dodge 1-2) PGU-28 (200), Chaff (120), Flare (60), AIM-9X (2)

Blue Assets

2 X F-15E (Austin 1-2) PGU-28 (250), Chaff (120), Flare (60), AGM-88 (2), AIM-9M (4)

2 X F-16C (Buick 1-2) PGU-28 (510), Chaff (90), Flare (90), AIM-9M (4)

MATCH UP (BLUE)

Destroy the enemy's top-secret B-2 fighter, stored in a bomb-proof shelter. The only way to accomplish this mission is to land at the enemy base, taxi to the shelter and shoot the enemy plane through the shelter door.

Time   1200 HRS

Mission Type

Special Operation

Mission Description

Destroy a strategic Red airplane, stored in a highly protective hangar, and protect the Blue plane located in the Blue home base.

To destroy the plane, Blue planes must land at the Red airbase and shoot the airplane through the hangar door using the gun (press Shift S to use weapons on the ground).

Situation

Both the Blue and the Red side have recently acquired advanced strategic B-2 fighters with nuclear weapon deployment capabilities. Each side holds its B-2 in a specially designed hangar, protecting it from every possible way of attack except one — shooting through the hangar door. To destroy the other side's B-2 the fighters must land at the enemy base, taxi to the hangar, and when reaching a close enough range, shoot the enemy plane though the hangar door using the gun. Both sides have launched aerial attacks on each other's B-2.

Weather

Clear

Intel

Targets

One specially designed B-2 located in an attack-proof hangar at the end of Runway 06 Left in the Red Erding airbase (waypoint 4).

Threats

Two SA-6 batteries protecting the Red airbase — one located west of Erding runways (waypoint 3), the other at an unknown location.

Red F-16C and F-15E fighters are expected to simultaneously attack the Blue base and protect the Red base.

Primary Flights

Austin

Airframe	4 x F-16C
Task	SEAD (Suppression of Enemy Air Defense) & Strike
Target	Red SA-6, Red B-2
Loadout	AIM-9M, AGM-88

Buick

Airframe	4 x F-15E
Task	CAP (Combat Air Patrol)
Target	N/A
Loadout	AIM-9M

Tasking

Austin

Your mission is to locate and destroy the SAM sites protecting the Red Erding base, then land at the base, taxi to the end of Runway 06 Left and destroy the Red B-2 by shooting through the hangar door.

Buick

Your mission is to protect the Blue base against Red fighters attempting to land and destroy the Blue B-2.

Mission Objectives

Austin

1. Destroy the enemy's B-2.

Buick

2. Protect your B-2.

Mission Tips

♣ **Austin.** Try to divide your forces. One plane should try to land at the enemy base, while the others protect him.

Once on the ground, if you are shooting through the hangar door and the B-2 does not explode, get closer to the hanger for a better aim, and don't forget to press Shift S.

♣ **Buick.** Stay close to the home base. Do not engage in unnecessary dogfights.

Commander's Summary

You are actually faced with two separate missions. One is to protect our B-2, and the other is to destroy the enemy's B-2. Divide your forces wisely to achieve the maximum effect.

Please remember to press Shift S to activate your weapons while on the ground.

Blue Assets

4 X F-16C (Austin 1-4) PGU-28 (510), Chaff (90), Flare (90), AGM-88 (2), AIM-9M (2)

4 X F-15E (Buick 1-4) PGU-28 (250), Chaff (120), Flare (60), AIM-9M (1)

B-2 (in hangar)

Red Assets

4 X F-16C (Corvette 1-4) PGU-28 (510), Chaff (90), Flare (90), AGM-88 (2), AIM-9M (2)

4 X F-15E (Dodge 1-4) PGU-28 (250), Chaff (120), Flare (60), AIM-9M (2)

B-2 (in hangar)

MATCH UP (RED)

Destroy the enemy's top-secret B-2 fighter, stored in a bomb-proof shelter. The only way to accomplish this mission is to land at the enemy base, taxi to the shelter and shoot the enemy plane through the shelter door.

Time 1200 HRS

Mission Type

Special Operation

Mission Description

Destroy a strategic Blue airplane, stored in a highly protective hangar, and protect the Red plane located in the Red home base.

To destroy the enemy plane, Red planes must land at the Blue airbase and shoot the airplane through the hangar door using the gun (press [Shift][S] to use weapons on the ground).

Situation

Both the Blue and the Red side have recently acquired advanced strategic B-2 fighters with nuclear weapon deployment capabilities. Each side holds its B-2 in a specially designed hangar, protecting it from every possible way of attack except one — shooting through the hangar door. To destroy the other side's B-2 the fighters must land at the enemy base, taxi to the hangar, and when reaching a close enough range, shoot the enemy plane though the hangar door using the gun. Both sides have launched aerial attacks on each other's B-2.

Weather

Clear

Intel

Targets

One specially designed B-2 located in an attack proof hangar at the end of Runway 27 Right in the Blue Landsberg airbase (waypoint 4).

Threats

Two SA-6 batteries protecting the Blue airbase — one located east of Landsberg runways (waypoint 3), the other at an unknown location.

Blue F-16C and F-15E fighters are expected to simultaneously attack the Red base and protect the Blue base.

Primary Flights

Corvette

Airframe	4 x F-16C
Task	SEAD (Suppression of Enemy Air Defense) & Strike
Target	Blue SA-6, Blue B-2
Loadout	AIM-9M, AGM-88

Dodge

Airframe	4 x F-15E
Task	CAP (Combat Air Patrol)
Target	N/A
Loadout	AIM-9M

Tasking

Corvette

Your mission is to locate and destroy the SAM sites protecting the Blue Landsberg base, then land at the base, taxi to the end of Runway 27 Right and destroy the Red B-2 by shooting through the hangar door.

Dodge

Your mission is to protect the Red base against Blue fighters trying to land and destroy the Red B-2.

Mission Objectives

Corvette

1. Destroy the enemy's B-2.

Dodge

2. Protect your B-2.

Mission Tips

✦ **Corvette.** Try to divide your forces. One plane should try to land at the enemy base, while the others protect him.

Once on the ground, if you are shooting through the hangar door and the B-2 does not explode, get closer to the hanger for a better aim, and don't forget to press ⌈Shift⌉⌈S⌉.

✦ **Dodge.** Stay close to the home base. Do not engage in unnecessary dogfights.

Commander's Summary

You are actually faced with two separate missions. One is to protect our B-2, and the other is to destroy the enemy's B-2. Divide your forces wisely to achieve the maximum effect.

Please remember to press ⌈Shift⌉⌈S⌉ to activate your weapons on the ground.

Red Assets

4 X F-16C (Corvette 1-4) PGU-28 (510), Chaff (90), Flare (90), AGM-88 (2), AIM-9M (2)

4 X F-15E (Dodge 1-4) PGU-28 (250), Chaff (120), Flare (60), AIM-9M (2)

B-2 (in hangar)

Blue Assets

4 X F-16C (Austin 1-4) PGU-28 (510), Chaff (90), Flare (90), AGM-88 (2), AIM-9M (2)

4 X F-15E (Buick 1-4) PGU-28 (250), Chaff (120), Flare (60), AIM-9M (1)

B-2 (in hangar)

HILL 247 (BLUE)

In this mission each side must prevent the other side's convoy from reaching a strategic point, designated Hill 247.

Time   1200 HRS

Mission Type

CAS (Combat Air Support)

Mission Description

Each side should prevent the other side's convoy from reaching Hill 247.

Situation

Hill 247 is a strategic point for ground operations, and the side that captures it first will have an advantage over the other side in the ensuing ground war.

Therefore, two convoys, Red and Blue, are rushing forward to the hill. Each convoy consists of tanks and a mobile SA-6 battery. Each side has two aircraft to try to stop the other side's convoy. Each aircraft has air-to-air missiles, HARM missiles, and CBUs for attacking the convoy.

Our mission is to stop the Red convoy from reaching Hill 247.

Weather

20000' scattered, visibility unlimited

Euphrates River

Intel

Targets

Red Convoy.

Threats

Red F-16.

SA-6.

AAA Gundish, ZSU-23x4.

Primary Flights

Austin

Airframe	F-16C
Task	CAS
Target	Red Convoy
Loadout	AIM-9M, AGM-88, CBU-87

Corvette

Airframe	F-16C
Task	CAS
Target	Red Convoy
Loadout	AIM-9M, AGM-88, CBU-87

Tasking

Austin

You are the leading aircraft and the closest to the convoys.

Corvette

Backup flight if Austin gets shot down or out of ammunition.

Mission Objectives

1. Destroy the Red convoy before they reach Hill 247.

In Addition

✈ Blue convoy reaches Hill 247 and achieves firing positions.

Squadron Commander's Summary

The mission is to stop the convoy. Use your weapons arsenal wisely. Deal with the targets one by one according to their threat — aircraft, SAMs and tanks. Do this and you shall be victorious.

Blue Assets

F-16C (Austin 1) PGU-28 (510), Chaff (120), Flare (90), AGM-88 (2), AIM-9M (2), CBU-87 (6), Small Fuel Tank

F-16C (Corvette 1) PGU-28 (510), Chaff (120), Flare (90), AGM-88 (2), AIM-9M (2), CBU-87 (6), Small Fuel Tank

Red Assets

F-16C (Buick 1) PGU-28 (500), Chaff (120), Flare (90), AGM-88 (2), AIM-9M (2), CBU-87 (6), Small Fuel Tank

F-16C (Dodge 1) PGU-28 (510), Chaff (90), Flare (60), AGM-88 (2), AIM-120 (2), AIM-9M (2), CBU-87 (6), Small Fuel Tank

HILL 247 (RED)

In this mission each side must prevent the other side's convoy from reaching a strategic point, designated Hill 247.

Time 1200 HRS

Euphrates River

Mission Type

CAS (Combat Air Support)

Mission Description

Each side should prevent the other side's convoy from reaching Hill 247.

Situation

Hill 247 is a strategic point for ground operations, and the side that captures it first will have an advantage over the other side in the ensuing ground war.

Therefore, two convoys, Red and Blue, are rushing forward to the hill. Each convoy consists of tanks and a mobile SA-6 battery. Each side has two aircraft to try to stop the other side's convoy. Each aircraft has air-to-air missiles, HARM missiles, and CBUs for attacking the convoy.

Our mission is to stop the Blue convoy from reaching Hill 247.

Weather

20000' scattered, visibility unlimited

Intel

Targets

Blue Convoy.

Threats

Blue F-16.

SA-6.

AAA Gundish, ZSU-23x4.

Primary Flights

Buick

Airframe	F-16C
Task	CAS
Target	N/A
Loadout	AIM-9M, AGM-88, CBU-87

Dodge

Airframe	F-16C
Task	CAS
Target	N/A
Loadout	AIM-9M, AGM-88, CBU-87

Tasking

Buick

You are the leading aircraft and the closest to the convoys.

Dodge

Backup flight if Buick gets shot down or out of ammunition.

Mission Objectives

1. Destroy the Blue convoy before they reach Hill 247.

In Addition

✈ Red convoy reaches Hill 247 and achieves firing positions.

Commander's Summary

The mission is to stop the convoy. Use your weapons arsenal wisely. Deal with the targets one by one according to their threat — aircraft, SAMs and tanks. Do this and you shall be victorious.

Red Assets

F-16C (Buick 1) PGU-28 (500), Chaff (120), Flare (90), AGM-88 (2), AIM-9M (2), CBU-87 (6), Small Fuel Tank

F-16C (Dodge 1) PGU-28 (510), Chaff (90), Flare (60), AGM-88 (2), AIM-120 (2), AIM-9M (2), CBU-87 (6), Small Fuel Tank

Blue Assets

F-16C (Austin 1) PGU-28 (510), Chaff (120), Flare (90), AGM-88 (2), AIM-9M (2), CBU-87 (6), Small Fuel Tank

F-16C (Corvette 1) PGU-28 (510), Chaff (120), Flare (90), AGM-88 (2), AIM-9M (2), CBU-87 (6), Small Fuel Tank

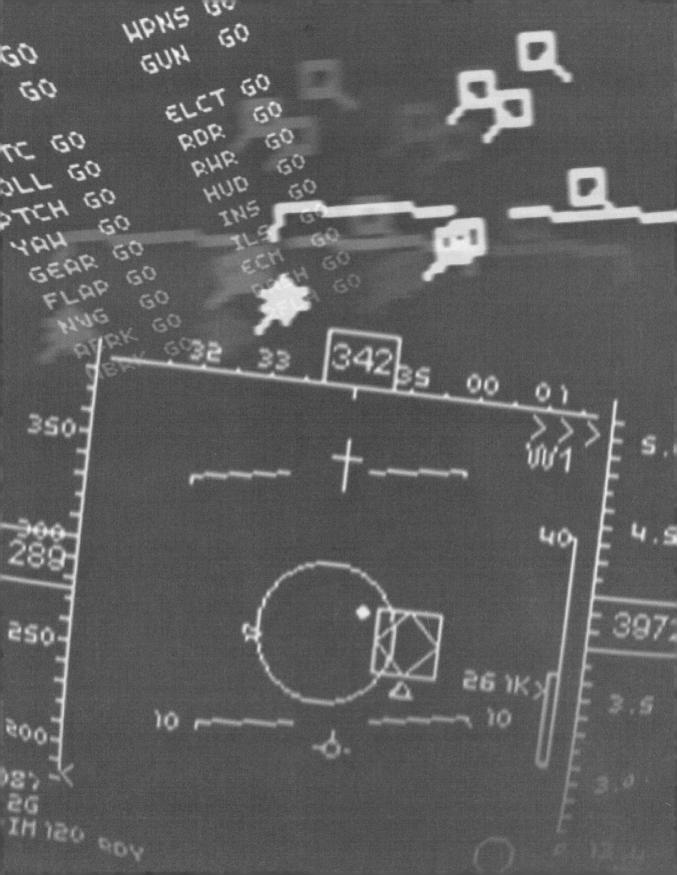

44T

400

350

10

10

HISTORICAL CAMPAIGNS
Desert Storm
Vietnam

M6S8

IM9M

2

120

K84

T10

AIM9M

20NT

GUN 1000

4 X MRM

3 X SRM

DESERT STORM

FIRST KILL

On 17 January, the first night of the war, an F-15C flight of the 58th TFS, 33rd TFW, took off and scored the first A/A kill in Desert Storm — a MiG-29 Fulcrum.

Date 17 JAN 1991

Time 0520 HRS

Mission Type

CAP (Combat Air Patrol)

Mission Description

Provide CAP for USAF strikers in Baghdad.

Situation

It's the first night of 'Desert Storm.' Numerous strikes are taking place over the Baghdad area. Austin, a 4-ship flight of F-15Cs, is flying CAP south of the city, in case Iraqi fighters take off and threaten coalition strike packages.

Weather

20,000' scattered, unlimited visibility with a full moon

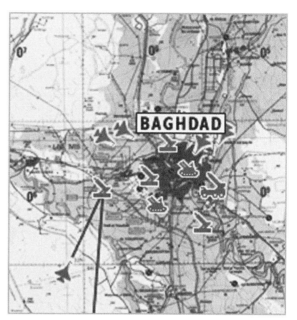

Intel

Targets

N/A

Threats

The Baghdad area is defended by SA-2, SA-3, SA-6, and Roland SAMs.

ZSU-23x4 'Gun Dish' AAA vehicles are also present.

MiG-29 and Mirage F-1 fighters are likely to scramble from all Iraqi airfields.

Primary Flights

Austin

Airframe   4 x F-15C
Task   CAP
Target   N/A
Loadout   AIM-9M, AIM-7F

Supporting Flights

T-bird

Airframe   2 x F-117A
Task   Strike
Target   Strategic Sites
Loadout   GBU-27

Stingray

Airframe   2 x F-111F
Task   Strike
Target   Strategic Sites
Loadout   AIM-9M, Mk 83

Ford

Airframe   2 x F-117A
Task   Strike
Target   Strategic Sites
Loadout   GBU-27

Olds

Airframe   2 x F-4G
Task   SEAD
Target   SA-6 sites
Loadout   AGM-88, AIM-7M, Mk 82

Shell

Airframe   KC-135R
Task   Tanker
Target   N/A
Loadout   N/A

Buckeye

Airframe   E-3C AWACS
Task   AWACS
Target   N/A
Loadout   N/A

Tasking

Austin

Fly CAP over waypoint 1, south of the city. Receive tasking from AWACS if any Iraqi fighters scramble against our forces.

T-Bird, Stingray and Ford (non-controllable)

Strike various strategic targets in and around Baghdad.

Olds (non-controllable)

Perform SAM strikes in the vicinity of Baghdad.

Mission Objectives

Austin

1. Shoot down all Iraqi aircraft (up to 7).

Mission Tips

✈ To accomplish this mission you must avoid the SAM-defended zone. You can see it on your JTIDS as a red circle.

✈ Use radar missiles for long-range shooting and heat missiles for close range.

✈ Use ⑴ to toggle between your A/A weapons.

✈ Utilize your wingmen by using wingman commands:

Alt E "Engage My Target," to send your wingmen to the target you are locked onto.

Alt W "Engage The Other One," to send your wingmen to another target of the same class as yours.

Alt P "Protect Me," to send your wingmen to your nearest threat.

✈ Use F11 to watch your missiles.

✈ Don't forget to use your wingmen.

Commander's Summary

We want zero casualties. If you're intercepted by Iraqis, take them out. We have longer-range missiles than they do. Be very careful to identify friend from foe with the IFF TD Box indicator. There are a lot of friendly aircraft out there. Let's do this right. Good hunting!

Assets & Opposition

Assets

4 X F15C (Austin 1-4) PGU-28 (600), Chaff (120), Flare (120), AIM-7F (4), AIM-9M (4), Fuel Tank

2 X F111F (Stingray 1-2) PGU-28 (500), Chaff (60), Flare (30), AIM-9M (2), Mk 83 (12)

2 X F117A (Ford 1-2) Chaff (80), Flare (60), GBU-27 (2)

2 X F117A (T-bird 1-2) Chaff (80), Flare (60), GBU-27 (2)

F-4G (Olds 1) M61 Vulcan (510), Chaff (90), Flare (60), AGM-88 (2), AIM-7M (4), Mk 82 (6)

F-4G (Olds 2) M61 Vulcan (510), Chaff (90), Flare (60), AGM-88 (2), AIM-7M (4), Mk 82 (12)

KC-135R (Shell)

E-3C (Buckeye)

Opposition Aircraft

2 X F-1 GSh-301 (301), Chaff (30), Flare (30), AA-8 (2)

F-1 GSh-301 (300), Chaff (60), Flare (60)

F-1 30mm (300), Chaff (60), Flare (30)

MiG-29 GSh-301 (300), Chaff (60), Flare (60), AA-10 (2)

5 X MiG-29 GSh-301 (300), Chaff (60), Flare (60), AA-8 (2)

SHOWDOWN

17 January 1991 marked the start of the Desert Storm air campaign. USAF forces attacked air defenses and other strategic facilities in Baghdad, showing the world the devastating effectiveness of superior technology. You now have a chance to participate in this historical attack.

Date   17 JAN 1991

Time   0230 HRS

Mission Type

Interdiction, Strike, SEAD (Suppression of Enemy Air Defense)

Mission Description

Strike Iraqi defense systems and key targets in and around Baghdad.

Situation

It is the opening night of 'Desert Storm.' The Coalition forces' goal is to knock out strategic facilities in the Baghdad area.

Weather

Clear, with unlimited visibility

Intel

Targets

USAF fighters will target strategic facilities in the vicinity of Baghdad. These will be the ITC (Iraqi Telecommunications) building, the Baghdad TV station, and the Scud HQ site.

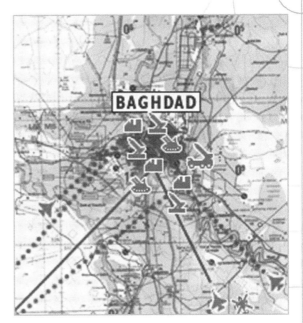

Threats

The Baghdad area is defended by a heavy SAM belt, which consists of SA-2, SA-3, SA-6, Roland and various AAA vehicles.

Iraqi MiG-29s and Mirage F-1s are on 5-minute alert. We don't know if they will be scrambled against us.

ITC TV Station

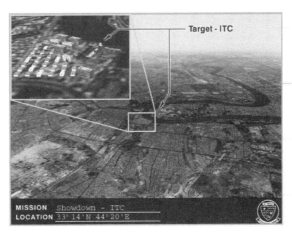

MISSION   Showdown - ITC
LOCATION 33° 14'N 44° 20'E

Scud HQ building

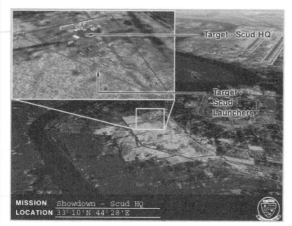

MISSION Showdown - Scud HQ
LOCATION 33°10'N 44°28'E

AT&T Building

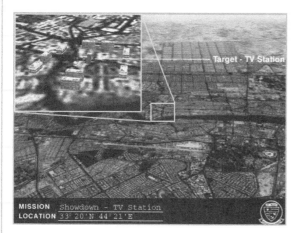

MISSION Showdown - TV Station
LOCATION 33°20'N 44°21'E

Primary Flights

Austin

Airframe	2 x F-16C
Task	SEAD + Strike
Target	SA-6 site, ITC
Loadout	AGM-88, GBU-12D, AIM-9M, AIM-120

Buick

Airframe	2 x F-117A
Task	Strike
Target	TV station
Loadout	GBU-27

Corvette

Airframe	2 x F-15E
Task	Strike
Target	Scud HQ
Loadout	AGM-88, GBU-24, CBU-93, AIM-9M, AIM-120

Supporting Flights

Normandy

Airframe	4 x Apache AH-64A
Task	Strike
Target	EWR site
Loadout	Hellfire

Ford

Airframe	F-111F
Task	Strike
Target	Electric Plant
Loadout	AIM-9L, Mk 83

Olds

Airframe	F-15E
Task	Strike
Target	Oil Refinery
Loadout	AIM-120, AIM-9M, Mk 84, CBU-93

T-bird

Airframe F-117A
Task Strike
Target Sadaam International Airfield
Loadout Mk 84

Stingray

Airframe F-117A
Task Strike
Target Communication Center
Loadout Mk84

Texaco

Airframe KC-135R
Task Tanker
Target N/A
Loadout N/A

Buckeye

Airframe E-3C AWACS
Task AWACS
Target N/A
Loadout N/A

Tasking

The first missile in the campaign will be launched by Task Force Normandy: AH-64 Apache helicopters from Al Jouf. The force will destroy an Iraqi EWR (Early Warning Radar) site.

Austin

You will be five miles behind Normandy, providing cover from Iraqi fighters and SAMs.

Launch two AGM-88 HARM radar-seeking missiles at the two SA-6 sites en route to the ITC building. These are not primary mission objectives.

After that, switch to laser-guided munitions, GBU-12D, and launch one bomb on the Iraqi Telecommunication Center building, dubbed the AT&T Building. It is located at waypoint 2. You have two GBU-12D bombs, and you must destroy the building.

Austin 2 will target the AAA site near the building.

After finishing task, egress to waypoint 3.

Buick

Locate the TV station at waypoint 2. Destroy it using GBU-27 laser bombs.

After the target is destroyed, egress to waypoint 3.

Corvette

Your target is the fixed Scud HQ, south of the city, located at waypoint 2.

Launch AGM-88 missiles at any SAM site in the vicinity, and then drop a GBU-24 laser-guided bomb on the main Scud HQ, designated by a 'T' on your HUD.

After the target is destroyed, use CBU-93 cluster bombs to destroy the Scud launchers, one mile south of the HQ building. After hitting the targets, egress to waypoint 3.

All aircraft are equipped with night vision systems.

There are other flights in and around the city.

Mission Objectives

Austin

1. Destroy AT&T Building.

Buick

2. Destroy ITC TV Station.

Corvette

3. Destroy Scud HQ building.

4. Destroy Scud launchers.

Mission Tips

✦ After completing a flight's objective, press [Shift][1]/[Shift][2]/[Shift][3]/[Shift][4] to switch to the next flight: Austin/Buck/Corvette/Dodge.

✦ At mission start you can lock onto the choppers and watch them perform their job by pressing [F4].

✦ Press [Ctrl][N] to turn on Night Vision.

✦ Find the ITC building by switching to Ground Radar ([R]) and selecting Map Mode ([Q]). Select the GBU-12 bomb by pressing [↑].

✦ Make sure that you are locked onto the correct building, by pressing [F4]. This will allow you to view your current radar target.

✦ All targets have a 'T' marking on the HUD.

✦ Use Object ID in the Preferences if you're not sure about what target to hit.

✦ **Austin.** Hit the second SA-6 site that comes up on HARM MFD.

✦ **Buick.** Do not lose altitude. There's a lot of AAA at the target.

✦ **Corvette.** Don't forget to use your HARMs to take out SAMs and AAA.

Commander's Summary

Well, this is it. We've trained, waited, trained, and waited some more. Now it's our turn. The President sends his good luck and best wishes to all of us about to go to war in the Gulf, so let's do this right. We don't know how the Iraqis will react, so be prepared for surprises. I don't want any heroes here today, just pros. We go in, do our job and get the hell out. If the Iraqis try to engage us, well, that's their tough luck. Give them their wishes and help them die for their country.

Assets

2 X F-16C (Austin 1-2) PGU-28 (510), Chaff (90), Flare (60), 2100lb (1), AGM-88 (2), AIM-120 (2), AIM-9M (2), GBU-12D (2)

2 X F-117A (Buick 1-2) Chaff (80), Flare (60), GBU-27 (2)

F-15E (Corvette 1) PGU-28 (600), Chaff (120), Flare (60), AGM-88 (2), AIM-9M (2), CBU-93 (4), GBU-24 (3)

F-15E (Corvette 2) PGU-28 (600), Chaff (120), Flare (60), AGM-88 (2), AIM-120 (2), CBU-93 (4), GBU-24 (3)

4 X AH-64A (Normandy 1-4) 30mm (500), Chaff (50), Flare (50), Hellfire (8)

F-111F (Ford) 30mm (200), Chaff (90), Flare (60), AIM-9L (2), Mk 83 (8)

F-111F (Olds) PGU-28 (600), Chaff (120), Flare (90), AIM-120 (2), AIM-9M (2), CBU-93 (4), Mk 84 (3)

F-117A (T-bird) PGU-28 (500), Chaff (80), Flare (60), Mk 84 (2)

F-117A (Stingray) PGU-28 (500), Chaff (80), Flare (60), Mk 84 (2)

KC-135R (Texaco)

E-3C (Buckeye)

4 X F-15E (Hawk 1-4) PGU-28 (250), Chaff (120), Flare (60), AIM-120 (2), AIM-9M (2), CBU-93 (4), Mk 84 (2)

2 X F-117A (Sky 1-2) Chaff (80), Flare (60), Mk 84 (2)

F-16C (York 1) PGU-28 (510), Chaff (90), Flare (90), 2100lb (1), AIM-120 (2), AIM-9M (2), CBU-87 (12)

3 X F-16C (York 2-4) PGU-28 (510), Chaff (90), Flare (90), 2100lb (1), AIM-120 (2), AIM-9M (2), CBU-87 (6), Mk 83 (6)

No Opposition Aircraft

WHERE IT HURTS MOST

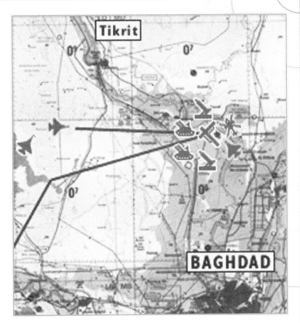

Along with the F-117 attacks on Baghdad in the early morning hours of the first and second day of Desert Storm, other packages struck airfields throughout Iraq. In this mission you will take part in one of these sorties, striking Balad Airbase north of Baghdad.

Date   17 JAN 1991

Time   1200 HRS

Mission Type

Airfield Strike

Mission Description

Strike Balad Airfield, north of Baghdad.

Situation

Along with the massive air strikes on Baghdad, other strike packages are being sent to Iraqi airfields in an attempt to cripple Iraq's air power and gain air superiority. This attack is directed at Balad Airfield, just north of Baghdad.

Weather

20,000' scattered, visibility unlimited

Intel

Targets

Balad Airfield is home to MiG-29 fighters, helicopters and transport squadrons. It also contains other valuable targets.

The northern fuel depot is a distinctive fuel tank, located in the northern part of the airfield. The runway intersection must be hit in order to stop activity in the airfield. All aircraft in the two flight lines must be destroyed, as well as the eastern control tower. Note that the western tower is a dummy.

Threats

The Iraqis will most likely scramble their fighters once they realize that the airfield itself is our target. The SAM and AAA crews will also be scrambled to action. The airfield is defended by SA-3 and SA-6 SAMs. Mirage F-1 and MiG-29s are on alert. Massive AAA is expected.

Balad Airfield

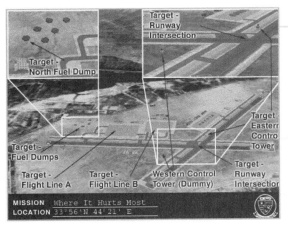

Primary Flights

Austin

Airframe	4 x F-16C
Task	SEAD, Strike
Target	Runway intersection, SAMs
Loadout	AGM-88, Mk 84, AIM-9M, AIM-7M

Buick

Airframe	4 x F-15E
Task	CAP, Strike
Target	Fuel Depots
Loadout	Mk 84, AIM-120, AIM-9M

Corvette

Airframe	4 x A-10A
Task	Strike
Target	Flight Line A, Flight Line B, Control Tower
Loadout	AGM-65B, CBU-87

Supporting Flights

Olds

Airframe	2 x F-15C
Task	Sweep
Target	N/A
Loadout	N/A

Buckeye

Airframe	E-3C AWACS
Task	AWACS
Target	N/A
Loadout	N/A

Shell

Airframe	KC-135R
Task	Tanker
Target	N/A
Loadout	N/A

Tasking

Austin

Approach the airfield and launch HARM missiles at the SAM sites.

Pull up and strike the runway intersection. After hitting, egress to waypoint 3 and clear the target area for Buick.

Buick

Perform a fighter sweep, strike the Fuel Dumps, and remain on CAP above the airfield, covering Corvette. Buick 1 will target the Northern Fuel Depot. Buick 2, 3, and 4 will target the others.

Corvette

Enter target area and take out all aircraft on flight lines A & B, as well as the Eastern Control Tower.

Mission Objectives

Austin

1. Destroy the runway intersection.

Buick

2. Destroy the fuel depot.

Corvette

3. Destroy all aircraft in flight line A.

4. Destroy all aircraft in flight line B.

5. Destroy the eastern control tower.

Mission Tips

✦ To launch an AGM-88 (HARM) anti-radiation missile, toggle A/G armament using [ ] until 'AGM-88' is displayed on your HUD.

✦ When the right MFD shows 'In Range,' at about 10 miles from target, you can launch the radar-homing missile. Press [Ctrl][Enter] to toggle targets in the HARM display.

- You may load Buick with Mk 84 iron bombs instead of the GBU-24 laser bombs to strike the fuel dumps.

- The AGM-65B 'Maverick' locks onto the target that the radar, in Map mode, is currently locked onto. If this is the desired target, just press the pickle! You can view the missile flight with F11.

- You may also optically lock onto the target with the AGM-65. To do this, press Z to bring the MFD to full screen. Using Ctrl +joystick, position the crosshairs over the desired target until the optical eye locks onto the contrast.

- The best way to avoid AAA is to stay high above its firing range.

- **Austin.** You can bomb the runway and the tower in one pass.

- **Buick.** Take extra bombs for the pass on the fuel tanks.

- **Corvette.** Use cluster bombs to bomb the flight lines.

Commander's Summary

A lot of aircraft are going to attack Balad Airfield today in close intervals. Keep your eyes open for each other. We don't need any accidents today.

Assets & Opposition

Assets

F-16C (Austin 1) PGU-28 (510), Chaff (100), Flare (80), AGM-88 (2), AIM-7M (2), AIM-9M (2), Mk 84 (3)

F-16C (Austin 2,4) PGU-28 (510), Chaff (90), Flare (60), AIM-7M (2), AIM-9M (2), Mk 84 (3)

F-16C (Austin 3) PGU-28 (510), Chaff (90), Flare (90), AGM-88 (1), AIM-7M (2), AIM-9M (2), Mk 84 (3)

2 X F-15E (Buick 1-2) PGU-28 (600), Chaff (120), Flare (60), AIM-120 (4), AIM-9M (2), Mk 84 (3)

2 X F-15E (Buick 3-4) PGU-28 (600), Chaff (120), Flare (60), AIM-120 (4), AIM-9M (4), Mk 84 (3)

4 X A-10A (Corvette 1-4) PGU-14B (600), Chaff (90), Flare (60), AGM-65B (8), AIM-9M (4), CBU-87 (2), Fuel Tank

2 X F-15C (Olds 1-2) PGU-28 (600), Chaff (90), Flare (60), Fuel Tank

KC-135R (Shell)

E-3C (Buckeye)

Opposition Aircraft

4 X F-1 30mm (600), Chaff (60), Flare (60), AA-8 (2)

MiG-23 GSh-301 (100), Chaff (40), Flare (20), AA-8 (4)

MiG-23 GSh-301 (100), Chaff (40), Flare (20), AA-6 (2), AA-8 (2)

3 X MiG-23 GSh-301 (100), Chaff (40), Flare (20), AA-8 (2)

MiG-23 GSh-301 (300), Chaff (40), Flare (20), AA-8 (4)

MiG-23 GSh-301 (300), Chaff (40), Flare (20), AA-8 (2)

MiG-29 GSh-301 (301), AA-10 (4), AA-11 (4)

2 X MiG-29 GSh-301 (300), Chaff (60), Flare (60), AA-8 (4)

2 X MiG-29 GSh-301 (300), Chaff (60), Flare (60)

2 X MiG-29 GSh-301 (300), Chaff (60), Flare (60), AA-8 (2)

5 X MiG-29 GSh-301 (300), Chaff (60), Flare (60), AA-10 (4), AA-8 (4)

2 X Mi-8

2 X Mi-24

2 X Il-76

SCUD BUSTING

Hitting Scud surface-to-surface missile launchers was a major USAF task in Desert Storm, and a difficult one at that. Scuds are very hard to locate when camouflaged. They operate mostly at night, and never stay in one place for long. In this mission, USAF Strike Eagles will locate and destroy several of these launchers located in Western Iraq. If at all possible, get them before they fire their missiles.

Date 19 JAN 1991

Time 0530 HRS

Mission Type

Strike

Mission Description

Destroy mobile Scud ballistic-missile launchers.

Situation

Iraqi Scuds have been hitting civilian targets in Saudi Arabia and Israel, as well as US forces stationed in the area. The Iraqi tactics are to hide the Scud launchers by day, pull them out at night for firing and run to a camouflaged hiding site. The launchers are constantly on the move between their refueling area and the launch area, and should be hit before they launch.

Several British SAS Special Forces are out in the desert and will assist in pinpointing and designating the targets.

We'll orbit near the IP (Initial Point), and wait for the ground force guidance. Once contact is made, the best way to locate the launcher is to lock onto a laser spot initiated by a UAV or Special Ops commando. If that is not available we will use our Ground Map radar to find the launcher.

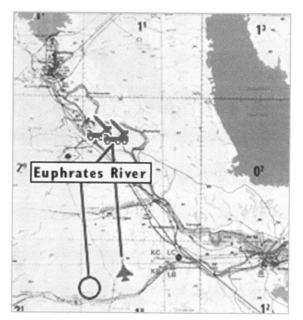

Euphrates River

Weather

10000' scattered, unlimited visibility

Intel

Targets

The Scud launchers are mobile and their location is currently unknown.

Threats

Possible Iraqi fighters of all types. Possible AAA integral defense at the Scud launch area.

Primary Flights

Austin

Airframe	4 x F-15E
Task	Strike
Target	Scud Site
Loadout	GBU-12, AIM-120, AIM-9M

Supporting Flights

Buckeye

Airframe E-3C AWACS

Task AWACS

Target N/A

Loadout N/A

Tasking

Austin

Ingress from the south towards the target area, and receive directions from the British SAS Special Forces. The force will laser-designate the targets, so you can pick them up on your LANTIRN system.

Destroy the targets using LGBs and Mk 20 'Rockeye' cluster bombs. If you can't destroy the launcher before it launches, destroy it afterwards, so that the Iraqis won't be able to launch again.

Mission Objectives

Austin

1. Destroy two Scud sites.

2. No Scud may launch.

In Addition

♣ Two Mi-8s must be destroyed.

Mission Tips

♣ Once the ground force reports that it is designating the targets, look for the target designation symbol on your HUD.

Your LANTIRN system will slave to the designated target.

Switch to GBU-12 bombs (Press ⌷), approach the target, and drop the laser bomb on the target area. The bomb will home on the laser spot and hit.

♣ You can also search for ground targets by selecting Ground radar (R), and toggling the various modes by pressing Q.

♣ View the target by pressing F4 .

♣ If you see that the launcher is erect, it means the missile is about to be launched. This is a high-priority target!

♣ Be careful of the ZSU-23 by the second Scud. Wait for the first Scud to slow down and stop before you attack.

Commander's Summary

It's another night of this frustrating job of looking for a needle in a haystack. Don't give up. We're flying the best aircraft in the world for this mission, using the latest technologies. Stay alert, and let's try to find those suckers.

Assets & Opposition

Assets

F-15E (Austin 1-4) PGU-28 (600), Chaff (60), Flare (60), AIM-120 (2), AIM-9M (2), Fuel Tank (3), GBU-12 (12)

E-3C (Buckeye)

Opposition Aircraft

2 X MiG-29 GSh-301 (301), Chaff (60), Flare (60), AA-10 (4), AA-11 (4)

2 X Mi-8

WARTHOG TO THE RESCUE

On January 21st, 1991, Lt. Devon (Devil) Jones and his back-seater, Lt. Harry (Snake) Slade, bailed out of their F-14 Tomcat during an escort mission, after being hit by an SA-2 missile. After a short time, a heroic rescue mission starring two Special Ops MH-53J helicopters was underway. The helicopters got to the area 2 hours after the ejection. Enemy MiGs came out for them but were chased out by RESCAP F-15 Eagles. Lt. Jones was brought safely home. Lt. Slade was not located and was taken prisoner.

Date   21 JAN 1991
Time   1630 HRS

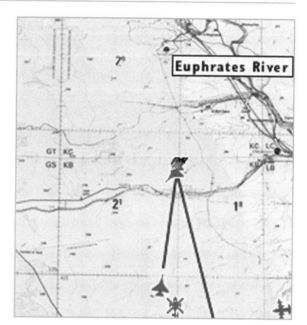

Mission Type

SAR (Search and Rescue)

Mission Description

Rescue a downed F-14 crew.

Situation

An F-14 went down this morning after being hit by an SA-2 missile, north of the Amman-Baghdad road. An A-10 flight will try to contact the downed jocks. Two Pave Low helicopters will do the pick-up, and a pair of Eagles will provide CAP over the rescue area. The Eagles will dispatch any enemy fighters nearing the rescue area, and the A-10 Warthogs will take care of any ground threats. The downed pilot's callsign is Slate 4-6 Alpha. The Radar Intercept Officer (RIO) is Slate 4-6 Bravo.

Weather

Clear, with unlimited visibility

Intel

Targets

N/A

Threats

Possible air threats such as MiG-29 and Mirage F-1 fighters.

Various AAA are scattered around the area. The downed pilot is vulnerable to any ground threat.

Primary Flights

Austin

Airframe   2 x A-10A
Task   CAS, SAR
Target   N/A
Loadout   AGM-65B, AIM-9M

Buick

Airframe   4 x F-15C
Task   Escort.
Target   N/A
Loadout   AIM-9M, AIM-7F

Supporting Flights

Pave Low
Airframe   2 x MH-53J
Task   SAR
Target   N/A
Loadout   N/A

Shell
Airframe   KC-135R
Task   Tanker
Target   N/A
Loadout   N/A

Buckeye
Airframe   E-3C AWACS
Task   AWACS
Target   N/A
Loadout   N/A

Tasking

Austin
Keep the path of the Pave Lows' clear of ground threats.

Pay attention to the radio during the flight — it will assist you to understand which threats are the most dangerous to the SAR helicopters.

Buick
Clear out all enemy MiGs from the rescue area.

Mission Objectives

Austin
1. Protect the Pave Low SAR helicopter from all ground threats.

Buick
2. Protect the Pave Low SAR helicopter from all ground threats.

Mission Tips
+ In this mission you should switch between Austin and Buick according to the relevant threat.

+ AGM-65B, or 'Maverick,' locks onto the target that the radar, in Map mode, is locked onto (view the target by pressing F4).

+ If this is the desired target, just press pickle! You can view the missile flight by pressing F11 .

+ You may also lock optically onto the target with the AGM-65. To do this, press Z to bring the MFD to full screen. Press Ctrl and move the joystick to point at the desired target with the crosshairs, till the optical eye locks onto the contrast.

+ Use your wingmen wisely.

+ **Austin.** Save 1 AGM-65 from your stores for a surprise.

+ **Buick.** Save some AIM-7s for a later use.

Commander's Summary
Two of our Navy buds are down and need help fast. Slate 4-6 Alpha is out there counting on you. Keep in mind that you may be in his position tomorrow, so don't let him down.

Assets & Opposition

Assets
2 X A-10A (Austin 1-2) PGU-14B (500), Chaff (100), Flare (80), AGM-65B (8), AIM-9M (4), Fuel Tank

4 X F-15C (Buick 1-2) PGU-28 (600), Chaff (90), Flare (60), AIM-7F (4), AIM-9M (4), Fuel Tank

2 X MH-53J (Pave Low 1-2)

E-3C (Buckeye)

KC-135R (Shell)

Opposition Aircraft
2 X MiG-29   GSh-301 (300), Chaff (60), Flare (60), AA-10 (2), AA-8 (2)

2 X MiG-23   GSh-301 (300), Chaff (40), Flare (20), AA-8 (2)

4 X F-1 GSh-301 (600), Chaff (60), Flare (60), AA-8 (2)

2 X Mi-24 30mm (480), Chaff (30), Flare (30), Rocket (20)

HEAVY METAL

One of the primary missions in Desert Storm was HVAA (High Value Airborne Asset) protection. In this mission, F-15C Eagles of the 58th TFS/33RD TFW perform an escort mission, defending two high value assets — an E-3 Sentry AWACS and a KC-135 Stratotanker.

Date 25 JAN 1991

Time 1200 HRS

Mission Type

Escort

Mission Description

HVAA (High Value Airborne Asset) protection. Defend two precious aircraft: an E-3C Sentry AWACS and a KC-135 Stratotanker.

Situation

Coalition strikes are still going on in the Baghdad area. Austin and Buick's mission is to provide cover for the E-3C Sentry AWACS, and the KC-135 tanker.

Weather

10000' scattered, 12000' broken, unlimited visibility below

Intel

Targets

N/A

Threats

Iraqi MiG-23s and MiG-25s. Possible MiG-29s and Mirage F-1s.

SAM and AAA are surrounding the city of Baghdad.

Primary Flights

Austin

Airframe 4 x F-15C
Task Escort
Target N/A
Loadout AIM-9L, AIM-7F

Buick

Airframe 4 x F-15C
Task Escort
Target N/A
Loadout AIM-9L, AIM-7F

Supporting Flights

Buckeye

Airframe E-3C AWACS
Task AWACS
Target N/A
Loadout N/A

Shell

Airframe KC-135R
Task Tanker
Target N/A
Loadout N/A

Tasking

Austin

Provide escort and cover for the E-3 AWACS south of Baghdad.

Buick

Provide escort and cover for the KC-135 tanker west of Baghdad.

Mission Objectives

Austin

1. AWACS must survive.

Buick

2. KC-135 must survive.

Austin and Buick

3. All enemy fighters (up to 10) must be destroyed.

Mission Tips

✈ If you lock onto a friendly aircraft you will see an 'X' on the TD (Target Designation) Box on your HUD.

✈ **Austin and Buick.** Engage early to keep the MiGs from attacking AWACS.

Commander's Summary

OK, the war goes on. Let's do our escort, keep your eyes and ears open, and if any Iraqi gets the idea to intercept any of our forces, show them why it's a mistake. Their last mistake.

Assets & Opposition

Assets

4 X F-15C (Austin 1-4) PGU-28 (600), Chaff (60), Flare (60), AIM-7F (4), AIM-9L (4), Fuel Tank

4 X F-15C (Buick 1-4) PGU-28 (600), Chaff (60), Flare (60), AIM-7F (4), AIM-9L (4), Fuel Tank

E-3C (Buckeye)
KC-135R (Shell)

Opposition Aircraft

MiG-29 GSh-301 (300), Chaff (60), Flare (60), AA-8 (2)

5 X MiG-29 GSh-301 (300), Chaff (60), Flare (60), AA-10 (2), AA-8 (2)

2 X MiG-29 GSh-301 (500), Chaff (60), Flare (60)

2 X MiG-23 GSh-301 (300), Chaff (60), Flare (60), AA-8 (2)

KILLER SCOUTS

During Desert Storm, some F-16 Pilots were tasked with a specialized mission. They flew near Iraqi tank concentrations, pinpointed the valuable targets among the dead ones, and directed other flights to strike them. They were nicknamed "Killer Scouts." In this mission you are to locate these targets, communicate with the scouts, and hit those targets hard.

Date   10 FEB 1991

Time   1700 HRS

Mission Type

CAS

Mission Description

Destroy Iraqi ground targets, located by F-16C Fighting Falcons.

Situation

The Iraq-Kuwait border area is scattered with hundreds of small mobile targets — tanks, artillery and AAAs. Many of the targets are of high value, but it is hard to determine the valuable ones from the junk. Another problem is that when pilots hit the targets, it is hard to tell from the air if they have been destroyed due to their small size.

The tactic we are going to use today is to send out F-16C Falcon fighters as "Killer Scouts," to the area of the Baghdad-Amman road, where Iraqi tank reinforcements are on their way to the front. The Vipers will take the role usually performed by the O/A-10s. They will fly low and fast and locate the valuable targets. They will relay their position to us, and we'll go in for the kill with bombs or Mavericks.

Weather

10000' scattered, with unlimited visibility

Intel

Targets

Iraqi armor such as T-55, T-62, and T-72 tanks.

Threats

ZSU-23X4 AAA. Probable Iraqi MiG-23s.

Primary Flights

Austin

Airframe	4 x A-10A
Task	Strike
Target	Iraqi armor
Loadout	AGM-65B, AIM-9M, Mk 82

Buick

Airframe	4 x F-16C
Task	Strike
Target	Iraqi armor
Loadout	AGM-65B, Mk 84, AIM-9L, AIM-7M

Supporting Flights

Scout 1
Airframe 2 x F-16C
Task Scout
Target N/A
Loadout AIM-9L

Shell
Airframe KC-135R
Task Tanker
Target N/A
Loadout N/A

Buckeye
Airframe E-3C AWACS
Task AWACS
Target N/A
Loadout N/A

Tasking

Austin

Ingress from the south, receive directions from Scout 1, and destroy the targets that you receive from him using AGM-65B Mavericks. The targets you receive from the Scout are top priority, regardless of their type.

If you locate any other mobile targets you may destroy them as well. There might be targets that are already hit so don't waste time and armament on them. You can use your guns if necessary, but watch out for ZSU-23X4 'Gundish' AAA.

Buick

Ingress from the south and refuel from Shell (while you fly Austin formation). After that, ingress to target area, and attack the command vehicles located in the small base at waypoint 3.

Mission Objectives

Austin and Buick

1. All the targets given by the Scout 1 must be destroyed. (There may be as many as five targets.) The rest are a bonus.

Mission Tips

✈ Press Ctrl R to start the refueling process, and switch to Refuel mode.

✈ Press A twice in Refuel mode to engage the auto refuel.

✈ Cluster bombs are better than Mk-82s.

✈ **Austin.** Many tanks are a bonus. Watch out for the SA-8 by the campsite.

✈ **Buick.** You can use your wingmen to engage the MiGs while you take the ground targets.

Commander's Summary

Pay attention to the Scouts' directions — they're watching the targets and the guns. There are lots of destroyed targets around the live ones, so double-check that the target you're about to blow away is the one the Scouts want killed. Use your radar in Map mode for verification.

Assets & Opposition

Assets

A-10A (Austin 1) PGU-14B (1200), Chaff (60), Flare (60), AGM-65B (8), AIM-9M (4), Mk 82 (4)

A-10A (Austin 2) PGU-14B (1198), Chaff (100), Flare (80), AGM-65B (8), AIM-9M (4), Mk 82 (4)

A-10A (Austin 3) PGU-14B (1000), Chaff (100), Flare (80), AGM-65B (8), AIM-9M (4), Mk 82 (4)

A-10A (Austin 4) PGU-14B (1000), Chaff (100), Flare (80), AGM-65B (7), AGM-65D (1), AIM-9M (4), Mk 82 (4)

4 X F-16C (Buick 1-4) PGU-28 (510), Chaff (90), Flare (90), AGM-65B (12), AIM-7M (2), AIM-9L (2), Mk 84 (1)

2 X F16C (Scout 1 1-2) PGU-28 (510), Chaff (90), Flare (60), AIM-9L (2)

Opposition Aircraft

6 X MiG-23 GSh-301 (100), Chaff (40), Flare (20), AA-6 (2), AA-8 (2)

RUNAWAYS

On the final days of the air campaign, Iraqi pilots started pointing their aircraft east and fleeing to Iran. So far, about 150 Iraqi aircraft have been flown to Iran during the war. This mission's targets are the Iraqi runaway aircraft.

Date   28 JAN 1991
Time   1200 HRS

BAGHDAD

Mission Type

CAP (Combat Air Patrol)

Mission Description

Shoot down Iraqi aircraft fleeing for Iran.

Situation

At this stage of the operation, desperate Iraqi pilots are trying to fly their aircraft to Iran. They prefer doing so rather than being shot down by coalition fighters or being executed by Saddam's men. USAF aircraft will CAP west of Baghdad in an attempt to locate these aircraft. Takeoff is expected from Balad Airfield, and Baghdad International Airfield. All airfields are north of the CAP points. You are strictly forbidden to cross latitude line 44' 40". This is getting close to Iranian territory and a major issue is to keep Iran out of the game for now.

Weather

10000' scattered, with unlimited visibility

Intel

Targets

N/A

Threats

Probable MiG-29s, Mirage F-1 fighters, and Su-24 bombers amongst the escaping flights. Enemy runaway fighters are expected to react offensively

if challenged. Around the Iranian border are multiple, highly efficient SAM sites. Stay out of their firing envelope.

Primary Flights

Austin

Airframe	4 x F-15C
Task	CAP
Target	N/A
Loadout	AIM-9L, AIM-7M

Buick

Airframe	4 x F-15C
Task	CAP
Target	N/A
Loadout	AIM-9L, AIM-7M

Supporting Flights

Shell

Airframe	KC-135R
Task	Tanker
Target	N/A
Loadout	N/A

Buckeye

Airframe E-3C AWACS
Task AWACS
Target N/A
Loadout N/A

Tasking

Austin

Orbit west of Baghdad.

Engage as many Iraqi aircraft as you can before they cross the border. If five or more bandits reach the border you will fail the mission. You will receive a message from AWACS when the amount of aircraft has exceeded the allowed limit.

Notice that you are NOT ALLOWED to chase the bandits across the border. If you do, you may be hit by the SAMs defending the border, and you'll surely fail the mission.

Iraqi 707 civilian airliners are also around. Do not harm them! Engage only after VID (Visual Identification — press F4). There is also an IL-76 transport that you should shoot down.

When you are out of loadout, switch to Buick and continue the mission.

Buick

Orbit 20NM south of Austin for backup.

Mission Objectives

Austin and Buick

1. No more than five Iraqi aircraft may cross the border.
2. All bandits in the Iraqi area are destroyed.
3. Civilian aircraft may not be harmed.
4. You must not enter the DMZ area.
5. Il-76 must be destroyed.

Mission Tips

- Switch to TWS radar mode by pressing Q. This will display all aircraft on the radar screen, even if you are locked onto one.

- Occasionally switch to the Tactical Display by pressing Esc.
- You must not cross the border in any case.
- Check out the enemy aircraft positions on the Tactical Display. If necessary, switch from Austin to Buick and vice-versa by pressing 'Austin' or 'Buick' on the Tactical Display Screen, and then press 'Fly.'
- You may also switch between flights using Shift 1 and Shift 2.
- Use your wingmen before you use your missiles.

Commander's Summary

The Iraqis are trying to hide their planes in Iran, and then bring them back for the next confrontation. Uncle Sam says "no way, José," so go shoot those sitting ducks. Remember that these guys are desperate — they have nothing to lose. Let's turn what's left of their air force into junk.

Assets & Opposition

Assets

4 X F-15C (Austin 1-4) PGU-28 (600), Chaff (60)
Flare (60), AIM-7M (4), AIM-9L (4)
4 X F-15C (Buick 1-4) PGU-28 (600), Chaff (60)
Flare (60), AIM-7M (4), AIM-9L (4)

KC-135R (Shell)

E-3C (Buckeye)

Opposition Aircraft

6 X MiG-29 GSh-301 (300), Chaff (60),
Flare (60), AA-10 (4), AA-8 (4)
2 X F-1 30mm (600), Chaff (60), Flare (60),
AIM-9M (2)
2 X Su-24) M61 Vulcan (510), Chaff (90),
Flare (60), AA-6 (2)
2 X MiG-23
2 X Su-22
Il-76

Commercial Aircraft

Iraqi Boeing (do not harm)

SUMMER HEAT

On January 17, coalition fighters set out for Tikrit, north of Baghdad, to search for Saddam Hussein. USAF aircraft went for the Saddam's summer palace. The strike was successful, but unfortunately the Iraqi leader was elsewhere.

Date   17 JAN 1991

Time   1200 HRS

Mission Type

Strike

Mission Description

Strike Saddam Hussein's Summer Palace.

Situation

Coalition forces are attempting to achieve a psychological advantage by hitting Iraqi high-value targets, like the Iraqi leader Saddam Hussein's Summer Palace. Targeting Iraqi leadership was a high priority during the campaign, as it was believed that this would demoralize the enemy, and bring about a quick end to the campaign.

Weather

10000' scattered, with unlimited visibility

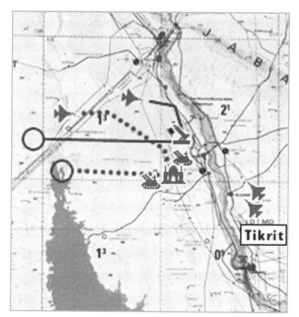

Intel

Targets

The Summer Palace is a complex located in the city of Tikrit. Your primary target is the distinctive Main Dome.

Threats

Probable MiG-29s defending the area. Probable ZSU-23X4 and SAMs in the Palace area.

Saddam Hussein's Palace

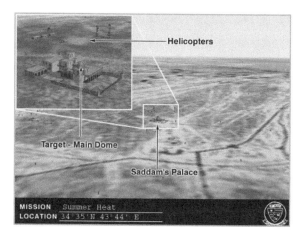

Primary Flights

Austin

Airframe	4 x F-16C
Task	Strike
Target	SA-2 radar
Loadout	Mk 84, AGM-65B, AIM-7M, AIM-9L

Buick

Airframe	4 x F-15E
Task	Strike
Target	Saddam's Palace
Loadout	Mk 84, GBU-15, AIM-120, AIM-9L

Supporting Flights

Snake

Airframe	2 x F-111F
Task	Strike
Target	SAM sites
Loadout	Mk 82, AIM-9L

Shell

Airframe	KC-135R
Task	Tanker
Target	N/A
Loadout	N/A

Buckeye

Airframe	E-3C AWACS
Task	AWACS
Target	N/A
Loadout	N/A

Tasking

Austin

Ingress from the north towards the target area. Destroy the SA-2 radar (positioned northeast of the palace), using AGM-65B A/G missiles, and then provide CAP for the remainder of the mission. None of these are primary mission objectives.

Buick

Ingress from the west and destroy Saddam Hussein's palace using a GBU-15 TV bomb.

Snake

This F-111 (non-controllable) flight is the first flight to ingress to the target area and attack the SAM sites around the palace.

Mission Objectives

Austin

1. Destroy SA-2 radar (not a primary mission objective).

Buick

2. The palace main dome must be destroyed.

Mission Tips

- Targets are designated by a 'T' on the HUD.
- After launching the GBU-15 TV bomb, toggle to the next waypoint by pressing [W] and press [A] twice to get into autopilot NAV. You can also turn back and press [A] once to engage autopilot level.
- After autopilot is engaged you will have the time to control the TV bomb.
- Press [Z] to view the TV bomb in full screen.
- Use [Ctrl] + [↑], [↓], [←], [→] to control the TV bomb while in flight.
- Press [Shift][C] to jettison your bombs and fuel tanks when entering a dogfight.
- Beware the ZSU by the bunker. Take out the bunker with your GBU-15s.

Commander's Summary

This guy is a madman. Maybe he'll get the hint when we shake his house a little.

If you find yourself engaged at close range with Iraqi fighters, jettison your bombs. Good luck!

Assets & Opposition

Assets

F-16C (Austin 1) PGU-28 (600), Chaff (60), Flare (60), AGM-65B (4), AIM-7M (2), AIM-9L (2), Mk 84 (2), Small Fuel Tank

F-16C (Austin 2) PGU-28 (510), Chaff (90), Flare (60), AGM-65B (2), AIM-7M (2), AIM-9L (2), Mk 84 (2), Small Fuel Tank

2 X F-16C (Austin 3-4) PGU-28 (510), Chaff (90), Flare (90), AGM-65B (6), AIM-7M (2), AIM-9L (2), Mk 84 (2), Small Fuel Tank

2 X F-15E (Buick 1-2) PGU-28 (250), Chaff (120), Flare (60), AIM-120 (2), AIM-9L (2), GBU-15 (2), Mk 84 (3)

2 X F-15E (Buick 3-4) PGU-28 (250), Chaff (120), Flare (60), AIM-120 (2), AIM-9L (2), GBU-15 (2), Mk 84 (5)

2 X F-111F (Snake 1-2) 30mm (200), Chaff (30), Flare (15), AIM-9L (2), Mk 82 (12)

KC-135R (Shell)

E-3C (Buckeye)

Opposition Aircraft

4 X MiG-29 GSh-301 (300), Chaff (60), Flare (60), AA-10 (4), AA-11 (2), AA-8 (2)

2 X Mi-24 30mm (300), Chaff (50), Flare (50), Rocket (20)

PUTTING OUT THE FIRE

Preventing an environmental disaster is of the utmost importance to the coalition forces. In this mission, USAF aircraft assist with putting out burning oil wells.

Date   01 FEB 1991

Time   1710 HRS

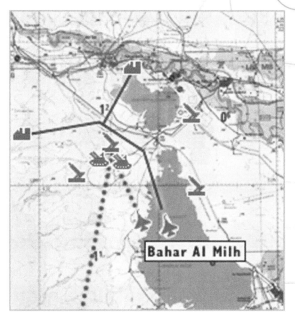

Mission Type

Oil Well Strike

Mission Description

Destroy burning oil pipes and piping stations.

Situation

As one of his final efforts, Saddam Hussein is now opening oil wells in Kuwait. Some of them are pouring into the Persian Gulf, others have been set on fire. Hussein is threatening to burn all of Kuwait and the Persian Gulf.

In this mission USAF aircraft are called to stop Hussein's actions. Destroying the oil pipes will stop some of the burning.

Weather

10000' cloudy, visibility 12 miles

Intel

Targets

Austin's targets are an SA-6 site and an SA-3 site on the way to the oil fields. The main targets are the radars, named SA-6 Radar-Target and SA-3 Radar-Target. Other flights will go for the oil

pumps: Oil Pump 1 in the eastern area and Oil Pump 2 in the western area. Destroying the oil pumps will extinguish the fire, due to lack of oxygen.

Threats

Possible ZSU-57X2 and ZSU-23X4 AAA. SA-3 and SA-6 SAMs are also present.

SA-6 Site

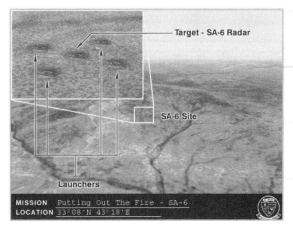

SA-3 Site

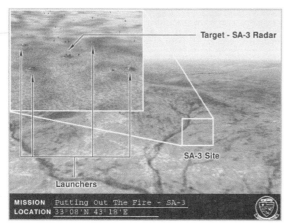

Oil Pump 1

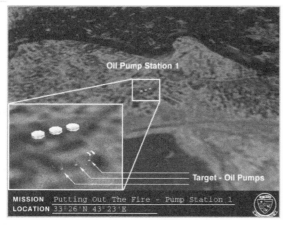

Oil Pump 2

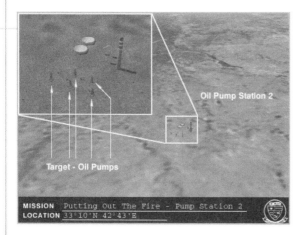

Primary Flights

Austin

Airframe   2 x F-16C
Task   SEAD
Target   SA-6 Site, SA-3 Site
Loadout   AGM-88, AIM-9L, AIM-120

Buick

Airframe   2 x F-15E
Task   Strike
Target   Oil Pump 1
Loadout   AIM-120, AIM-9M, Mk 84

Corvette

Airframe   2 x F-15E
Task   Strike
Target   Oil Pump 2
Loadout   AIM-120, AIM-9M, Mk 84

Tasking

Austin

Destroy the SA-6 and SA-3 sites on the way, and clear a path for Buick and Corvette.

Buick

Fly two minutes after Austin.

Your task is to destroy all the oil pumps in the oil pumping station nicknamed Oil Pump 1, using Mk 84 bombs.

Corvette

Escort Buick until your paths split, then ingress west toward Oil Pump 2 station in the western area. Destroy all oil pumps as well.

This is your last mission in the Gulf War, and there are abandoned Iraqi vehicles in the area. If you locate any of them, you are allowed to destroy them.

Don't forget that this is not your primary task!

Mission Objectives

Buick

1. Oil Pump 1 must be destroyed.

Corvette

2. Oil Pump 2 must be destroyed.

Mission Tips

✦ This is a multi-flight mission.

   After destroying the SA-6 and SA-3 sites, switch to Buick flight by pressing Shift 2.

   After destroying the oil pumps, switch to Corvette flight by pressing Shift 3. You will accomplish the mission after all targets have been destroyed.

✦ Pay special attention to incoming interceptors.

✦ Make sure you hit all the oil wells. Corvette flight can take out a convoy of Iraqi tanks for bonus points.

Commander's Summary

That madman has lost his mind. The burning oil is killing everything in the area, and hampering our operations. If we hit the designated spot the fire will be put out, so let's help Mother Earth on this one.

Assets & Opposition

Assets

2 X F-16C (Austin 1-2) PGU-28 (102), Chaff (90), Flare (60), AGM-88 (2), AIM-120 (2), AIM-9L (2)

2 X F-15E (Buick 1-2) PGU-28 (100), Chaff (120), Flare (60), AIM-120 (4), AIM-9M (2), Mk 84 (3)

2 X F-15E (Corvette 1-2) PGU-28 (100), Chaff (120), Flare (60), AIM-120 (4), AIM-9M (2), Mk 84 (3)

Opposition Aircraft

2 X MiG-29 GSh-301 (100), Chaff (60), Flare (60), AA-10 (2), AA-8 (4)

2 X MiG-23 GSh-301 (100), Chaff (40), Flare (20), AA-6 (2), AA-8 (2)

VIETNAM

FIRST AIRFIELD ATTACK

On 24 April 1967 eight F-105D 'Thuds' attacked Kep and Hoa Loc airfields in North Vietnam. Fourteen MiGs were destroyed on the ground. All USAF aircraft returned safely to their base.

Date   24 APR 1967

Time   1200 HRS

Mission Type

Strike

Mission Description

Attack Hoa-Loc airfield near Hanoi.

Situation

For quite a long time US Government has been denying the USAF field commanders the chance of attacking the MiG airfields and the MiGs on the ground. Today, at last, we have the opportunity to get them before they take off. Our target is the NVAF (North Vietnamese Air Force) airfield Hoa-Loc, at Hanoi.

Weather

7000' broken, unlimited visibility

Intel

Targets

Your initial targets are the two SA-2 batteries defending the airfields: an eastern battery and a

western battery. The primary target within each battery is the 'Fan Song' radar. Destroying it will disable the battery.

The targets in the airfields are the runway intersection, the control tower and all MiGs on the ground.

MiG-17s

MiG-21s

Airfield Control Tower

Western SA-2 Battery

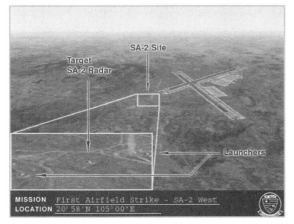

Eastern SA-2 Battery

Threats

All NVAF aircraft are likely to scramble. These will include MiG-21s and MiG-17s. The Hanoi area is well defended by SA-2. Hand-held SA-7s may also be present.

Possible AAA integral defense at the target's area.

Primary Flights

Austin

Airframe	4 x F-4E
Task	CAP
Target	N/A
Loadout	AIM-7B, AIM-9B

Buick

Airframe	2 x F-4E
Task	Wild Weasel
Target	SA-2 Batteries
Loadout	AGM-45, AIM-7B

Corvette

Airframe	4 x F-105D
Task	Airfield Strike
Target	Runway Intersection, Parked MiGs, Control Tower
Loadout	Mk 84, Mk 82, napalm

Tasking

Austin

Escort Buick, which is right ahead of you. Buick will call 'Approaching Targets' when approaching the IP (Initial Point, last waypoint before the strike). The airfield is located at waypoint 3.

Buick

Destroy the SA-2 radars at waypoint 2, using AGM-45 Shrike missiles. This will eliminate Corvette's threat and allow it to attack its target safely.

Corvette

You will attack the runway intersection at waypoint 3.

Corvette 3 and 4 will go for the control tower using general-purpose Mk 84 bombs. After the strike you should look for the parked MiGs and destroy them using rockets, bombs or plain guns. Remember to bug out as soon as you complete the strike. MiGs are likely to scramble from all around you.

Mission Objectives

Buick

1. Destroy two SA-2 batteries.

Corvette

2. Hit the runway intersection.

3. Destroy the airfield control tower.

4. Destroy at least 12 MiGs on the ground.

Mission Tips

+ Learn your target photos well. All targets are in place.

+ Switch to Buick when it calls 'IP Inbound.' This is the time to strike the SA-2 radar. Switch to Buick by pressing (Shift)(2).

+ The AGM-45 'Shrike' is a radar-homing missile. Select it by pressing (↑). If the targets are ahead, you will see a '2' display on the MFD.

+ Fly toward the target and wait for the 'in range' message to appear on the MFD. Launch the missile by pressing (Spacebar) or the Weapon Launch Button on your joystick.

+ Press (Alt)(E) to assign your radar target to your wingmen.

+ Press (Alt)(W) to assign your wingmen to attack other targets.

+ **Austin.** The MiG-17s come quick, so designate them with the air-to-air (A/A) radar and be ready with the AIM-7s.

+ **Buick.** Fly low over the hill before the airfield and be ready to take out the 2 SA-2s.

+ **Corvette.** Use napalm to take out the aircraft on the ground. It is quicker and very effective because of its wide spread, and it looks cool.

Commander's Summary

This is our first airfield strike in this war. NVAF are going to be caught by surprise so take advantage of it. Learn your targets well and hit them.

Assets & Opposition

Assets

4 X F-4E (Austin 1-4) M61 Vulcan (600), Chaff (60), Flare (60), AIM-7B (4), AIM-9B (4)

2 X F-4E (Buick 1-2) M61 Vulcan (600), Chaff (60), Flare (60), AGM-45 (2), AIM-7B (2)

4 X F-105D (Corvette 1-4) M61 Vulcan (1029), Chaff (100), Flare (80), Mk 82 (2), Mk 84 (1), Napalm (6)

Opposition Aircraft

2 X MiG-21 30mm (300), Chaff (60), Flare (60), AA-2D (4)

4 X MiG-17 30mm (300), AA-2D (2)

MiG-17 (grounded) 30mm (300), AA-6 (2), Mk 82 (6)

OPERATION BOLO

During this operation, USAF F-4s tricked North Vietnamese aircraft to think that the F-4s were bombers rather then fighters. They used this disguise to lure them into combat and shoot them down. Operation 'Bolo' was planned by Colonel Robin Olds, Wing Commander of the 8th TFW 'Wolfpack.' It was carried out on the morning of 2 January 1967 and ended up in 7 enemy MiGs down.

Date   02 JAN 1967

Time   1200 HRS

Mission Type

CAP (Combat Air Patrol)

Mission Description

USAF F-4s lure NVAF MiGs into combat. In this mission, you must destroy all of the MiGs in the vicinity.

Situation

Over the two first years of fighting, the North Vietnamese MiG pilots had generally avoided engaging F-4s, preferring to make hit-and-run attacks on bombers. The idea behind operation 'Bolo' is to try to convince the North Vietnamese that F-4s are bombers rather then fighters, and to lure them into combat before they could realize their mistake.

In some of the missions in this operation, USAF Phantoms are flying using Thud callsigns, and Thud flight patterns. They are also using the F-105 ECM pod — QRC 160.

Here we will be using our usual callsigns. The radio should be kept quiet until the MiGs are close enough to enter a dogfight. If you lock onto them further than 8-10 miles range they will ID your aircraft and flee.

Weather

10000' cloudy, visibility 15 miles

Intel

Targets

N/A

Threats

Expected MiG-21s, MiG-17s

Possible SA-2 SAMs and AAA — unknown

Primary Flights

Austin

Airframe	4 x F-4E
Task	Fighter Sweep
Target	N/A
Loadout	AIM-9B, AGM-45, AIM-7B

Buick

Airframe	2 x F-4E
Task	Fighter Sweep
Target	N/A
Loadout	AIM-9B, AGM-45, AIM-7B

Corvette

Airframe	2 x F-4E
Task	Fighter Sweep
Target	N/A
Loadout	AIM-9B, AGM-45, AIM-7B

Tasking

Austin

You will lead the intercepting package. Fly at 15,000' in close formation, in order to simulate a strike formation. Don't forget to stay silent at first. Don't lock onto any bandit until you are eight miles away, or they will run for it without leaving you a chance. You can switch to Buick when you are out of ammo, or if unfortunately, your flight goes down.

You are armed with AGM-45 Shrikes because there is a possibility of SAMs in the area. If you must use them, use them wisely.

Buick

Take over Austin's task in case Austin is in trouble.

Corvette

Assist Austin and Buick in the same task.

Mission Objectives

Austin, Buick and Corvette

1. All 12 MiGs must be downed.

Mission Tips

- ✈ Occasionally switch to the Tactical Display by pressing [Esc] and look around for Red MiGs. If you see any of them, press [Esc] again and fly in their direction. You can also switch to a closer flight and press Fly in the Tactical Display.

- ✈ If the SA-2 interferes with your mission, take it out using Shrikes. Do not forget, however, that this is not your primary mission.

- ✈ Wait for the AWACS to notify you of where to go and don't lock on to enemy targets until you are 8 miles out.

Commander's Summary

Hanoi is a hornet's nest. Get in there carefully. Look around for SAM and AAA, as well as bandits. Red Crown (the controller) will not help you much, but check out his calls. I want you all back here in one piece.

Assets & Opposition

Assets

4 X F-4E (Austin 1-4) 30mm (600), Chaff (60), Flare (60), AGM-45 (2), AIM-7B (2), AIM-9B (4)

2 X F-4E (Buick 1-2) 30mm (600), Chaff (60), Flare (60), AGM-45 (2), AIM-7B (2), AIM-9B (4)

2 X F-4E (Corvette 1-2) 30mm (600), Chaff (60), Flare (60), AGM-45 (2), AIM-7B (2), AIM-9B (4)

Opposition Aircraft

6 X MiG-17 30mm (300), AA-2D (2)

6 X MiG-21 30mm (300), Chaff (30), Flare (30), AA-2D (4)

THE DMZ DECEPTION

North Vietnamese MiGs used the DMZ (demilitarized zone) on the Chinese border as shelter to defend themselves from USAF aircraft, which were not allowed in that area. This mission challenges you to counter these hit-and-run tactics.

Date 03 JAN 1972
Time 1200 HRS

Mission Type

Strike

Mission Description

Attack an NVA (North Vietnamese Army) Headquarters building at Hanoi, as part of a USAF Strike Package.

Situation

The mission is to attack an important NVA HQ site in Western Hanoi. NV air defense and NVAF MiGs will attempt to prevent the attack at all costs.

The area close to the Vietnam-China border is defined by the US government officials as a DMZ (Demilitarized Zone, in which US military flights are restricted), in an attempt to leave China out of the Vietnam conflict. Entering this area is prohibited and will result in being grounded. NVAF MiGs are well aware of the USAF limitations and use this area as cover after unsuccessful intercepts.

Weather

Clear, with unlimited visibility

Intel

Targets

Your target is the NV Army HQ complex. The primary target in this complex is the communications center.

Threats

MiG-21 and MiG-17 fighters are on CAP, and more are likely to be scrambled from Hanoi, Kep, Hoa Loc and Phuc-Yen airfields. The North Vietnamese are aware of USAF DMZ limitations and are expected to attempt to fly north when threatened.

Hanoi is also defended by SA-2 SAM batteries.

Dogfights around Hanoi are very dangerous because of the massive air defense.

Communication Center

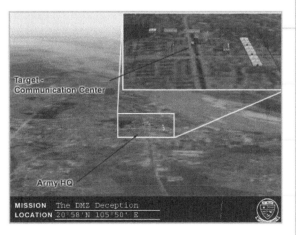

Primary Flights

Austin

Airframe	4 x F-105D
Task	Bombers
Target	Army HQ
Loadout	AIM-9B, Mk 84, Mk 82

Buick

Airframe	4 x F-4E
Task	CAP
Target	N/A
Loadout	AIM-7B, AIM-9B

Corvette

Airframe	4 x F-4E
Task	CAP
Target	N/A
Loadout	AIM-7B, AIM-9B

Tasking

Austin

You are the package leader. You should perform a quick bombing run on your targets at waypoint 2, and leave the city area as fast as possible to avoid the SAM.

Buick

You will be stationed on CAP east of Hanoi, watching for MiG takeoffs from Phuc-Yen airfield (east of Hanoi).

Corvette

Provide CAP west of Hanoi.

Mission Objectives

Austin

1. The Army HQ building must be destroyed.

Buick and Corvette

2. Down all MiGs (up to 10).

Mission Tips

✈ **Austin.** Take out the MiG-21s first — they have A/A missiles.

✈ Switch to **Corvette** to get the targets to south.

✈ **Buick.** Use Buick to mop up the remaining planes after you've run out of weapons in your other flights.

Commander's Summary

Destroying the target is our primary mission. Don't let the MiGs drag you into dogfights around Hanoi. They'll try to get you into the DMZ and I have very strict orders on how to deal with you if you go in there. Good luck guys.

Assets & Opposition

Assets

3 X F-105D (Austin 1,3,4) M61 Vulcan (1029), Chaff (100), Flare (80), AIM-9B (2), Mk 84 (3)

F-105D (Austin 2) M61 Vulcan (1029), Chaff (100), Flare (80), AIM-9B (2), Mk 82 (6), Mk 84 (1)

4 X F-4E (Buick 1-4) M61 Vulcan (600), Chaff (60), Flare (60), AIM-7B (4), AIM-9B (4)

3 X F-4E (Corvette 1,2,4) M61 Vulcan (600), Chaff (60), Flare (60), AIM-7B (4), AIM-9B (4)

F-4E (Corvette 3) M61 Vulcan (600), Chaff (60), Flare (60), AIM-7B (3), AIM-9B (5)

Opposition Aircraft

4 X MiG-17 30mm (300), AA-2D (2)

4 X MiG-21 30mm (300), Chaff (20), Flare (20), AA-2D (2)

2 X MiG-21 30mm (300), Chaff (60), Flare (60), AA-2D (4)

THE 11 DAY WAR

Operation 'Linebacker II' was dominated by the 'Buffs' — B-52s striking strategic targets in the Hanoi and Hai-Phong areas. This Linebacker mission involves striking a radar station, in downtown Hanoi, and the Gia-Lam Airfield.

Date   27 DEC 1972

Time   1710 HRS

Mission Type

Strike

Mission Description

Attack targets in Hanoi, and Escort B-52s attacking the area.

Situation

B-52s of the 307th Strategic Wing at U-Tapao are assigned to destroy Radcom Station 11 in downtown Hanoi, as well as the Gia-Lam Airfield. The strike packages will consist of two waves of B-52s, callsign Rhino. Each wave will consist of two bombers flying in a trail formation. The F-4E flights will escort the Buffs. The F-4E formations will attack SA-2 sites in target proximity, and provide cover against VC MiGs.

Weather

20000', scattered, good visibility

Intel

Targets

Austin's target is SA-2 Site A, near the Radcom station.

Buick's target is the SA-2 Site B, near the Gia-Lam Airfield.

Threats

Probable MiG-21s and SA-2 SAMs threatening the fighter and bomber flights.

Possible AAA integral defense at target area.

SA-2 Site A

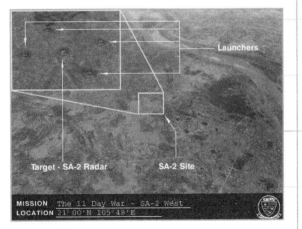

MISSION The 11 Day War - SA-2 West
LOCATION 21°00'N 105°48'E

SA-2 Site B

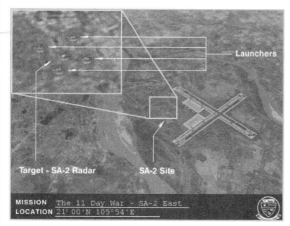

Launchers

Target - SA-2 Radar   SA-2 Site

MISSION The 11 Day War - SA-2 East
LOCATION 21°00'N 105°54'E

Communication Center

Communication
Center

MISSION The 11 Day War - Communication Center
LOCATION 21°07'N 105°44'E

Gia-Lam Airfield

MISSION The 11 Day War - Gialam Airfield
LOCATION 21°00'N 105°55'E

Primary Flights

Austin

Airframe	4 x F-4E
Task	Strike, Escort
Target	SA-2 A
Loadout	AIM-9B, AIM-7B, CBU-87

Buick

Airframe	4 x F-4E
Task	Strike, Escort
Target	SA-2 B
Loadout	AIM-9B, AIM-7B, CBU-87

Supporting Flights

Rhino 1,2

Airframe	2 x B-52
Task	Strike
Target	Radcom Station 11
Loadout	80 x Mk 83

Rhino 3,4

Airframe	2 x B-52
Task	Strike
Target	Gia-Lam Airfield
Loadout	80 x Mk 83

Tasking

Austin

Strike the SA-2 site, targeting the radar of course. Then provide cover for Rhino 1 and 2 against MiGs. After Rhino egresses from the Hanoi area, Austin flight will egress as well, and clear the area for the next flight.

Buick

Destroy the SA-2 radar near the Gia-Lam Airfield. Then provide cover for Rhino 3 and 4 until they are safely out of the Hanoi area.

Mission Objectives

Austin

1. Destroy SA-2 Site A.

2. Rhino 1 and 2 must perform their mission and survive.

Buick

3. Destroy SA-2 Site B.

4. Rhino 3 and 4 must perform their mission and survive.

Mission Tips

★ **Austin and Buick.** Take out the ground threats and get back to the bombers. The MiG-17s will go after the bombers.

★ To be safe (but receive fewer points) tell your wingmen to go after the ground targets by pressing Alt E.

Commander's Summary

The B-52s are sitting ducks for the NV forces. We must give them cover from the NV SAMs and MiGs. Yesterday we lost two BUFFs over Hanoi, and I'm fed up with these guys' sneak attacks! I want you to blow them back to Kingdom Come! Let's give those BUFFs the opportunity to throw their iron down there, and bring this war to a stop!

Assets & Opposition

Assets

4 X F-4E (Austin 1-4) M61 Vulcan (600), Chaff (120), Flare (60), AIM-7B (2), AIM-9B (2), CBU-87 (6), Fuel Tank (3)

4 X F-4E (Buick 1-4) M61 Vulcan (600), Chaff (120), Flare (60), AIM-7B (4), AIM-9B (4), CBU-87 (6), Fuel Tank

4 X B-52 (Rhino 1-4) Chaff (50), Flare (50), Mk 83 (18)

Opposition Aircraft

6 X MiG-21 30mm (300), Chaff (30), Flare (30), AA-2D (4)

2 X MiG-21 30mm (300), Chaff (60), Flare (60), AA-2D (4)

2 X MiG-21 30mm (300), Chaff (60), Flare (60), AA-6 (4)

2 X MiG-17 30mm (300), Chaff (20), Flare (20), AA-2D (2)

2 X MiG-17 30mm (300), Chaff (20), Flare (20), AA-6 (2)

YOU'RE NEVER ALONE

This SAR (Search and Rescue) mission calls you to assist the rescue operation of a downed B-52 crew, shot down during a Linebacker mission. The HH-53C Super Jolly helicopter is on its way, and A-1 'Sandies' will assist in the rescue.

Date 27 DEC 1972

Time 1700 HRS

Mission Type

SAR (Search And Rescue)

Mission Description

Rescue a downed B-52 crew.

Situation

The downed B-52 crew, callsign 'Minnesota,' parachuted into the jungle area between Vinh and the village of Ban Nape. The FAC (Forward Air Controller) is sending us the target location, and an HH-53 Super Jolly SAR (Search And Rescue) helicopter is on its way to the area. The Jolly is escorted by two A-1E 'Sandies.' The Sandies were on their way back from another mission, and were left without ammunition.

Austin flight, 2 F-105 'Thuds,' are assigned to accompany the rescue mission, and to clear the path from any VC threats which might arise along the route.

It is also possible that other tasking will come up during the mission, since there are numerous Army and Marine 'sweeps' taking place in VC villages in that area. If any of them need assistance, their FAC will call us.

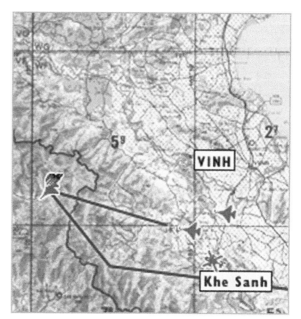

Weather

12,000' scattered, visibility 10 miles, light showers

Intel

Targets

N/A

Threats

The area is swarming with VC forces, positions unknown. We know they have mobile 85 mm AAA guns that are constantly on the move. They also possess some PT-76 tanks and trucks.

Possible fighter interception by MiG-17s.

Primary Flights

Austin

Airframe 2 x F-105D

Task SAR, CAS

Target N/A

Loadout AIM-9B, BLU-27 'napalm' dispensers, rockets

Supporting Flights

Nail 7-5

Airframe	Cessna
Task	FAC
Target	N/A
Loadout	N/A

Jolly

Airframe	HH-53C
Task	SAR
Target	N/A
Loadout	N/A

Sandy

Airframe	2 x A-1E
Task	Escort
Target	N/A
Loadout	N/A

Tasking

Austin

Take out any threats to the Jolly Greens and the downed pilots in the jungle.

Mission Objectives

Austin

1. The Super Jolly must perform the rescue, and egress safely back to Da-Nang.

2. Protect the downed pilots from any incoming threats.

3. Perform any tasks during the mission.

Mission Tips

✦ Listen to the Jolly rescue helicopter's reports on the radio.

✦ If the Jolly reports threats, switch to air-to-ground radar, lock and destroy.

✦ AAA is likely to fire from the jungle. Don't spend too much time on them or you will delay the mission.

✦ When you contact enemy fighters, lock one of them and send your wingman to hit the others by using the wingman command "Engage the other one" (Alt W).

✦ Send your wingman to take out the MiG-17. 85mm are your first two main targets. Follow the waypoints and take out the targets marked with yellow smoke. Forget bombs — napalm is your best friend.

Commander's Summary

Our boys are in the bush. Let's try to spare them the pleasure of checking in at the Hanoi Hilton. React swiftly to all possible threats along the way — watch your six and those bullets coming from the jungle. It's another hot day in 'Nam, let's see it ending with our boys back in the PX.

Assets & Opposition

Assets

2 X F-105D (Austin 1-2) M61 Vulcan (1029), Chaff (100), Flare (80), AIM-9B (2), Napalm (3), Rocket (22)

UH-1
HH-53C
2 X A-1E

Opposition Aircraft

MiG-17	30mm (300), Chaff (20), Flare (20), 2100lb (1), AA-2D (2)
MiG-21	30mm (300), Chaff (30), Flare (30), AA-6 (4)

LINEBACKER AT SEA

North Vietnam used merchant vessels for the transport of AAA shells and SAM missiles. This mission tasks you with disabling these transports that have just entered the beautiful bay of Hai-Phong.

Date   03 JAN 1972
Time   0700 HRS

Mission Type

Air-to-Sea Strike

Mission Description

Search and destroy NVA merchant boats smuggling armament into North Vietnam.

Situation

The NVA is using merchant vessels to smuggle SAM missiles and AAA ammo into North Vietnam, in an attempt to avoid US Navy boats patrolling in the Gulf of Tonkin.

We have received reliable intelligence stating that two of these ships are on their way to the Bay of Hai-Phong.

Weather

15,000' scattered, visibility unlimited

Intel

Targets

We have been informed of 2 armed merchant boats in the harbor. The boats are currently approaching Hai-Phong Harbor. The harbor is full of civilian merchant boats which look similar to the targets. Under no circumstances are the civilian boats to be hit. Each armed boat may carry up to 50 tons of ammo. US Navy boats will be attempting to detect the enemy boats amongst the civilians.

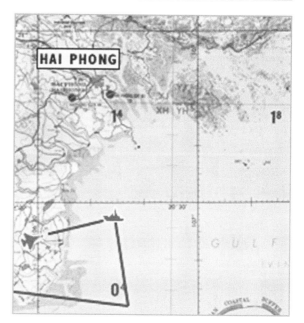

There is a 57mm gun on the beach. It is recommended that this be destroyed, although it is not a primary mission target.

Threats

MiG-21s and MiG-17s are patrolling the area.

Possible AAA fire from enemy boats.

Possible North Vietnamese Navy patrol vessels in the bay.

A 57mm gun site is located on the beach.

57mm site

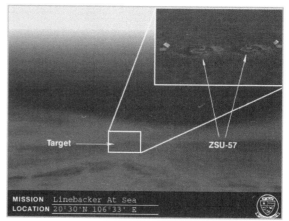

Primary Flights

Austin

Airframe 4 x F-4E
Task Strike
Target Merchant boats
Loadout AIM-9B, AIM-7B, AGM-62, Mk 82

Buick

Airframe 4 x F-4E
Task Backup
Target Merchant boats
Loadout AIM-9B, AIM-7B, AGM-62, Mk 82

Tasking

Austin

Strike the two NVA smuggler ships.

Buick

Buick formation serves as backup for Austin. The mission can be completed with Austin flight only.

Mission Objectives

Austin and Buick

1. The smuggler merchant boats must be destroyed.

2. Civilian ships must not be harmed.

Mission Tips

- You may launch after positive VID (Visual IDentification), and only at vessels that fire at you.

- It is recommended that you destroy the 57mm site and any patrol vessels if they interfere with your mission.

- Listen carefully to your radio for tips regarding target location.

- After detecting an enemy target, turn away from it first before beginning a long, steady bombing run.

- Switch to Ground Radar–MAP mode by pressing [R] and then [Q].

- Lock onto the target by pressing [Enter].

- Select AGM-62 'Walleye' TV bomb by pressing [ ].

- Launch the missile by using [Spacebar] or the joystick.

- **Austin.** Fly to waypoint 1 and take out the MiGs with AIM-7s.

- **Buick.** Use your bombs to take out the northern and southern merchants' ships. Fly high and dive-bomb to assure a hit.

Commander's Summary

The situation is sensitive enough without you taking out a civilian ship, so just don't. Now get out there and stop those ammo shipments from reaching the beach.

Assets & Opposition

Assets

4X F-4E (Austin 1-4) M61 Vulcan (600), Chaff (60), Flare (60), AGM-62 (2), AIM-7B (4), AIM-9B (4), Mk 82 (3)

4 X F-4E (Buick 1-4) M61 Vulcan (600), Chaff (60), Flare (60), AGM-62 (2), AIM-7B (4), AIM-9B (4), Mk 82 (3)

Opposition Craft

6 X MiG-21 30mm (300), Chaff (60), Flare (60), AA-2D (4)

2 X MiG-17 30mm (300), AA-2D (2)

2 X Armed Boat Missile (1), AAA (20)

Armed Boat Rocket (20)

THE KHE-SANH SIEGE

On January 1968, the Marine Corps base at Khe-Sanh was set under siege. A remarkable US effort was made to ensure a flow of supplies into the base, and to keep it safe from North Vietnamese attacks. In this mission you will take part in another day of survival in Khe-Sanh.

Date   02 FEB 1968

Time   0630 HRS

Mission Type

CAS (Combat Air Support)

Mission Description

Provide CAS for the Khe-Sanh Marine base.

Situation

The Marines at Khe-Sanh are under constant bombardment from the NVA 325C and 304 Divisions. Last night was especially harsh, and an ammo dump was hit. Supplies are running low, and we have reports on wounded Marines waiting for evacuation.

Today, like any other day, we're concentrating our efforts on bringing in supplies, and bringing out the wounded. Trouble is, the VC are shooting at every aircraft trying to land in Khe-Sanh, and yesterday they got an HH-53 helicopter. In the base we have a Forward Air Controller (FAC), callsign 'Sky-Dog,' and he knows best what the immediate needs are, who's landing, who's threatening, and where. Lately the Marines are marking the targets with orange smoke bombs, so it will be easier for us to pinpoint the exact threat, and to take them out.

We'll be sending a supply cargo plane this morning, a C-130A, callsign Olds 1, and HH-53 helicopters will be flying all day carrying supplies and evacuating. It's up to us to see they make it in and out safely.

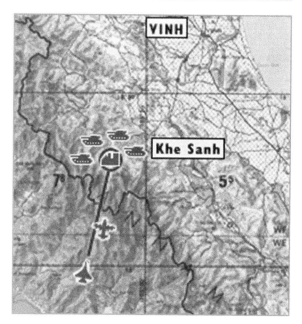

Intelligence warns us that the VC will try to launch a frontal attack on the base today, and break into the base perimeter. The VC have PT-76 tanks, and if they manage to reach the base's inner perimeter line, the whole base will be in danger of falling into their hands. This attack could possibly come from north, where the 325C NVA Division is formed, or from the west, where the 304 NVA Division have set positions. Other flights will be all around, including A-1s and B-52s.

In conclusion, this day is important in the holding-out combat we're fighting. The FAC will direct you according to the immediate threats to the base, assisting with orange smoke indicators near the designated target.

Weather

14000' scattered clouds, with light showers

Intel

Targets

N/A

Threats

VC may possess 85mm AAA vehicles.

Primary Flights

Austin

Airframe	2 x F-105D
Task	CAS
Target	N/A
Loadout	BLU-27 'napalm' dispensers, Mk 82

Supporting Flights

Olds

Airframe	C-130H
Task	Supply
Target	N/A
Loadout	N/A

Dallas

Airframe	HH-53C
Task	Supply
Target	N/A
Loadout	N/A

Stingray

Airframe	2 x B-52H
Task	CAS
Target	N/A
Loadout	Mk 83

T-bird

Airframe	2 x A-1E
Task	CAS
Target	N/A
Loadout	BLU-27 'napalm' dispensers, AIM-9B, Mk 82

Tasking

Austin

Destroy the targets assigned by the FAC at Khe-Sanh, in order to assure the survival of the transport planes and helicopters, and the overall survival of the camp.

Mission Objectives

Austin

1. Destroy all the targets marked with orange smoke as assigned by the FAC — 'Skydog.'

In Addition

✦ Olds, Dallas and the communications center must survive.

Mission Tips

✦ There are a lot of targets near Khe-Sanh. Preserve your loadout for the targets you will get from the FAC on the radio.

✦ The relevant targets will be marked by orange smoke.

✦ You don't have to see the target itself — just aim at the smoke.

✦ **Austin.** Take out the 85mm — they're the primary targets. Listen to the Sandies and bomb the yellow smoke marked targets.

Commander's Summary

Another day in Hell. Oh well. But seriously, the Marines are hanging on bravely, under constant fire, and the supply planes are under heavy fire all the time, from landing till take-off. The NVA have concentrated two divisions there, and that's a lot of firepower. It's up to us to try and ease the pressure, and help our boys hang in there yet another day. Let's go.

Assets

2 X F-105D (Austin 1-2) M61 Vulcan (1029), Chaff (100), Flare (80), Mk 82 (2), Napalm (9)

2 X B-52 (Stingray) Mk 83 (36)

2 X A-1E (T-bird) PGU-28 (300), Chaff (60), Flare (60), AIM-9B (2), Mk 82 (9), Napalm (6)

HH-53C (Dallas)

C-130H (Olds)

No Opposition Aircraft

BUSTING THE BRIDGE

The Paul Doumer Bridge at Hanoi was a primary USAF target during the Vietnam War. It was never seriously damaged until this mission. On 10 May, 1972, USAF F-4s proved the efficiency of laser-guided weapons and scored direct hits on the bridge, leaving it in ruins.

Date   10 MAY 1972

Time   0700 HRS

Mission Type

Strike

Mission Description

Strike Paul Doumer Bridge, east of Hanoi.

Situation

All prior attacks on the Paul Doumer Bridge failed in cutting off this major railway and highway link to Hanoi. This was due to insufficient hits while using "dumb bombs."

Our mission today is to strike the Bridge using GBU-12 (Laser Guided Bombs) and AGM-62 'Walleye' TV missiles, and destroy it.

Weather

10000' cloudy, visibility 15M

Intel

Targets

The primary target is the Paul Doumer Bridge. The designated impact points are the eastern tip and the western tip of the bridge. The bridge is located along Corvette's route, at waypoint 5.

Destroying both sides of the bridge will cut the major transportation link to Hanoi.

Threats

Numerous SA-2 sites are located along Buick's route, near waypoint 3, waypoint 4, and north of waypoint 4. AAA are located along Buick's route, near waypoint 4 defending the bridge and around the SAM sites.

MiG-17s and MiG-21s are on alert in Hanoi, at the Gia-Lam Airfield east of the bridge, and at Hoa Lac Airfield west of the bridge. They are most likely to take off and intercept our strikers.

Paul Doumer Bridge

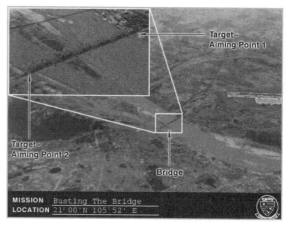

Primary Flights

Austin

Airframe	2 x F-4E
Task	CAP
Target	N/A
Loadout	AIM-7B, AIM-9B

Buick

Airframe	2 x F-4E
Task	SEAD
Target	SA-2 Site
Loadout	AGM-45, AIM-9B, CBU-87

Corvette

Airframe	2 x F-4E
Task	Strike
Target	Eastern side of the Paul Doumer Bridge, western side of the Paul Doumer Bridge
Loadout	GBU-12, AGM-62, AIM-7B, AIM-9B, Mk 82, AVQ-26 Designation Pod

Supporting Flights

Ford

Airframe	2 x F-4E
Task	Laser Designation
Target	Eastern side of the Paul Doumer Bridge, western side of the Paul Doumer Bridge
Loadout	AIM-9B, AIM-7B, Mk 82, AVQ-26 Designation Pod

Tasking

Austin

Perform a Fighter sweep against all enemy fighters, covering Buick, Corvette and Ford while performing their tasks.

Buick

Launch AGM-45 Shrike missiles and destroy the SAM sites around waypoints 3 and 4. Destroy hostile AAA around the Paul Doumer Bridge in order to clear a path for Corvette.

After hitting the SAMs and AAA, egress northwest to waypoint 5, and clear the target area for Corvette.

Ford

Approach the target from a distance and laser-designate both ends of the bridge.

After initiating target designation, Ford will contact Corvette lead, and clear the flight for him to ingress. Ford will stay south of the target area.

Corvette

Ingress to the target area at waypoint 5 after the SAMs have been destroyed, and after Ford reports it is starting target designation.

Both sides of the bridge will be designated. You must destroy them both.

After destroying the bridge, clear the area according to your route (heading waypoint 6).

Mission Objectives

Corvette

1. Destroy the eastern side of the Paul Doumer Bridge.

2. Destroy the western side of the Paul Doumer Bridge.

Mission Tips

+ This is a multi-flight mission. Switch between flights by pressing Shift 1, Shift 2, Shift 3.

+ Buick should fly to waypoints 3 and 4, designated by a 'T' on the HUD.

+ Switch to AGM-45 Shrike missiles by pressing ↑. Make sure you're locking onto the correct target using the F4 key.

+ When the MFD shows 'In Range,' at about 10 miles from target, you may launch the radar-homing missile.

+ Toggle targets in the Shrike display by pressing Ctrl Enter.

+ When flying Corvette, press ↑ to toggle to the Laser Bomb. You will see the Laser Pod video source on your MFD (Multi Function Display).

   Switch your radar to A/G–MAP mode using R and Q, and lock.

   In this stage the Laser Pod will lock onto the target and the HUD will mark the position of the designated target.

   When the CCIP sight is in the target area, release the bomb.

+ You may need more than one pass in order to blow up both sides of the bridge.

+ Follow the waypoints and the Paul Doumer is the first bridge you come upon. Bomb both ends of the bridge to succeed. Put Mk-82 on Austin, then you can do this mission in one flight.

Commander's Summary

I have already stopped counting the unsuccessful attacks on this bridge. This time you're getting the best weapons there are, Laser Bombs. Get those bombs working and wipe out that bridge.

Assets & Opposition

Assets

2 X F-4E (Austin 1-2) M61 Vulcan (600), Chaff (100), Flare (100), AIM-7B (2), AIM-9B (4), Fuel Tank

2 X F-4E (Buick 1-2) M61 Vulcan (600), Chaff (100), Flare (100), AGM-45 (4), AIM-9B (2), CBU-87 (6), Fuel Tank

F-4E (Corvette 1) M61 Vulcan (600), Chaff (60), Flare (60), AGM-62 (1), AIM-7B (2), AIM-9B (1), Fuel Tank, GBU-12 (3), LANTIRN Pod

F-4E (Corvette 2) M61 Vulcan (600), Chaff (60), Flare (60), AGM-62 (1), AIM-7B (2), AIM-9B (1), GBU-12 (3), LANTIRN Pod, Mk 82 (6)

2 X F-4E (Ford 1-2) M61 Vulcan (600), Chaff (60), Flare (60), AIM-7B (2), AIM-9B (5), LANTIRN Pod, Mk 82 (12)

Opposition Aircraft

3 X MiG-17 30mm (300), Chaff (20), Flare (20), AA-2D (2), Mk 82 (6)

MiG-17 30mm (300), Chaff (20), Flare (20), AA-6 (2), Mk 82 (6)

2 X MiG-21 30mm (300), Chaff (60), Flare (60), AA-2D (4)

FUTURE CAMPAIGNS
Red Arrow
Sleeping Giant

RED ARROW

The Red Arrow training campaign involves two opposing sides — Blue and Red. The objective of the campaign is to simulate a disadvantageous opening situation for the Blue side, in a surprise attack by air and ground. The Red side's objective is to conquer the simulated city of Colorado, built especially for this campaign, representing a Blue ground asset. The Blue side's objective is to prevent Red from succeeding. A DMZ area where no military forces are to be found separates both sides. Along the Red border there are multiple Red ground forces, including two armored divisions in the north and three artillery divisions in the south. Various commando and support units are spread all over the Red area, east of the border, stretching out to the Red airfield and Red nuclear facility, which closes the Red area from east. The Blue airfield is Nellis AFB, and the Blue ground forces are spread out to the west of Colorado City. Should the Red ground forces attack, the Blue side will have a short time to try and stop them in the DMZ before they achieve key attack positions on Colorado City. The present status of the campaign opening is one of quiet tension, in which the Blue side does not want to enter an all-out conflict with the Red side. Blue is directed to avoid any hostile action until provoked to do so. The Blue side starts with a given resource situation and can resupply lost aircraft by choosing Aircraft Supply Missions during the campaign. A Weapon Supply Mission can also be delivered. You are limited to two supply missions of each kind.

Campaign Supplies

You have a finite amount of supplies available in the two future campaigns, Red Arrow and Sleeping Giant. If you run out of a type of aircraft or munition, you must choose another aircraft or a different loadout.

If you start losing aircraft and pilots, you can fly a 'deploy aircraft' mission, which involves four F-15Cs and two F-22As. Whatever new aircraft sur-

vive the mission and arrive at your base are added to your available aircraft, and their pilots join your flight roster.

A 'weapon supply' mission restores all munitions to 80% of their original quantities. If you have not expended more than 20% of a particular type of weapon, your stores of that weapon are not affected.

You can only fly two of each type of resupply mission ('deploy aircraft' and 'weapon supply').

You begin the Red Arrow campaign with the following quantities:

Pilots 45

Aircraft

A-10A	10	F-16C	16
F-15C	16	F-22A	16
F-15E	12	F-117A	4

Air-to-Ground Munitions

AGM-45	. .10	GBU-10	12
AGM-62	. .10	GBU-12	12
AGM-65B	.50	GBU-12D	20
AGM-65D	.50	GBU-15	7
AGM-88	. .20	GBU-24	12
AGM-130	. .8	GBU-27	12
AGM-142	. .4	GBU-30	8
CBU-52	. . .15	Mk 20	15
CBU-54	. . .15	Mk 82	25
CBU-58	. . .12	Mk 83	30
CBU-87	. . .75	Mk 84	35
CBU-89	. . .12	BLU-27	20
CBU-93	5	LAU61 Hydra Rocket	.176

Air-to-Air Munitions

AIM-7B	. . .30	AIM-9L	40
AIM-7F	. . .20	AIM-9M	80
AIM-7M	. . .40	AIM-9P	20
AIM-9B	. . .20	AIM-9X	40
AIM-9D	. . .20	AIM-120	120

SCRAMBLE

There is no evidence of Red ground movement. During the night Intelligence has discovered some activity at the Red airfield and some helicopter flights moving across the Red area. Not much more is known.

There are several aircraft on high alert at Nellis AFB. The pilots are in a 5-minute scramble status. We have recently lost contact with one of our flights, which was flying CAP, 50 miles east of Nellis AFB.

Date   27 MAR 2004

Time   0545 HRS

Mission Type

Air-to-Air

Mission Description

Five minute air-defense alert.

Situation

There appears to be some Red force movement during the past few days. USAF command has raised the alert situation to a higher notch, and directed a five-minute-to-takeoff state of readiness for the Nellis air-to-air squadrons, just in case. If Red fighters attempt to attack our HQ in Colorado City, you will be notified to make this your first priority tasking! Colorado City is at waypoint 2.

Weather

Clear, with unlimited visibility

Intel

Targets

N/A

Threats

MiG-29 fighters, Su-24 bombers.

Primary Flights

Austin

Airframe 4 x F-22A

Task   Alert

Target   N/A

Loadout   AIM-120

Buick

Airframe 4 x F-15C

Task   CAP

Target   N/A

Loadout   AIM-9M, AIM-120

Tasking

Austin

You are on five-minute alert and will receive further instructions during the mission.

Buick

Provide CAP west of Colorado City.

Mission Objectives

Austin and Buick

1. Our HQ in Colorado City (waypoint 2) must not be hit by any incoming bombers.

In Addition

✦ All Su-24s must be destroyed.

Mission Tips

✦ When you receive a radio message about Reds approaching Colorado City, switch to Buick (Shift 2) and take them down.

✦ **Austin.** Press Shift S (safety off) to be able to attack targets while taking off. After reducing enemy attack on Nellis airfield, quickly switch to Buick flight.

✦ **Buick.** Stay around Colorado City and don't let any enemy aircraft get close — they may try to destroy our headquarters building.

Commander's Summary

Stay alert. Remember that Colorado City is our most important asset in this campaign. It must NOT be hit!

Assets & Opposition

Assets

F-22A (Austin 1) PGU-28 (510), Chaff (120), Flare (90), AIM-120 (3), AIM-9X (3)

2 X F-22A (Austin 2-3) PGU-28 (510), Chaff (90) Flare (60), AIM-120 (3), AIM-9X (3)

F-22A (Austin 4) PGU-28 (200), AIM-120 (3), AIM-9X (3)

2 X F-15C (Buick 1-2) PGU-28 (500), Chaff (120), Flare (60), AIM-120 (4), AIM-9M (2)

2 X F-15C (Buick 3-4) PGU-28 (600), Chaff (90), Flare (60), AIM-120 (4), AIM-9M (4)

Opposition Aircraft

MiG-29 30mm (600), Chaff (90), Flare (90), AA-8 (2)

MiG-29 30mm (600), Chaff (90), Flare (90)

2 X MiG-29 GSh-301 (300), Chaff (60), Flare (60), AA-8 (2)

2 X MiG-29 GSh-301 (600), Chaff (90), Flare (90), AA-8 (2)

2 X MiG-23 GSh-301 (100), Chaff (40), Flare (20), Mk 83 (2)

2 X MiG-23 GSh-301 (300), Chaff (60), Flare (60), Mk 82 (2)

Su-22 30mm (300), Chaff (60), Flare (60), Mk 83 (6)

Su-22 30mm (300), Chaff (60), Flare (60), AA-6 (2), Mk 83 (6)

2 X Su-24 30mm (300), Chaff (60), Flare (60), Mk 83 (6)

2 X Su-24 AA-6 (2), Mk 83 (6)

2 X Su-24 PGU-28 (500), Chaff (90), Flare (60), Mk 83 (6)

Su-24 30mm (500), Chaff (60), Flare (60), AA-6 (1), Mk 83 (6), AA-6 (1)

Su-24 30mm (500), Chaff (60), Flare (60), AA-6 (2), Mk 83 (6)

2 X Su-35 GSh-301 (300), Chaff (60), Flare (60), Mk 82 (6)

BLUE BLOCK

It has been a few hours since the first massive Red dawn strike, and information is starting to pour in, allowing us to try to assess the situation.

The initial Red air attack on Nellis AFB and on Colorado City has been met with quick and massive Blue resistance, preventing the Red side from reaching their goals, namely that of destroying most of our aircraft by catching us off guard. This air strike came together with a vast Red ground advancement into the DMZ, and it is obvious that the enemy wanted to neutralize our air power in order to ease their ground operation.

Our assessment of the present situation is that about 30 enemy aircraft (mostly bombers) have been shot down in the first two hours of their attack. They appear to be concentrating their fighter deployment over their ground forces to give them cover while they try to rush across the DMZ to the Blue border. Our side has sustained heavy losses — 17 aircraft have been shot down, and numerous assets, mainly at Nellis AFB, have been destroyed. However, we are still in a fully operational status, and Colorado City has not been heavily hit.

USAF aircraft are instructed to stop a combined air and ground attack on the major Blue town, Colorado City.

Date   MAR 27, 2004

Time   1200 HRS

Mission Type

CAS (Combat Air Support)

Mission Description

Stop the Red air and ground assault on Colorado City.

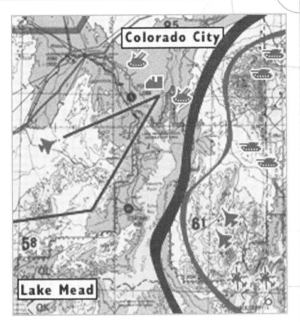

Situation

After the initial Red surprise attack on Nellis, the Red main attack force is converging on Colorado City with fighters, helicopters, tanks and artillery.

We have managed to survive the first assault due to quick reflexes, and managed to prevent the annihilation of our air power. We have enough resources yet to launch a defensive air attack and stop the Red assault before they enter Colorado City, but we must do it quickly.

Intelligence has managed to construct a fuzzy picture about the main Red efforts. It seems that there will be some attempt to land commando units behind our lines in an effort to cut off the city from the west, and a major ground effort is coming from the east.

Weather

20000' scattered, with unlimited visibility

Intel

Targets

From the initial intelligence data we can infer that the Red tanks will make a push from east of Colorado City, and that artillery forces will be arriving from the southeast, in order to achieve firing positions on Colorado City. We don't know any more than that, but will give you further instructions in the air. Expect M-60 tanks and various artillery and helicopters.

Threats

Probable SA-8 and SA-6 SAMs, various AAA.

MiG-29s and MiG-23s are the expected air threats.

Mi-24 gunships may go after our ground forces and choppers, and Mi-8 helicopters may be airlifting enemy commandos.

Primary Flights

Austin

Airframe	4 x F-22A
Task	CAP
Target	Any fighters and helicopters
Loadout	AIM-120, AIM-9X

Buick

Airframe	4 x A-10A
Task	CAS
Target	M-60 Tanks
Loadout	AGM-65B, AIM-9M, CBU-87

Corvette

Airframe	4 x F-16C
Task	CAS
Target	M-109 Artillery
Loadout	CBU-87, AGM-65B, AIM-9M, AIM-120

Supporting Flights

T-bird

Airframe	2 x F-15C
Task	Sweep
Target	N/A
Loadout	AIM-9M, AIM-120, AIM-9L

Stingray

Airframe	2 x F-15C
Task	Sweep
Target	N/A
Loadout	AIM-9M, AIM-120

Shell

Airframe	KC-135R
Task	N/A
Target	N/A
Loadout	N/A

Big Bird

Airframe	E-3C AWACS
Task	AWACS
Target	N/A
Loadout	N/A

Tasking

Austin

Perform an initial fighter sweep, and down any Red helicopters bringing in commando troops.

Buick

You are armed with AGM-65B Maverick missiles and CBU-87 cluster bombs. You are tasked to stop the Red tank advancement from the east. After launching all your weapons, egress! Corvette flight will verify that all the tanks are destroyed if Buick does not handle all of them.

Corvette

You are armed with AGM-65B missiles and CBU cluster bombs. You are tasked to stop any other ground advancement — most likely, artillery from the southeast.

Mission Objectives

Austin

1. All the enemy helicopters must be shot down.

Buick

2. All enemy tanks must be destroyed.

Corvette

3. All enemy artillery vehicles must be destroyed.

In Addition

✦ The Blue com center and watch tower must survive.

Mission Tips

✦ Take off from Nellis in Austin flight and head for Colorado City.

✦ If you run into fighters, shoot them down. Use your wingmen. If you run out of missiles against the helicopters, use your gun. Slow down to about 350 knots for convenient aiming runs.

✦ **Buick** flight will approach Colorado City from the west. Use your A/G radar in Map mode to locate your targets, then choose AGM-65B A/G missiles which will be slaved to your radar target. Launch at will.

✦ Corvette should do the same with their targets. You also have CBU (cluster bombs) to take out convoys or groups of targets.

✦ **Austin.** Switch to Buick flight right after taking out enemy choppers.

✦ **Buick.** Take out M-60 tanks first — they are the main threat to Colorado City. To make this task easier, turn on "object ID on TD box" in the Gameplay section of Preferences.

✦ **Corvette.** Destroy all M-109 artillery vehicles to get mission success.

Commander's Summary

We don't know the exact targets we're going to attack, so stay alert and be ready to receive tasking from Mission Control, who have the overall picture. Always define the most relevant threat at any given time. Let's be flexible and improvise. You may not have always have the best ordinance to kill a target, but we have to stop them any way we can. The most important thing is to give hell to those Red troops and stop them in their tracks.

Assets & Opposition

Assets

4 X F-22A **(Austin 1-4)** PGU-28 (600),
Chaff (120), Flare (90), AIM-120 (3),
AIM-9X (3)

4 X A-10A **(Buick 1-4)** PGU-14B (500),
Chaff (100), Flare (80), AGM-65B (8),
AIM-9M (4), CBU-87 (2)

2 X F-16C **(Corvette 1-2)** PGU-28 (510),
Chaff (90), Flare (60), 2100lb (1),
AGM-65B (6), AIM-120 (2),
AIM-9M (2), CBU-87 (6)

2 X F-16C **(Corvette 3-4)** PGU-28 (510),
Chaff (90), Flare (90), AGM-65B (6),
AIM-120 (2), AIM-9M (2),
CBU-87 (6)

2 X F-15C **(Stingray 1-2)** PGU-28 (600),
Chaff (120), Flare (60), AIM-120 (4),
AIM-9M (4)

2 X F-15C **(T-bird 1-2)** PGU-28 (600),
Chaff (60), Flare (60), AIM-120 (4),
AIM-9L (2), AIM-9M (2), Fuel Tank

KC-135R **(Shell)**

E-3C **(Big Bird)**

Opposition Aircraft

6 X MiG-23 GSh-301 (100), Chaff (40),
Flare (20), AA-6 (2), AA-8 (2)

4 X MiG-29 GSh-301 (300), Chaff (60),
Flare (60), AA-10 (4), AA-8 (4)

2 X MiG-29 30mm (600), Chaff (90),
Flare (90), AA-10 (4), AA-8 (4)

4 X Mi-8

5 X Mi-24

THE LEADING FORCE

It is the second day of the campaign. After the fierce fighting yesterday and into the night, we can safely state that the enemy has been literally stopped in their tracks. The Red side has sustained heavy damage so far, but has not lost its teeth. All through the night, our ground forces went through a vast reorganization operation. The Blue Force Commander had directed that this campaign switch from defensive to offensive ASAP, while the Red side is trying to catch its breath. The idea is to try to wedge our forces between Colorado City and the Red ground forces, and start pushing them back east.

USAF aircraft are called to provide CAS for Blue ground troops attempting to get into attack positions between Colorado City and the enemy ground forces.

Date 28 MAR 2004

Time 1705 HRS

Mission Type

CAS (Combat Air Support)

Mission Description

Destroy Red choppers and ground targets.

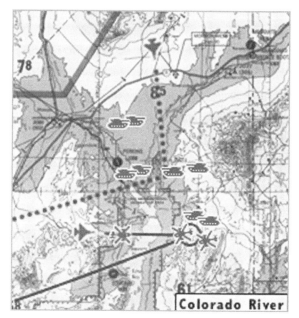

Colorado River

Situation

Mission Ops has directed us to provide full CAS for the first Blue offensive. The plan is to launch a three-pronged attack on the Red forces.

From the north, armor and artillery divisions are directed to attack the relatively weak defense the Red side has put there, and we will provide support for the ground troops by clearing away major enemy pockets in the way of our forces.

The second effort will concentrate on maneuvering our forces into the valley between Colorado City and the enemy's massive concentration of armor just to the east.

The third effort is in the south and consists of landing Airborne and Marine forces on the eastern bank of the river. In order to accomplish this landing, we must provide cover for the main task force, consisting mainly of helicopters and landing vessels.

Weather

CAVU (Clear and Visibility Unlimited)

Intel

Targets

Intelligence informs us that Mi-24 gunships and M-60 tanks were last seen two hours ago near the Jolly Green's planned landing area.

There is an ongoing battle in the northern area, and the Red Tanks are all over the eastern bank of the river.

The landing area

Northern Frontline

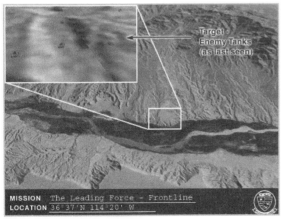

Threats

Possible AAA integral defense with ground forces. Possible mobile SAMs such as SA-8 and SA-6.

Primary Flights

Austin

Airframe	4 x F-16C
Task	Escort
Target	Choppers and Tanks
Loadout	CBU-87, AIM-9M, AIM-120

Buick

Airframe	4 x A-10A
Task	CAS
Target	Red Forces
Loadout	Mk 83, AGM-65D, AIM-9M

Supporting Flights

Jolly Green

Airframe	2 x MH-53J
Task	Commando airlift
Target	N/A
Loadout	N/A

Comanche

Airframe	2 x RAH-66 'Comanche'
Task	Escort
Target	N/A
Loadout	N/A

Tasking

Austin

Escort the Jolly Green flight to the landing area, and destroy any Mi-24 helicopters and tanks threatening it.

Buick

Destroy any artillery and tanks in the northern area over the eastern bank of the river, assisting the ground forces advance.

Mission Objectives

Austin

1. The MH-53 Jolly Green must deliver the commando troops safely to the landing area.

Buick

2. Destroy at least ten red tanks.

3. Comply with any requests in the air.

In Addition

✦ Jolly Green and at least five Blue tanks must survive.

Mission Tips

✦ For an efficient tank attack, use AGM-65 Mavericks at long range, and CBU-87 cluster bombs when closer to the targets. The CBU-87 has a large damage radius.

✦ Utilize your wingmen in this mission. They will be very useful.

✦ Be prepared for any new tasks during flight. Don't waste your ammo.

✦ Use your JTIDS. It will be useful.

✦ **Austin.** Destroy all enemy helicopters and switch to Buick flight.

✦ **Buick.** Destroy at least 10 enemy tanks on the eastern side of a river, then head upriver towards the bridge and be prepared to stop a secondary ground attack on Colorado City. Listen carefully to air requests.

Commander's Summary

Well, here we go. Till now we've taken losses but been able to successfully defend our assets. It's payback time, and you had better be on the ball to assist our men down there. It's time to change the nature of this war from a defensive one to an offensive one. This is our chance, and I expect each one of you to give them hell and protect our boys down on the ground. As usual, they are depending on us. Good luck to you all.

Assets & Opposition

Assets

4 X F-16C (Austin 1-4) PGU-28 (600), Chaff (60), Flare (60), AIM-120 (2), AIM-9M (4), CBU-87 (6)

2 X A-10A (Buick 1-2) PGU-14B (270), Chaff (80), Flare (60), AGM-65D (6), AIM-9M (4), Fuel Tank, Mk 83 (4)

2 X A-10A (Buick 3-4) PGU-14B (270), Chaff (100), Flare (80), AGM-65D (6), AIM-9M (4), Fuel Tank, Mk 83 (4)

2 X RAH-66 (Comanche 1-2) 30mm (500), Chaff (50), Flare (50), Rocket (20)

2 X MH-53J (Jolly Green)

3 X RAH-66 Chaff (30), Flare (30), Rocket (20)

Opposition Aircraft

Mi-24 30mm (600), Chaff (50), Flare (50), Rocket (20)

2 X Mi-24 Chaff (50), Flare (50), Rocket (20)

UMBILICAL CORD

Our effort in achieving key attack positions along the front has been costly, but successful. Our ground forces have established a new, closed front to the east of Colorado City, and are now facing the enemy in close quarters. Both sides are heavily exhausted, and are digging in for the night. High Command is worried that this campaign may bog down for a lengthy time and wear our forces out. Therefore, before night falls, there will be a last effort on our side to wear the enemy down and exhaust their supplies, which are continuously streaming in from the east.

USAF aircraft are assigned to cut the enemy's supply lines running through the Colorado River by air, ground and stream.

Date 28 MAR 2004

Time 1700 HRS

Mission Type

CAS (Combat Air Support)

Mission Description

Destroy transports, choppers and enemy forces.

Situation

Intelligence has discovered Red force supply lines approaching us across the Colorado River by air and ground. USAF aircraft are being sent to cut these lines. The targets assigned for destruction are "the heavies" — helicopters, enemy buildings and convoys around the Colorado River.

Weather

12000' scattered, visibility 17 miles

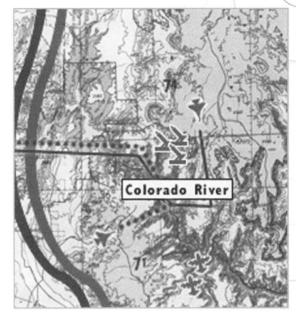

Intel

Targets

The Red Camp (photos on next page).

Threats

Probable AAA integral defense with the ground forces. Probable mobile SAMs such as SA-8 and SA-6.

Probable enemy air defending enemy forces.

Camp

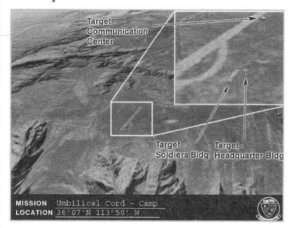

SA-6 East

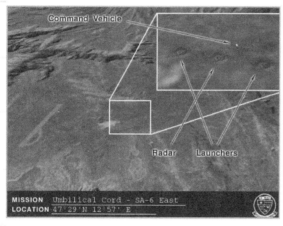

SA-6 West

Primary Flights

Austin

Airframe 4 x F-16C
Task CAS
Target Transports, Red Camp
Loadout AIM-9M, Mk 83, AIM-120

Buick

Airframe 4 x F-15E
Task CAS
Target Red Camp
Loadout Mk 82, CBU-93, AIM-9M, AIM-120

Tasking

Austin

Shoot down two enemy air transports before they land in the Red Camp. Afterwards locate the Red Camp at waypoint 4, where you are to destroy the headquarters building and the soldiers' quarters around the temporary dirt runway.

Buick

Hold position until called in to assist Austin in destroying the Red Camp buildings. Your target is the communication center in the camp.

All flights are armed with a variety of weapons, so that you should be prepared for any contingency.

Mission Objectives

Austin

1. Both enemy transports must be downed.

2. The headquarters building next to the runway must be destroyed.

3. The soldiers' quarters building next to the runway must be destroyed.

Buick

4. The communication center next to the runway must be destroyed.

Austin and Buick

5. Comply with any requests in the air. (Destroy the Red convoy.)

Mission Tips

✦ When launching AIM-120 AMRAAM missiles it is not necessary to stay locked onto the aircraft. The AMRAAM is a semi-active fire-and-forget missile. You can launch it and then lock onto another aircraft.

✦ **Austin.** Take care of all air targets. Your primary targets are the enemy transports.

✦ **Buick.** Destroy all ground structures (except hangar) around Red Camp, then pay attention to air requests.

Commander's Summary

I know you are all tired, but so are the grunts down there. If we manage to find and cut those supply lines it will shorten this war, and we'll all be able to hit the rack. But business first. Stay alert, don't fall asleep in the cockpit. Keep your eyes and ears open for surprises. While the Intel is poor and we don't know the exact location of their supply routes or supply bases, we need to find them and knock them out of business. Good luck!

Assets & Opposition

Assets

4 X F-16C (Austin 1-4) PGU-28 (600), Chaff (90), Flare (90), AIM-120 (2), AIM-9M (2), Mk 83 (6)

2 X F-15E (Buick 1-2) PGU-28 (700), Chaff (90), Flare (90), AIM-120 (2), AIM-9M (2), CBU-93 (2), Mk 82 (12)

2 X F-15E (Buick 3-4) PGU-28 (250), Chaff (120), Flare (60), AIM-120 (2), AIM-9M (2), CBU-93 (2), Mk 82 (12)

Opposition Aircraft

2 X MiG-29 GSh-301 (300), Chaff (60), Flare (60), AA-8 (4)

2 X MiG-29 GSh-301 (300), Chaff (60), Flare (60), AA-10 (4), AA-8 (4)

2 X MiG-23 GSh-301 (100), Chaff (40), Flare (20), AA-8 (2), Mk 83 (2)

3 X Mi-8

2 X Il-76

BLACK EYE

The Red ground assault force is in near chaos. The destruction of the supply lines was successful and delivered immediate results. The Red troops are getting hungry, thirsty, short of ammo, and beaten down by the constant bombardment from our artillery and bombers. It is apparent that their time is up. In some areas retreat is evident, and there is a feeling that the Red 'wall' is cracking. Headquarters is eager to move our offense deeper, and to strike at the core of the Red army's assets, including airfields, electric power plants, headquarters and command centers.

A night mission, in which USAF fighters and helicopters make use of TV-guided missiles to destroy the Red side's SA-10 defense.

Date   28 MAR 2004

Time   0200 HRS

Mission Type

SEAD (Suppression of Enemy Air Defense)

Mission Description

Night SAM Strike.

Situation

The JFACC has directed us to launch a night SEAD mission, which will consist of a preemptive strike to take out the enemy's long-range SAMs before the main strike at dawn. The objective of this night mission is to blow open a hole in the Red SAM defenses, which consist mainly of long range SA-10 missiles placed to guard the Red strategic assets.

Weather

Night, clear with unlimited visibility

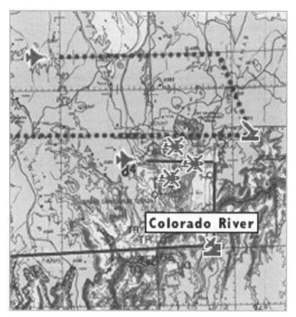

Colorado River

Intel

Targets

The primary target, which is to be destroyed by Buick, is the SA-10 site.

Threats

MiG-29 fighters, ZSU-23X4 'Gundish,' and AAA are our major threats tonight. The Gundish has an accurate radar and good night capabilities.

SA-10 site

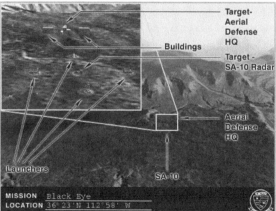

Primary Flights

Austin

Airframe 2 x F-16C
Task CAP
Target N/A
Loadout AIM-120, AIM-9L

Buick

Airframe 2 x F-15E
Task SEAD
Target SA-10 site and the aerial defense HQ
Loadout AGM-130, Mk 84, AIM-120, AIM-9L

Tasking

First wave to go in will be Atlanta, four AH-64 'Apache' helicopters assigned to destroy the Early Warning Radar sites in the area.

Austin

Provide CAP for Atlanta, against enemy air threats, fighters and attack helicopters as well.

Buick

Enter the target area and destroy the SA-10 site and the HQ located near the site, using a TV-guided AGM-130 missile.

Mission Objectives

Austin

1. Secure the Apaches and destroy all air-to-air threats. (Air-to-air threats include two Mi-24s and two or four MiG-29s.)

Buick

2. Destroy the SA-10 site and the HQ.

Mission Tips

✦ For night vision, press Ctrl N.

✦ Use the A/A radar in TWS mode to find air targets. Press Q to toggle radar modes.

✦ **Austin.** Destroy enemy helicopters quickly.

✦ **Buick.** To get a mission success, destroy the SAM site and the com center next to it.

Commander's Summary

Let's take advantage of the dark and bore some holes in their defense systems, so that come dawn, we can blow away the strategic assets that they really need to continue the war. So, let's fly smart, cover those choppers, and blow away this SA-10 site. Your success will make it a cake walk for our strikers to cream 'em at dawn.

Assets & Opposition

Assets

2 X F-16C (Austin 1-2) PGU-28 (600), Chaff (60), Flare (60), AIM-120 (4), AIM-9L (2), Small Fuel Tank

2 X F-15E (Buick 1-2) PGU-28 (250), Chaff (120), Flare (60), AIM-120 (6), AGM-130 (2), AIM-9L (2), Mk 84 (1)

4 X AH-64A (Atlanta 1-4) 30mm (500), Chaff (50), Flare (50), Rocket (20)

Opposition Aircraft

2 X Mi-24 30mm (500), Chaff (50), Flare (50), Rocket (20)

4 X MiG-29 GSh-301 (300), Chaff (60), Flare (60), AA-10 (4), AA-8 (4)

EAGLE EYES

After the night activity in which most of the peripheral Red targets have been dealt with, the Blue Command decides there is no point in wasting any more time. The conditions are right for an all-out strike at the Reds' heart, the Red airfield itself. Attacking the Red airfield moves the air campaign from a defensive situation to the offensive, and hopefully will begin to reduce the Reds' air power, which has been continuously hampering our air and ground movements.

The Blue side deploys its fighters in a strike on the Red airfield.

Date   29 MAR 2004

Time   0630 HRS

Mission Type

Strike

Mission Description

Blue aircraft strike the Red airbase.

Situation

In order to strike the well defended Red airfield, the two surviving SA-10 sites defending the airfield must be destroyed. Once the two sites are destroyed, AWACS will declare the target area clear, allowing Corvette flight of F-15Cs to perform a fighter sweep over the airfield against the defending MiGs. Following will be Dodge flight of F-15Es, who will attack the runways and A/C shelters.

Weather

15000' feet scattered, unlimited visibility

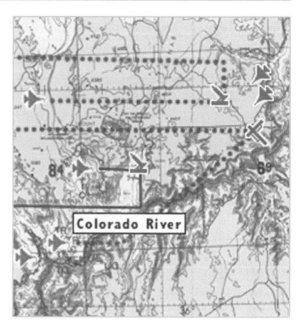

Colorado River

Intel

Targets

Runway Intersection.

Threats

Red MiG-29s may be scrambled. ZSU-23X4 AAA are defending the airfield, as well as the SA-10 sites.

Runway Intersection

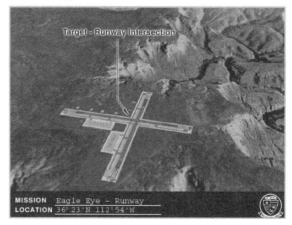

Target - Runway Intersection

MISSION   Eagle Eye - Runway
LOCATION 36° 23'N 112° 54'W

SA-10 site defending Red Base

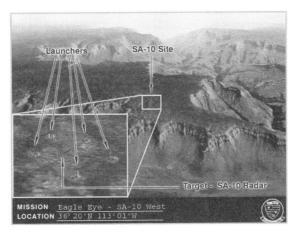

Eastern SA-10 site

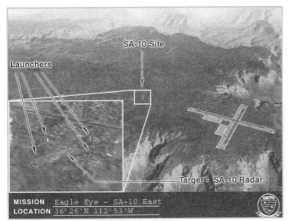

Primary Flights

Austin

Airframe	2 x F-16C
Task	SEAD
Target	SA-10 radar
Loadout	AGM-130, AIM-9L, AIM-120

Buick

Airframe	2 x F-16C
Task	SEAD
Target	SA-10 radar
Loadout	AGM-130, AIM-9L, AIM-120

Corvette

Airframe	2 x F-15C
Task	Sweep
Target	N/A
Loadout	AIM-120, AIM-9M

Dodge

Airframe	2 x F-15E
Task	AG
Target	Runway intersection
Loadout	Mk 84, AIM-120, AIM-9M

Tasking

Austin

Ingress from the west and destroy the SA-10 radar site that is positioned close to the runway, using AGM-130 TV-guided bomb.

Buick

Destroy the Eastern SA-10 radar, using AGM-130 TV-guided bomb. This should be done right after Austin destroys its target.

Corvette

Provide CAP for Dodge formation. Most enemy fighters are predicted to be on the ground, but some might have already taken off.

Dodge

Ingress from the west, and destroy the runway intersection using Mk 84 'dumb bombs.'

Mission Objectives

Austin and Buick

1. The two SA-10 radars must be destroyed.

Dodge

2. The runway intersection must be destroyed.

Mission Tips

✦ The AGM-130 TV-missile is launched like an ordinary bomb.

✦ To access full-screen MFD, press Z.

✦ To steer the missile, use Ctrl + ↑, ↓, ←, →.

✦ While in the full-screen MFD, pressing W and A (twice) will automatically fly the plane to the next waypoint, away from the SA-10 launch range.

Commander's Summary

OK, now's our chance to turn this campaign around. Until now we've been trying to keep our heads above the water preventing the Reds from getting the advantage. Now we're going into the lions' den, their primary airfield, which has puked out a lot of sorties against us. But revenge aside, this mission calls for cool heads. We're going in with AGMs, stealth and Strike Eagles, our top technology. Let's do this like professionals and take this campaign to their home drome and make them remember this day. Good luck!

Assets & Opposition

Assets

2 X F-16C (Austin 1-2) PGU-28 (510), Chaff (60), Flare (60), AGM-130 (2), AIM-120 (2), AIM-9L (4), Small Fuel Tank

2 X F-16C (Buick 1-2) PGU-28 (510), Chaff (90), Flare (60), AGM-130 (2), AIM-120 (2), AIM-9L (4), Small Fuel Tank

2 X F-15C (Corvette 1-2) PGU-28 (600), Chaff (100), Flare (100), AIM-120 (4), AIM-9M (4), Fuel Tank

2 X F-15E (Dodge 1-2) PGU-28 (250), Chaff (120), Flare (60), AIM-120 (2), AIM-9M (2), Mk 84 (7)

Opposition Aircraft

4 X MiG-29 GSh-301 (300), Chaff (60), Flare (60), AA-10 (4), AA-8 (4)

4 X MiG-29

TAKE AIM

The Red side has all but capitulated. Our forces have overrun nearly all the Red tactical positions, and our aircraft have landed and set up operations on the Red airfield. The campaign is nearly over, but the JFACC is keen to destroy a few more Red strategic targets before someone declares a cease-fire. If we don't do the job now we will have to pay the consequences of leaving the enemy with the potential for power in the future. Therefore, there is a last effort on our side to destroy three Red strategic installations before the cease-fire is declared:

1) The main Red headquarters.

2) Aircraft manufacturing facility.

3) Nuclear manufacturing and storage facility.

A final attack on the enemy nuclear facility. You are tasked with the destruction of the Red Side's nuclear core.

Date 30 MAR 2004

Time 1200 HRS

Mission Type

Strike and CAP (Combat Air Patrol)

Mission Description

Destroy the Red side's nuclear reactor core.

Situation

Blue Force has been assigned to destroy the Red nuclear facility and leave it inoperative for the next decade. A flight of B-2s will take out the SAMs around the nuclear plant. Other USAF flights will perform SEAD (Suppression of Enemy Air Defense) and fighter sweeps.

Weather

CAVU (Clear and Visibility Unlimited)

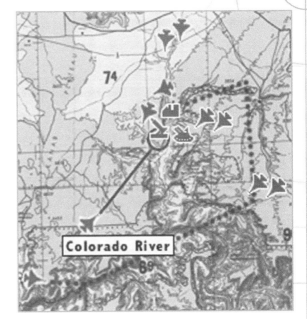

Intel

Targets

Dodge's target is the control center of the main reactor. This is a small building surrounded by two chimneys. Accurate aiming is vital. Guns are an appropriate weapon for this target since it is a small building and requires precision aiming.

Threats

Possible AAA and SAMs around the plant. Massive air defense in the area.

Control Center

Primary Flights

Austin

Airframe	4 x F-22A
Task	Sweep
Target	N/A
Loadout	AIM-9X, AIM-120

Buick

Airframe	4 x F-15C
Task	Sweep
Target	N/A
Loadout	AIM-9M, AIM-120

Corvette

Airframe	4 x F-16C
Task	Sweep
Target	N/A
Loadout	AIM-9M, AIM-120

Dodge

Airframe	2 x F-16C
Task	Strike
Target	Control center of the main reactor
Loadout	AIM-9M, AIM-120

Supporting Flights

Olds

Airframe	2 x F-16C
Task	Sead
Target	SA-6
Loadout	AGM-88, AIM-9M

Tasking

Austin

Perform an early sweep to clear enemy aircraft from the path to the plant.

Buick

Join Austin and engage the rest of the enemy aircraft.

Corvette

Provide backup for Austin and Buick.

Dodge

Take out the control center of the main reactor. This mission is a butt-kicker, because the building is located between two chimneys. Only this building can be destroyed. Around this building there are nuclear reactors that will create an environmental disaster if you hit them, and the main generator building houses many civilian workers. In order to succeed you'll have to attack in the direction of 250 degrees, which is the only direction you'll see the target. You must not hit any other buildings in the nuclear plant.

Pay attention to an exact STRF, or you'll hit other buildings. It will be easier to attack from a steep angle.

Mission Objectives

Dodge

1. Control center of the main reactor must be destroyed.

2. The nuclear core must not be hit.

3. The generator must not be hit.

Mission Tips

✦ Use [Shift][S] to disable the armament safety switch and launch while on the ground.

✦ Hitting any other building in the plant will cause an environmental disaster.

✦ Make sure you have locked onto the control center by checking the target view using [F4].

Commander's Summary

This is the final and most important mission of this campaign. We have won all the battles, but without the destruction of the nuclear plant, we won't be able to secure our future. Lets make it happen for mom, the kids and our future.

Assets & Opposition

Assets

2 X F-22A (Austin 1-2) PGU-28 (600), Chaff (90), Flare (90), AIM-120 (3), AIM-9X (2)

2 X F-22A (Austin 3-4) PGU-28 (200), Chaff (90), Flare (90), AIM-120 (3), AIM-9X (2)

4 X F-15C (Buick 1-4) PGU-28 (600), Chaff (60), Flare (60), AIM-9M (4), AIM-120 (4), Fuel Tank

4 X F-16C (Corvette 1-4) PGU-28 (200), Chaff (90), Flare (90), AIM-9M (4), AIM-120 (2), Small Fuel Tank

2 X F-16C (Dodge 1-2) PGU-28 (600), Chaff (90), Flare (90), AIM-9M (2), AIM-120 (2), Small Fuel Tank

2 X F-16C (Olds 1-2) PGU-28 (600), Chaff (90), Flare (90), AIM-9M (2), AGM-88 (2)

Opposition Aircraft

4 X MiG-23 GsH 301 (100), Chaff (40), Flare (20), AA-8 (2), AA-6 (2)

4 X MiG-29 GsH 301 (300), Chaff (60), Flare (60), AA-8 (4), AA-10 (4)

2 X Su-27 30mm (300), Chaff (20), Flare (20), AA-6 (2)

2 X Su-35 30mm (500), Chaff (40), Flare (40), AA-8 (4), AA-10 (4), AA-11 (2)

2 X Su-35 30mm (600), Chaff (30), Flare (30), AA-8 (4), AA-11 (4), AA-10 (4)

LOAD AND SUPPLY

Escort a new supply of weapons arriving at Nellis. You may fly this mission up to twice during the Red Arrow campaign.

Mission Type

Escort

Mission Description

Escort a package of cargo planes bringing in a new supply of weapons into Nellis AFB.

Situation

The 57th Wing/CC is worried about the quantity of weapons left in the armament bunkers, and has issued a request for a weapon supplementary.

This request has been approved at HQ, and a flight of three cargo planes carrying a full supply of weapons is flying into Nellis AFB.

Nellis HQ has issued two flights of F-22s to intercept and escort the cargo planes safely to our base in order to prevent trouble with any possible enemy air threats.

Weather

10000' scattered, visibility unlimited

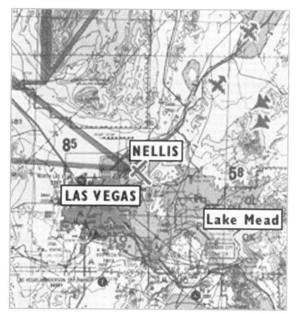

Intel

Targets

N/A

Threats

MiG-29 and Su-35 fighters are likely to contact Blue forces.

Mi-24 combat helicopters.

Primary Flights

Austin

Airframe   2 x F-22A
Task   CAP
Target   N/A
Loadout   AIM-120

Buick

Airframe   2 x F-22A
Task   CAP
Target   N/A
Loadout   AIM-120

Supporting Flights

Grizzly 1-3

Airframe   3 x C-17A
Task   Weapon supply
Target   N/A
Loadout   N/A

Tasking

Austin

Escort Grizzly 1-3 to their safe landing.

Buick

You will begin on the runway lineup, and take off when needed.

Mission Objectives

Austin and Buick

1. All three C-17s must land and taxi safely to the flight line.

    If the C-17As land safely, all your munitions are restored to 80% of their original quantities.

Commander's Summary

Well, you pulled today's milk run, so hopefully you can relax a bit from all the fighting, and just make sure the heavies make it safely home. If, and I say if because it seems unlikely, the Red guys try to intercept the heavies, give them hell and make sure that our guys land safely. We really need the weapons they're bringing in.

Assets & Opposition

Assets

2 X F-22A (Austin 1-2) PGU-28 (600), Chaff (90), Flare (90), AIM-120 (6)

F-22A (Buick 1) PGU-28 (600), Chaff (90), Flare (90), AIM-120 (6)

F-22A (Buick 2) PGU-28 (600), AIM-120 (6)

3 X C-17A (Grizzly 1-3)

Opposition Aircraft

2 X MiG-29 30mm (600), Chaff (90), Flare (90), AA-8 (2), Mk 83 (6)

2 X MiG-29 Mk 83 (6)

4 X Su-27 30mm (600), Chaff (90), Flare (90)

2 X Su-35 30mm (600), Chaff (90), Flare (90), 2100lb (1), 2100lb (1), AA-8 (4)

3 X Mi-24 Chaff (50), Flare (50), Rocket (20)

DEPLOY TO NELLIS

A new batch of USAF aircraft is deployed to Nellis AFB. You may fly this mission up to twice during the Red Arrow campaign.

Mission Type

CAP (Combat Air Patrol)

Mission Description

Deploy aircraft to Nellis AFB.

Situation

The continuing Red Arrow campaign is inflicting lots of casualties. The number of USAF pilots and aircraft is decreasing. HQ has sent a special request to deploy extra fighters to join the forces up front. Six aircraft have taken off from several airbases in the US to meet landing slot times at Nellis AFB at 1740, every three minutes.

Weather

Clear, visibility unlimited

Intel

Targets

N/A

Threats

Enemy radar is following all air traffic incoming to Nellis and will probably try to intercept them. Enemy fighters stand in high alert.

Primary Flights

Austin

Airframe	4 x F-15C
Task	Deploy
Target	N/A
Loadout	AIM-9M, AIM-120

Buick

Airframe	2 x F-22A
Task	Deploy
Target	N/A
Loadout	AIM-9X, AIM-120

Tasking

Austin

You are arriving from Alaska, and will refuel at the beginning of the mission, in order to make it safely into Nellis AFB. After refueling, head into Nellis AFB. If you encounter any enemy fighters on the way to Nellis, you may engage them, then go to landing. After landing, switch to Buick.

Buick

You are arriving from Edwards AFB in California, and will approach Nellis AFB from the west. Follow radio instructions, and land at Nellis.

Mission Objectives

Austin and Buick

1. Land all aircraft safely at Nellis.

    Those that land are added to your flight line. The pilots who flew them in are added to your roster.

Commander's Summary

OK, this is today's milk run, but it's not that easy. The Reds will probably try to intercept us, and cut down on our aircraft resource. Let's make them wish they hadn't!

Assets & Opposition

Assets

4 X F15C (Austin 1-4) PGU-28 (600), Chaff (120), Flare (60), AIM-120 (4), AIM-9M (4)

2 X F-22A (Buick 1-2) 30mm (900), Chaff (120), Flare (90), AIM-120 (3), AIM-9X (3)

2 X F-16C (Ford 1-2) PGU-28 (510), Chaff (90), Flare (90), 2100lb (1), AIM-120 (4), AIM-9M (2)

KC-135R (Shell)

E-3C (Big Bird)

Opposition Aircraft

MiG-23   30mm (800), Chaff (90), Flare (90), AA-8 (2)

3 X MiG-23 GSh-301 (100), Chaff (40), Flare (20), AA-8 (2)

MiG-29   GSh-301 (300), Chaff (60), Flare (60), AA-10 (2)

MiG-29   GSh-301 (300), Chaff (60), Flare (60), AA-8 (2)

MiG-29   30mm (600), Chaff (90), Flare (90), AA-10 (2), AA-8 (2)

MiG-29   30mm (600), Chaff (90), Flare (90), AA-8 (2)

2 X MiG-29 30mm (600), Chaff (90), Flare (90)

2 X Su-27 30mm (500), Chaff (60), Flare (60), AA-10 (2), AA-8 (2)

Su-35   30mm (600), Chaff (60), Flare (60), AA-10 (2), AA-8 (4)

Su-35   30mm (600), Chaff (60), Flare (60), AA-11 (1), AA-8 (2)

3 X Mi-8

SLEEPING GIANT

With an ailing Boris Yeltsin continuing to see his power base erode in the year 2000, the liberal reform government in Russia found it impossible to maintain a popular majority. The Russian army — previously a force of social cohesion, having helped Yeltsin avert a coup in the 1990s — now found itself deeply divided along political lines. With Russian citizens unhappy at the slow pace of market reform, hard-liners saw their chance to return to power. After much political infighting, a charismatic new army commander named Sergey Damidov was elected President by the Russian Duma, which had seen most of its reform-minded members systematically purged during the past several years. General Damidov was a Russian nationalist whose overriding goal was "a strong Russia" that would stand up to the West.

Damidov announced to an elated populous that Russia was no longer willing to accept its "second-rate" status in the world community and would once again claim its rightful place as a nuclear superpower. The next four years saw a severe weakening in NATO as events in the Balkans had Greece and Italy threatening to resign from the treaty organization. At the same time, there was increasing pressure at home for the US to reassess their Cold War strategy of being so closely linked to the defense of Europe. When a second Iran-Iraq war caused a dramatic jump in the price of crude oil, Russian export revenues increased dramatically. Damidov used this hefty windfall to embark Russia on an ambitious rearmament program, reorganizing their forces and upgrading their huge arsenal of tanks and aircraft. This economic expansion brought about by the large increase in military spending greatly solidified Damidov's domestic popularity as a strong leader.

Concerned about Russia's growing military might, Estonia, Latvia, and Lithuania urged NATO in 2004 to accept their countries as full members of the alliance. Worried Europeans and Americans were looking for an excuse to geographically isolate Russia and agreed to accept all three Baltic States. (This was but an expansion of a military guarantee provided to the Baltic States in 1998). The Russians immediately protested and launched an invasion of the Baltics, claiming that their use of force was justified in order to "prevent NATO's criminal attempt to cut off Russia's link with the Kaliningrad oblast." (The Kaliningrad oblast is a 100 km–wide Russian enclave on the Baltic Sea, an important military and commercial base which the Russians can only access via rail lines through Lithuania and Belarus.)

With no choice but to protect its newest member nations, NATO promptly declared war even though adequate forces were not in place. Sensing weakness in NATO's resolve, the Russians elected for a forward defense by advancing into Poland, where their much modernized army still had a tough time against Poland's western-equipped forces. Believing that dramatic victories on the borders of Germany and Austria might cause a serious fracture in NATO's willingness to liberate the Baltic States, the Russians committed more forces and pressed their advance into the Czech Republic. On May 27, 2005, the Russians launched a three-pronged attack. The southern group headed toward Austria with the northern group moving against Berlin and a central thrust into the heart of Germany. NATO is hurriedly putting together the ground forces necessary to repulse the Russian offensive. But in the meantime, the USAF must stop the Russian tanks from overrunning all of Central Europe.

Campaign Supplies

You have a finite amount of supplies available in the two future campaigns, Sleeping Giant and Red Arrow. If you run out of a type of aircraft or munition, you must choose another aircraft or a different loadout.

If you start losing aircraft and pilots, you can fly a 'deploy aircraft' mission, which involves six F-15Es, four F-16Cs and four F-22As. Whatever new aircraft survive the mission and arrive at your base are added to your available aircraft, and their pilots join your flight roster. (The two-crew F-15Es each add *two* pilots to your roster.)

A 'weapon supply' mission restores all munitions to 80% of their original quantities. If you have not expended more than 20% of a particular type of weapon, your stores of that weapon are not affected.

You can only fly two of each type of resupply mission ('deploy aircraft' and 'weapon supply').

You begin the Sleeping Giant campaign with the following quantities:

Pilots 45

Aircraft

A-10A 10		F-16C 12	
F-15C 8		F-22A 16	
F-15E 16		F-117A 4	

Air-to-Ground Munitions

AGM-45 10		GBU-10 12	
AGM-62 10		GBU-12 40	
AGM-65B . . .36		GBU-12D 20	
AGM-65D . . .36		GBU-15 7	
AGM-88 20		GBU-24 12	
AGM-130 8		GBU-27 12	
AGM-142 4		GBU-30 8	
CBU-52 15		Mk 20 15	
CBU-54 50		Mk 82 20	
CBU-58 12		Mk 83 30	
CBU-87 25		Mk 84 30	
CBU-89 12		BLU-27 20	
CBU-93 5		LAU61 Hydra Rocket .176	

Air-to-Air Munitions

AIM-7B 30		AIM-9L 16	
AIM-7F 20		AIM-9M 70	
AIM-7M 40		AIM-9P 20	
AIM-9B 20		AIM-9X 40	
AIM-9D 20		AIM-120 120	

RED ALERT

USAF aircraft are on the highest alert status, flying CAP, and waiting for the Russians to make their first move.

Date JUN 20 2005
Time 0630 HRS

Mission Type

CAP (Combat Air Patrol)

Mission Description

USAF aircraft are on CAP, anticipating a Russian invasion of any type.

Situation

NATO and USAF among them are holding a high state of alert, ready to meet the Russians' first move. USAF command has declared a high state of readiness, and has ordered a 24-hour CAP above USAF airfields. The general assessment is that the Russians will try to diminish NATO air power as a first move, by going after the airfields. Possible threats for this attack will be fighters, bombers and cruise missiles. There is also a lot of helicopter activity in the Russian side, indicating that a Commando Operation is not out of the question.

Weather

11000' cloudy, visibility 10 miles

Intel

Targets

N/A

Threats

The major threats are commando forces airlifted by Mi-8 'Hip' transport helicopters. These are likely to be escorted by MiG-29 and Su-27 sweeps, as well as Mi-24 'Hind' attack helicopters and Mi-8 'Hip' helicopters carrying commando troops. Cruise missiles are also expected.

MUNICH

Primary Flights

Austin

Airframe 4 x F-15C
Task Erding CAP
Target N/A
Loadout AIM-120, AIM-9M

Buick

Airframe 4 x F-22A
Task Landsberg CAP
Target N/A
Loadout AIM-120, AIM-9X

Supporting Flights

Big Bird

Airframe E-3C AWACS
Task AWACS
Target N/A
Loadout N/A

Shell

Airframe KC-135R
Task Tanker
Target N/A
Loadout N/A

Tasking

Austin

Refuel from the tanker, three miles ahead of you.

Should you get a report about Russian planes approaching, fly east to intercept them.

Your first priority are the Russian helicopters.

Buick

Assist Austin if the Russians target Erding AFB, while Austin will assist Buick if the target is Landsberg AFB.

Mission Objectives

Austin and Buick

1. Down all incoming Russian fighters, helicopters and cruise missiles. (There are up to four Mi-8s and four Mi-24s.)

In Addition

✈ Your com centers must survive.

Mission Tips

✈ Press [Ctrl][R] to start the refueling process.

✈ You may then refuel manually, or press [A], and the refueling will be done automatically.

✈ Send your wingmen to engage other targets. Press [Alt][E] to engage your radar target or [Alt][W] to engage other targets.

✈ When you run out of missiles choose guns, or switch to Buick by pressing [Shift][S].

Flythrough

✈ Austin flight is the best place to start — Austin will see most of the action and you don't want to miss out on that. Use your wingman keys to help you out. Send your wingman to take out the MiGs in the area, while you deal with the Mi-24s and Mi-8s that are headed to your airbase.

✈ After you have cleared the helicopters out of you airspace and there is no threat to your base from them you get a new message. This message will tell you that the enemy has launched two cruise missiles to take out your base. This is where your wingman commands will help you out a lot. Send the remaining wingman you have to take out one cruise missile while you take out the other. This is the best way to be a kick-butt pilot.

Commander's Summary

We're maintaining CAP on a 24-hour basis. Stay alert. If the Russians make a move, let's give them our full firepower, and send them back over the border. Good luck!

Assets & Opposition

Assets

4 X F-15C (Austin 1-4) PGU-28 (600), Chaff (120), Flare (60), AIM-120 (4), AIM-9M (4), Fuel Tank (3)

2 X F-22A (Buick 1-2) PGU-28 (600), Chaff (120), Flare (90), AIM-120 (3), AIM-9X (3)

2 X F-22A (Buick 3-4) PGU-28 (600), Chaff (90), Flare (60), AIM-120 (3), AIM-9X (3)

E-3C (Big Bird)

KC-135R (Shell)

Opposition Aircraft

MiG-29   GSh-301 (301), AA-10 (2), AA-8 (4)

MiG-29   30mm (600), Chaff (90), Flare (90), AA-8 (4)

2 X MiG-29   30mm (600), Chaff (90), Flare (90), AA-10 (2), AA-8 (4)

Su-27   GSh-301 (301), AA-8 (4)

Su-27   GSh-301 (301), AA-10 (2), AA-8 (4)

2 X Su-27   GSh-301 (300), Chaff (60), Flare (60), AA-8 (4)

2 X Su-27   AA-10 (2), AA-8 (4)

6 X Mi-8

6 X Mi-24

OPEN A CORRIDOR

After the initial Russian attempt to sabotage NATO's air assets, the battle has come to a standstill. Neither side wants to launch an all-out ground war, and use of nuclear arms is too risky for either side. What ensues is a strange situation of each side trying to hurt and sabotage the other side's assets, without playing their hands. A first attempt on these lines is the decision of NATO HQ to attack the strong SA-10 defense the Russians deployed in Austria, covering their main tank divisions and Austrian airports which the Russians have taken over and deployed their Air Force in. Destruction of these sites could open ingress routes for attacks on high value assets, as well as the possibility to begin some 'tank plinking' on the tank regiments on the border. The operation is a "rolling" kind, where each formation engages targets which are deeper than the formation before him, thus creating a corridor for the last formation to run through and destroy the main target.

USAF fighters have been assigned this extremely important mission. Blow open a hole in the Russian's SAM defense belt, in order to allow strike packages to ingress to strategic target areas.

Date   21 JUN 2005

Time   1600 HRS

Mission Type

SEAD (Suppression of Enemy Air Defense)

Mission Description

Destroy the SA-10 sites and Central Command Radar (CCR) in section A/12, and blow open a corridor for incoming NATO sweeps.

Situation

Section A/12 encompasses the area south of Salzburg, and is currently under Russian control. As a major ingress route, this area is monitored and controlled by CCR (Central Command Radar) 2B, and defended by two SA-10 sites: SA-10 North and SA-10 South. Destruction of these sites will allow B-2 bombers and other strike packages to ingress south to strategic targets in Austria, which the Russians are controlling for their war needs.

We will take out the two SA-10 sites using AGM-130 stand-off TV-guided missiles.

After the two sites are destroyed, a flight of Falcons will ingress to the CCR area and bomb the main CCR HQ building. Destruction of this building will leave the whole area defenseless for at least 48 hours.

Weather

20000' scattered, visibility 22 miles

SA-10 North Site

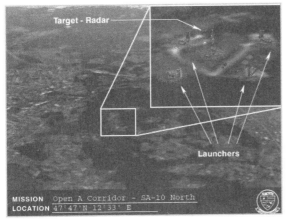

SA-10 South Site

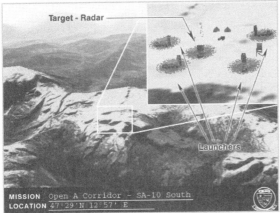

CCR Complex Site

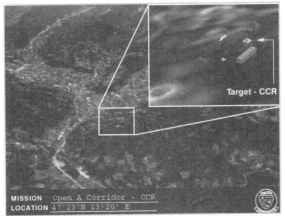

Intel

Targets

The first SA-10 site, SA-10 North, is located to the north of Bad Reichenhall on a hill.

The second SA-10 site, SA-10 South, is located on a very high alpine mountain, to the west of Bischofshofen.

The CCR is located on a hill between Sankt Johann and Radstadt.

The target in all SA-10 sites is the radar.

The target in the CCR complex is the main control building.

The CCR will be destroyed by ordinary bombs, since we are worried that the perimeter of the CCR is protected by jamming methods which might prevent use of any electronic methods. Two SA-6 sites and AAA protect the immediate vicinity of the CCR.

Threats

The major threat comes from the SA-10 batteries themselves. This advanced Russian SAM is effective for distances of up to 40 miles! Close to the CCR itself you will encounter SA-6 batteries defending it. Heavy SAM sites are defended by integral ZSU-23X4s for short range. Russian Su-27s and MiG-29s are patrolling in the vicinity of the front lines, and will scramble from the airfield to the east of SA-10 North.

Primary Flights

Austin

Airframe 2 x F-15E

Task SEAD

Target SA-10 North and SA-10 South

Loadout AIM-120, AIM-9M, AGM-130

Buick

Airframe 4 x F-16C

Task SEAD + Strike

Target CCR

Loadout AIM-120, AIM-9M, Mk 83, AGM-88

Supporting Flights

Olds

Airframe	4 x F-22A
Task	Sweep
Target	N/A
Loadout	N/A

Ford

Airframe	4 x B-2A
Task	Strike Mautendorf Factory
Target	N/A
Loadout	N/A

Stingray

Airframe	2 x F-15E
Task	Strike Mautendorf Power Plant
Target	N/A
Loadout	N/A

Big Bird

Airframe	E-3C AWACS
Task	AWACS
Target	N/A
Loadout	N/A

Tasking

Olds F-22 flight will perform an initial fighter sweep before Austin. Still, if any Russian fighter gets through to Austin, Austin 1 should send Austin 2 to engage.

Austin

Olds formation will be ahead of you but you will not be able to contact it on the radar due to F-22 stealth.

Pull up to 25,000 feet, launch an AGM-130 TV-guided missile on SA-10 North (waypoint 2), and turn north to waypoint 3, so as not to enter the deadly SA-10 range.

After hitting the SA-10 North radar, turn south to waypoint 4. Launch the second AGM-130 on SA-10 South, and turn north to waypoint 5 while guiding the TV missile home.

Then Switch to Buick (Shift 2).

Buick

Ingress to target area after the destruction of both SA-10 sites. At about 10 miles to target, you should launch two AGM-88 HARM missiles on the two SA-6 sites near the CCR, and then pull up and bomb the main building of the CCR with ordinary bombs, Mk 83.

Once this building is destroyed, it will be a 'go' for incoming strike packages to enter the area, en-route to their targets deeper in Austria.

Austin and Buick flights will be defended by F-22As and F-15Cs, but some enemy flights may get through, in which case we will engage them, dispatch, and continue with the mission.

Mission Objectives

Austin

1. Destroy SA-10 north site.
2. Destroy SA-10 south site.

Buick

3. Destroy the CCR complex site.

Mission Tips

✦ If the enemy's interceptors get close, send your wingman to deal with them (lock onto an enemy aircraft and order your wingmen to attack your target — Alt E).

✦ Strike the SA-10 using AGM-130 missiles.

✦ The AGM-130 TV missile is launched like an ordinary bomb.

To access full screen MFD, press Z.

To 'fly' the missile, use Ctrl + ↑, ↓, ←, →.

✦ After launching the bomb, fly your plane away from the target, activate Autopilot level (press A once), then press Z to display the full-screen MFD. Now, toggle waypoints be pressing W till you get the 'T' indicator on your screen. That's the target to hit!

✦ The target in any SAM site is the radar.

✦ AGM-88 HARM radar homing missile —
When you see the "In-Range" light up in the
MFD, you may launch. Toggle targets using
Ctrl Enter.

✦ Send number 3 or 2 to deal with the enemy's
interceptors — Alt E, Alt W, or Alt S.

Flythrough

✦ Study the map well, for it is very easy to get
sidetracked and lose sight of the targets.

✦ In Austin you will need to take out the northern SAM site and also the southern SAM site.

✦ After this you now need to go into your Buick
flight — make sure to take out any air targets
that are near you, then proceed to your target
area.

✦ When coming to your target area you will be
presented with two major problems. You have
SA-6s firing missiles at you, as well as two Su-
35s that don't seem to want you there. You
will have to be a crack pilot to get this one
done.

✦ After slipping by the enemy defenses, you have
to bomb the CCR building that is located on
a hill at your target location. The trick is that
the target is on the side of a hill, not on top.
There is no time limit here, so take your time
and make your shots count.

✦ If you follow the plan you will notice your ability to overcome your enemy getting better,
and you are starting to have a better under-
standing of how briefings work.

Commander's Summary

They asked for it. The ground war hasn't begun
yet. I think they're chicken, but this gives us an
edge now to pump some iron into the Russkies.
We're flying the best aircraft in the world, carrying
all ordnance, AA and AG, and we're going to show
them what this high-tech machine can do. This is
a precise standoff mission. Let's do this the quiet,
professional way!

Assets & Opposition

Assets

F-15E (Austin 1) PGU-28 (600), Chaff (120),
Flare (60), AGM-130 (2),
AIM-120 (6), AIM-9M (2)

F-15E (Austin 2) PGU-28 (600), Chaff (120),
Flare (60), AGM-130 (2),
AIM-120 (5), AIM-9M (3)

2 X F-16C (Buick 1-2) PGU-28 (600),
Chaff (120), Flare (60), AGM-88 (2),
AIM-120 (2), AIM-9M (2), Mk 83 (6)

F-16C (Buick 3) PGU-28 (510), Chaff (90),
Flare (90), AIM-120 (2), AIM-9M (2),
CBU-87 (6), Mk 83 (6)

F-16C (Buick 4) PGU-28 (510), Chaff (90),
Flare (90), AIM-120 (2), AIM-9M (2),
CBU-87 (6), Mk 83 (3), Mk 84 (1)

2 X F-22A (Olds 1-2) PGU-28 (510),
Chaff (90), Flare (60), AIM-120 (6)

2 X F-22A (Olds 3-4) PGU-28 (600), Chaff (90)
Flare (60), AIM-120 (3), AIM-9X (2)

4 X B-2A (Ford 1-4)

2 X F-15E (Stingray 1-2)

E-3C (Big Bird)

Opposition Aircraft

Su-27 GSh-301 (600), Chaff (90), Flare (90),
AA-10 (2), AA-8 (4)

Su-27 GSh-301 (600), Chaff (90), Flare (90),
AA-10 (2), AA-8 (2)

Su-27 30mm (600), Chaff (90), Flare (60),
AA-8 (4)

Su-27 30mm (600), Chaff (90), Flare (60),
AA-10 (2), AA-8 (4)

2 X Su-27 GSh-301 (301), Chaff (60), Flare (60),
AA-10 (2), AA-8 (2)

MiG-29 GSh-301 (301), Chaff (60), Flare (60),
AA-10 (4), AA-11 (4)

MiG-29 GSh-301 (301), AA-10 (4), AA-11 (4)

MiG-29 30mm (600), Chaff (90), Flare (90),
AA-10 (4), AA-8 (4)

2 X MiG-29 30mm (600), Chaff (90), Flare (90)

2 X MiG-29 30mm (600), Chaff (90),
Flare (90), AA-8 (2)

SPECIAL DELIVERY

In direct continuation with the last mission, as the SA-10 wall crumbles, waves of F-117A and B-2 bombers are sent in to strike at strategic targets. NATO's view is that disabling the enemy's stretched supply routes and facilities will cripple the Russians' long-range plans and prevent them from launching an all-out war. While the cruise missiles are doing a good job on their targets, they are not causing enough collateral damage, are too expensive, and are rapidly diminishing in amounts. Therefore, as opposed to safe standoff tactics adopted in the Gulf and Kosovo, USAF HQ and NATO believe more and more in delivering the goods personally, in the form of F-117 and B-2 bombers. F-22s are assigned to provide fighter cover for these bombers. F-16Cs are assigned to clear the way from SAM sites.

USAF fighters escort and assure that F-117s reach enemy strategic targets and bomb them.

Date   21 JUN 2005

Time   1730 HRS

Mission Type

Strike

Mission Description

Clear the way for the F-117As strike package assigned to destroy the Bruck Nuclear Reactor.

Situation

At the outset of the occupation of Austria, the Russians have harnessed all the Austrian facilities for their own use. One such facility is the Bruck Nuclear Plant. One of the finest nuclear facilities in the world, the Bruck plant was completed in February 2002, and was designed to pave the way

in the field of modern nuclear propulsion. Now, however, the Russians have harnessed this facility to meet their immediate needs, that of producing nuclear warheads for the coming struggle against the Western world.

Deprived of many of its resources in the last two decades, owing to mutual nuclear arms agreements with the US and NATO, Russia and the Russian leader Damidov thrive on assets such as this one. In a joint NATO conference, including the top scientific forum of the Western world, it was decided that we must take a loss on this fine facility, rather than letting it serve the enemy's dire plans. Therefore, in the broad sweep of bombings taking place this afternoon, after the SA-10 defense is down in most areas, the Bruck Nuclear Plant has been added to the list of targets. Guarding the facility are two SA-6 sites and AAA, and of course it is obvious that the Russians will scramble every available fighter to withstand this attack.

Weather

20000' cloudy, visibility 15 miles, light showers

Intel

Targets

Your targets are the two SA-6 sites defending the nuclear facility — SA-6 North and SA-6 South.

The Bruck nuclear facility.

SA-6 North site

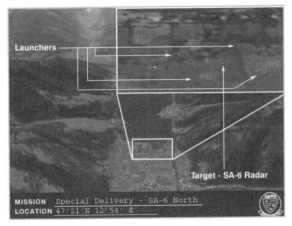

SA-6 South site

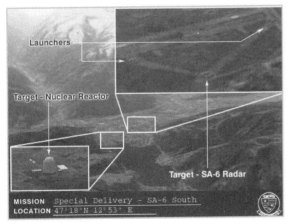

Threats

All available Russian fighters, including Su-27s and MiG-29s.

SA-6 sites pose a threat to all flights. Possible ZSU-23X4 en route and defending the SA-6.

Primary Flights

Austin

Airframe	4 x F-22A
Task	Sweep
Target	N/A
Loadout	AIM-120, AIM 9X

Buick

Airframe	4 x F-16C
Task	SEAD, Strike
Target	SA-6 North, SA-6 South
Loadout	AIM-120, AIM-9M, CBU-87

Corvette

Airframe	2 x F-117A
Task	Strike
Target	Bruck Nuclear Facility
Loadout	GBU-27

Supporting Flights

Ford

Airframe	2 x F-15C
Task	Escort
Target	N/A
Loadout	N/A

Olds

Airframe	2 x B-2A
Task	Strike
Target	Armament Factory
Loadout	Mk 84

Stingray

Airframe	2 x B-2A
Task	Strike
Target	Armament Factory
Loadout	Mk 84

Big Bird

Airframe	E-3C AWACS
Task	AWACS
Target	N/A
Loadout	N/A

Tasking

Austin

Precede the strike package and clear the area from all Russian fighters.

Buick

Ingress to target area at low altitude, find the northern SA-6 radar. Pop-up to 12,000 feet, and destroy the SA-6 radar.

After the target is destroyed, Buick flight will continue south to the target area, pop-up and bomb the Southern SA-6 radar.

After this, Buick can attack the two AAA sites near the target, Gundish-A and Gundish-B, using the remaining CBUs.

Both flights should stay alert for surprises. There is a chance that the Russians will deliver a strike of their own. We should provide cover for our F-117 and B-2s, while at the same time keeping an ear open for new developments!

Corvette

Ingress to target area, choose GBU-27 in your AG armament, and bomb the nuclear dome. Corvette 2 will bomb the laboratories near the dome.

Mission Objectives

Austin

1. Shoot down all Russian aircraft (up to 4 Su-35s).

Buick

2. Destroy SA-6 north site.

3. Destroy SA-6 south site.

Corvette

4. Destroy the Bruck Nuclear Reactor.

Mission Tips

✦ The target in any SAM site is the radar.

✦ When you hear the SAM launch warning, press [Insert] and [Delete] to deploy chaff and flare, turn 90 degrees from the missile (use [F5]), and break up or down.

✦ Press [F5] to view any missile that is being launched at you.

✦ To launch a GBU-27 laser guided bomb, choose it in the AG armament (press [ｉ]).

✦ Press [Ctrl][L] to activate the laser.

✦ Locate the target in the right MFD (Press [Z] for full screen), and lock on the target.

✦ You can locate the target in the AG radar, Map mode, and the laser will slave to it.

Flythrough

✦ Ok, by now you know how to bomb and take out air and ground threats at the same time. This mission is going to sharpen these skills. After the last mission you have paved a way to the primary target that you wanted in the first place. The primary target of this mission is the Nuke plant.

✦ Start off in Buick flight, as Austin will be able to fend off your air threat for you. Buick's main target for this mission are the SA-6 sites that are close to the Nuke plant. You will need to take these out before the B-2s can take out the generator and the surrounding buildings.

✦ Once you have neutralized the ground and air threat you are ready to hit the big one. Jump into Corvette and head to your primary target — this would be the Nuke plant. You are going to hit this building with two GBU-24s — make sure that when you drop your bombs that the piper is just at the bottom of the target or you will miss.

✦ After you've done this you might think that you're done. But one of those nasty little Su-35s has managed to slip by the damaging strike you just did. Switch to Austin flight and head after him. If he's still in the sky you will not finish this mission. Don't let him get back to warn the others.

Commander's Summary

Our last mission was successful. The SAM wall was burst open, allowing us to go in deep and strike at strategic targets. Well, we have this one with a nuclear reactor involved, so we better make sure the F-117s blow it to hell, or even our families back in the States won't be safe from this Damidov guy. Austin flight, show the Russkies why it's better to fly an F-22 than a MiG. Buick, you're flying at mud altitude in this mission, so watch your behinds, and give those SAM guys their ticket back home. Corvette, work quietly and professionally, and destroy that reactor! OK, we have work to do. Good luck!

Assets & Opposition

Assets

4 X F-22A (Austin 1-4) PGU-28 (600), Chaff (120), Flare (120), AIM-120 (3), AIM-9X (3)

4 X F-16C (Buick 1-4) PGU-28 (510), Chaff (120), Flare (60), AIM-120 (4), AIM-9M (2), CBU-87 (6), Small Fuel Tank

2 X F-117A (Corvette 1-2) M61 Vulcan, Chaff (80), Flare (60), GBU-27 (2)

2 X F-15C (Ford 1-2) PGU-28 (600), Chaff (60), Flare (60), AIM-120 (4), AIM-9M (4)

2 X B-2A (Olds 1-2) Chaff (30), Flare (20), Mk 84 (8)

2 X B-2A (Stingray 1-2)

E-3C (Big Bird)

Opposition Aircraft

2 X MiG-29 GSh-301 (300), Chaff (60), Flare (60)

2 X Su-27 GSh-301 (300), Chaff (60), Flare (60), AA-8 (2)

2 X Su-27 GSh-301 (600), Chaff (90), Flare (90)

Su-27 GSh-301 (300), Chaff (60), Flare (60), AA-8 (2)

Su-27 30mm (600), Chaff (90), Flare (90), AA-8 (2)

2 X Su-27 30mm (600), Chaff (90), Flare (90)

Su-35 GSh-301 (600), Chaff (90), Flare (90), AA-8 (4), Mk 82 (6)

Su-35 AA-8 (4), Mk 82 (6)

2 X Su-35 GSh-301 (600), Chaff (90), Flare (90), AA-8 (4), Mk 82 (8)

LOCK AND LOAD

While the deep strategic strikes are going well, NATO's attention is drawn back to the front line. Not because of any Russian troop movement, but because of the havoc played by the long-range surface-to-surface missiles and artillery the Russians are using against civilian targets. Many German villages and towns are taking heavy losses, and the roads are being filled with thousands of refugees, fleeing west from the shelling. This, (in addition to the humanitarian aspect, of course) is threatening to hamper NATO and US movement on the ground. Therefore, NATO HQ and USAF High Command have decided to deal with this threat without delay. They have given extra attention to the artillery side of the issue, as an element which can and must be dealt with prior to a ground attack, which most people are already seeing as inevitable.

USAF fighters launch an attack against Russian SS-21s.

Date   24 JUN 2005

Time   0630 HRS

Mission Type

CAP (Combat Air Patrol) and Strike

Mission Description

Strike Russian SS-21 launchers and artillery vehicles.

Situation

An SS-21 convoy has been spotted by JSTARS on its way north, in the valley south of Salzburg.

It is likely that these launchers are on their way from the arming and refueling area to the launch area. This is typical pre-launch behavior, and the convoy must be stopped before launch.

Special Ops have been assigned to send a laser-designating team into enemy territory, and work with us on this one. The team will be situated in key positions, and will call us on our frequency to start the designating sequence. We will be armed with GBU-24 laser bombs, which will pick up the designating team's signal, and ride the beam right to the target.

Weather

Clear, with unlimited visibility

Intel

Targets

The SS-21 launchers are the primary targets in the convoy. We do not have any info as to their current position.

Threats

MiG-29s are on CAP throughout the Salzburg. Possible AAA with the convoy.

Primary Flights

Austin

Airframe 4 x F-22A
Task Sweep
Target N/A
Loadout AIM-120, AIM-9X

Buick

Airframe 4 x F-15E
Task Strike
Target SS-21 Launchers
Loadout GBU-24, AIM-120, AGM-88

Tasking

Austin

Ingress from the west toward target area, and perform a fighter sweep, clearing the way from any enemy fighters that may be scrambled to the area. Remain on CAP for the rest of the mission.

Buick

Destroy the SS-21 launchers. Ingress from the north towards the target area (the valley between Salzburg and Hallein), find the convoy using your A/G radar. The ground force is located near waypoint 2. The ground force callsign is 'Lion.' They'll call you on our frequency, and will designate the targets one by one. Time of designation is limited so you must destroy them as soon as possible.

Mission Objectives

Buick

1. All SS-21 launchers must be destroyed.

Mission Tips

+ This is a multi-flight mission. If you are flying Austin and you hear Buick report "Approaching Targets," or if you hear the Ground Force call out the targets, switch to Buick ([Shift][2]).

+ Press [R] to switch to Ground Radar.

+ The Radar will be in GMT (Ground Moving Target) mode, and will only display moving targets. This will make it easier to locate moving targets.

Flythrough

+ Well, time to pull off some serious pilot stuff now. You have three flights of four MiG-29s headed to take out Austin, and Buick has a long way to the target. Just a small hint — if you set your radar to standby ([Shift][R]) the F-22 will be virtually invisible to radar.

+ Start in Austin flight and set the loadout for the F-22 to carry AIM-120s — this will give you some chance to take out the MiGs before they get close to you.

+ After you have taken out a few, turn that radar to standby. At this point start using guns; hopefully you have practiced your skills in this category.

+ After you've kept the MiGs occupied for a while and there are no more than ten of them left, switch back to Buick. Head to the primary target, which in this case are the SS-21 mobile missile launchers at waypoint 2.

+ Another bombing run here using the laser-guided bombs. You have ground troops that will target the ground targets for you, so don't worry about having your wingmen target them for you. After the ground troops have radioed you and said the target is lazed, you may begin to target them. Take out the ground targets around the area — if you neglect any ground targets you may find yourself parachuting to safety. After you have bombed the SS-21s, feel proud; you have just stopped them from destroying your airbase and costing lives.

Commander's Summary

We're up against the best planes the enemy has. Avoid getting into close dogfights. Use your long-range missiles, and your wingman!

Small tip — when bombing ground targets that are on the move, it's best to aim a little further up, to their future point of arrival.

It's very important to eliminate these targets. They're creating havoc every night.

Let's go in, do our job quickly, and egress out, lest they grasp what's shakin.' Then the MiGs will be wakin.'

Assets & Opposition

Assets

2 X F-22A (Austin 1-2) PGU-28 (150), Chaff (100), Flare (100), AIM-120 (3), AIM-9X (3)

2 X F-22A (Austin 3-4) PGU-28 (150), AIM-120 (3), AIM-9X (3)

2 X F-15E (Buick 1-2) PGU-28 (150), Chaff (100), Flare (100), AGM-88 (2), AIM-120 (2), GBU-24 (7)

2 X F-15E (Buick 3-4) PGU-28 (150), Chaff (120), Flare (60), AGM-88 (2), AIM-120 (2), GBU-24 (7)

Opposition Aircraft

MiG-29 GSh-301 (301), Chaff (30), Flare (30), AA-10 (4), AA-8 (4)

4 X MiG-29 GSh-301 (301), Chaff (50), Flare (50), AA-10 (4), AA-8 (4)

MiG-29 GSh-301 (301), Chaff (60), Flare (60), AA-10 (4), AA-8 (4)

2 X MiG-29 GSh-301 (301), Chaff (70), Flare (70), AA-10 (4), AA-8 (4)

2 X MiG-29 GSh-301 (301), Chaff (90), Flare (90), AA-10 (4), AA-8 (4)

MiG-29 GSh-301 (301), Chaff (30), Flare (30), AA-10 (2), AA-8 (4)

MiG-29 GSh-301 (301), AA-10 (4), AA-8 (4)

THE BATTLE OF SALZBURG

The Russian high command is worried about the time passage. NATO forces are creating havoc along the front lines and in deep strategic assets, and Damidov feels his hands are tied. To launch a ground war now, with NATO's immense air power, would be suicidal. On the other hand, waiting will wear out his forces, at least for this year. Therefore, Damidov decides on a huge air attack on German cities, with the true intent of luring NATO air power into a deadly air battle, trying to gain air supremacy as a priority before any ground movement. NATO recognized this intent at the last minute, and scrambled all the fighters right away. USAF Command has issued a directive in which the main targets are the Russian supply aircraft, the Ilyushin 76s. Downing these aircraft could well paralyze the Russian Air Force capability to launch any serious air campaigns in the future. It seems that the Battle of Salzburg will be the decisive one in this campaign.

USAF fighters bait the Russians into a large-scale air battle, in order to shoot down a Russian Il-76.

Date   26 JUN 2004

Time   1200

Mission Type

Strike and CAP (Combat Air Patrol)

Mission Description

Shoot down a Russian Il-76 Transport.

Situation

In order to down the Russian Il-76, we must lure away their air defense package. The package consists of MiG-29 and Su-27 fighters. The Il-76 transport is about 40 miles from them, monitoring their actions.

The bait that will cause the Russians to launch their defense package will be an A/G strike against their ground forces or air defense systems. Austin will come from the south and destroy EWR (Early Warning Radar) sites in the vicinity of Salzburg. At the same time, Buick F-22 flight will ingress from the west at low altitude. Buick will try to surprise the enemy by using its stealth and pull up to intercept the Il-76, behind the fighters. From prior intelligence we know that the Il-76 should be approximately on a route to the east of Salzburg, usually flying at an altitude of 20,000 feet and defended by fighters.

Weather

Storm, with scattered showers

Intel

Targets

Your two targets are Radar Station E-12 near Salzburg runways and the Il-76 transport aircraft.

Radar Station E-12

Target - Early Warning Radar   Radar Site

MISSION   The Battle Of Salzburg
LOCATION 47°43'N 12°29'E

Threats

Fighter planes of all types. Possible AAA integral defense around the Salzburg area.

Possible mobile SAMs, such as SA-8 and SA-13.

Primary Flights

Austin

Airframe 4 x F-15E
Task   Strike
Target   Radar Station E-12
Loadout   GBU-24, AIM-120, AIM-9L

Buick

Airframe 4 x F-22A
Task   CAP
Target   Il-76
Loadout   AIM-120, AIM-9X

Tasking

Austin

Ingress from the south inside the valley and destroy Radar Station E-12 near Salzburg Airfield's runways using GBU-24 laser bombs. The target will be designated for three minutes from the time you reach the target area.

Buick

Ingress from the west, at low altitude. Acquire the Il-76 by radar, and down it.

Mission Objectives

Austin

1. Radar Station E-12 must be destroyed.

Buick

2. The Il-76 must be destroyed.

Mission Tips

✦ Select the GBU-24 bomb to activate the LAN-TIRN display.

When the target is designated by a ground force, the display will be slaved to the closest designated spot.

You will see the laser spot displayed as a square on your HUD.

Release the GBU bomb when approaching the target. It will automatically fly to the designated spot.

Flythrough

✦ Now that you've taken out the mainstay of their air support, we've gotten word that they intend to re-supply an airfield. Your two main targets in this one are the IL-76 cargo supply plane and the P-14 radar. Time to use some of those bombing abilities again.

✦ In this one start off in Austin and head to the target location; you're looking for a radar station. This looks like a big satellite dish (a small hint — there are two of these).

✦ After bombing the targets it's time to address the Il-76 trying to supply the enemy. Now switch to Buick and head to the target waypoint. When you get close to the airfield that you just bombed there will be several target aircraft; keep in mind you can come back and finish them off later.

✦ Your primary target is the Il-76 and you will need your missiles for it. This cargo plane is far ahead of you so use your afterburners to catch up to it.

✦ On the way you may have some MiGs trying to shoot you down. Use your wingman commands to keep them busy while you go for the target. Once the Il-76 is downed you will get your 'pass mission' pop-up.

✦ If you wish to make a few extra points, continue and down a few more MiGs. This will give you those extra points for that new rank you're looking for.

Commander's Summary

Use your wingmen to shoot down the blocking fighters. This will leave you with some extra armament, which you're going to need once you reach that big Il-76!

Try to get around the fighters, and don't engage them. Remember that the objective is downing that Ilyushin, and not another MiG-29. Maintain high speed, and don't get mixed up in any 'turning' dogfights. You've got the best aircraft in the world, and this mission is a tough one. I'm counting on you — good luck!

Assets & Opposition

Assets

2 X F-15E (Austin 1-2) PGU-28 (600), Chaff (60), Flare (60), AIM-120 (4), AIM-9L (4), Fuel Tank, GBU-24 (2)

2 X F-15E (Austin 3-4) PGU-28 (250), Chaff (120), Flare (60), AIM-120 (6), AIM-9L (2), Fuel Tank, GBU-24 (2)

4 X F-22A (Buick 1-4) PGU-28 (200), Chaff (60), Flare (60), AIM-120 (3), AIM-9X (3)

Opposition Aircraft

4 X MiG-29 GSh-301 (300), Chaff (60), Flare (60), AA-10 (2), AA-8 (2)

2 X MiG-29 GSh-301 (300), Chaff (60), Flare (60), AA-8 (2)

2 X Su-35 30mm (600), Chaff (40), Flare (40), AA-8 (2)

2 X Su-35 30mm (500), Chaff (40), Flare (40), AA-8 (2)

2 X Su-35 AA-11 (2), AA-8 (2)

2 X Su-35 30mm (500), Chaff (70), Flare (70), AA-11 (2), AA-8 (2)

WATERSHIP DOWN

In the NATO debriefing at 2300, the Commander-in-Chief of NATO forces declared that the Russian air power has been destroyed for all practical purposes. In the Battle of Salzburg, NATO forces have summed up close to 562 Russian aircraft destroyed, as well as three Ilyushin 76 aircraft. This situation means that Damidov is backed into a corner, on one hand from NATO pressure, while on the other hand from restlessness within. The sheer number of Russian aircraft downed during the day caused Damidov to lose his main playing card, and to seek a fast and clever way to gain back some prestige, especially back home where dissident murmurs are growing louder and more widespread. NATO wishes to calm things down a bit and not continue the pressure, afraid that backing Damidov into a tighter spot will prompt him into using nuclear arms. NATO's directive is to continue on with strategic strikes, gnawing at assets which have significance if a total ground war ensues, and leave the front line alone for now.

USAF aircraft are assigned to destroy the bridges over the Danube (Donau), and any Russian naval force in the river, to hamper any ground movement in the future from the northern area of Linz to the south, and vice-versa.

USAF fighters are assigned to destroy the bridges on the Danube, as well as Russian naval forces in the river.

Date 27 JUN 2004

Time 1200

Mission Type

Strike and CAP (Combat Air Patrol)

Mission Description

Destroy the bridges over the Danube.

Situation

Intelligence has been updating that Russian forces may attempt to enter German territory by using the bridges over the Danube River. In order to diminish the possibility of this event, USAF aircraft are assigned to destroy the four major bridges over the Danube River. The secondary mission is to destroy any Russian naval force in the river and any ground forces along the river.

Weather

10000' scattered, visibility unlimited

Intel

Targets

Your targets are four bridges on the Danube River.

Threats

Possible OSA ships in the river. Probable Su-35 and Su-27 aircraft. Probable AAA.

Bridge 1

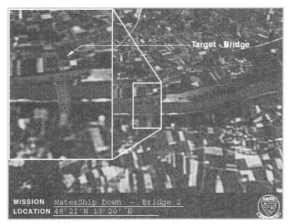

Bridge 2

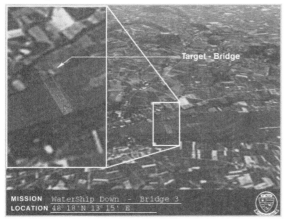

Bridge 3

Bridge 4

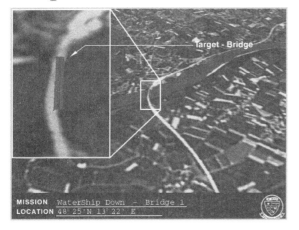

Primary Flights

Austin

Airframe	2 x F-15E
Task	Strike
Target	Bridges Site
Loadout	GBU-24, Mk 84, AIM-120, AIM-9M

Buick

Airframe	4 x F-22A
Task	CAP
Target	N/A
Loadout	AIM-120, AIM-9X

Corvette

Airframe	4 x A-10A
Task	CAS
Target	Ships and Ground Forces
Loadout	AGM-65B, Mk 82, AIM-9M

Supporting Flights

Shell

Airframe	KC-135R
Task	Tanker
Target	N/A
Loadout	N/A

Big Bird

Airframe	E-3C AWACS
Task	Control
Target	N/A
Loadout	N/A

Tasking

Austin

Destroy the four bridges over the river, starting from the southern bridge and progressing north.

Buick

Orbit west of the border, and make sure that Austin is able to complete its work safely.

Corvette

Attack all naval forces in the river and ground forces east of the river.

Mission Objectives

Austin

1.   All four bridge sites must be destroyed.

Corvette

2.   All enemy ships must be destroyed.

Mission Tips

✦ Remember to switch to Buick flight (Shift 2) when bandits close on you.

✦ Press I to toggle to the laser bomb. You will see the LANTIRN video source on your MFD (Multi-Function Display).

Switch your radar to A/G Map mode using R and Q.

Lock onto the target and make sure you are on the correct one by pressing F4.

Activate the laser designation using L.

In this stage the laser pod will lock onto the target and the HUD (Head up Display) will mark the position of the designated target.

Fly towards the target and climb to 10,000 feet above ground level.

When you reach 2.5 miles to target, lower your nose 20 degrees below the horizon, towards the target and release the bomb.

Flythrough

♣ Well, by now you've figured out that bombing is a very important weapon in war. Without it most of your planes would be lost to the enemy. In this mission you might want to give Buick some AGMs — you decide which ones.

♣ Start off in Austin. Head to your target waypoint. Your primary targets are the four bridges that cross the river. Make sure that you use one bomb for each — if you miss you might have a little problem on your hands.

♣ After you've successfully taken out the bridges, move on to Corvette flight. Buick flight is there to cover you, and they seem to do a good job of it. In Corvette flight, the A-10A is your weapon to fight the ground war, so let's get cracking. Off to the target location and you're looking for the OSA boats in the river. Now is when you will find that AGMs are your best friend.

♣ After the boats are taken out, you've successfully completed the mission. However, you might be tempted to go back and get rid of the rest of the enemy troops. Go ahead — your next mission is going to take more of this kind of targeting and flying, so you might as well get some practice.

Commander's Summary

Bridge bombing requires accurate aiming. This obligates a wide bombing run pattern.

Buick must be alert for Bandits trying to stand in the striker's way.

To avoid the AAA, fly high and don't scratch the ground. Good luck!

Assets & Opposition

Assets

2 X F-15E (Austin 1-2) PGU-28 (600), Chaff (120), Flare (60), AIM-120 (2), AIM-9M (2), GBU-24 (6), Mk 84 (1)

2 X F-22A (Buick 1-2) PGU-28 (600), Chaff (90), Flare (90), AIM-120 (3), AIM-9X (3)

2 X F-22A (Buick 3-4) PGU-28 (200), Chaff (120), Flare (60), AIM-120 (3), AIM-9X (3)

A-10A (Corvette 1) PGU-14B (270), Chaff (100), Flare (80), AGM-65B (12), AIM-9M (4), Fuel Tank, Mk 82 (4)

A-10A (Corvette 2) PGU-14B (270), Chaff (100), Flare (80), AGM-65B (9), AIM-9M (4), Fuel Tank, Mk 82 (7)

A-10A (Corvette 3) PGU-14B (270), Chaff (100), Flare (80), AGM-65B (12), AIM-9M (4), Fuel Tank, Mk 82 (4)

A-10A (Corvette 4) PGU-14B (270), Chaff (100), Flare (80), AGM-65B (9), AGM-65D (3), AIM-9M (4), Fuel Tank, Mk 82 (4)

KC-135R (Shell)

E-3C (Big Bird)

Opposition Aircraft

Su-27	30mm (600), Chaff (90), Flare (90), AA-11 (8)
2 X Su-27	30mm (600), Chaff (90), Flare (90), AA-11 (6)
Su-27	PGU-28 (300), Chaff (60), Flare (60), AA-11 (6)
Su-35	30mm (600), Chaff (90), Flare (90), AA-10 (4), AA-11 (2), AA-8 (2)
Su-35	30mm (600), Chaff (90), Flare (90), AA-11 (2), AA-8 (2)
2 X Su-35	AA-10 (4), AA-11 (2), AA-8 (2)

WATCH YOUR ASSETS

Damidov's hesitation is starting to unnerve NATO HQ, and it seems that the campaign is bogged down again. News from the captured Austrian and Czech republics is also distressing, detailing massive Russian exploitation of these countries' industrial and human resources to Russian Army needs, in a cruel way and with extreme measures. These cries of help, the cost of the operation, and the fatigue setting in all cause NATO to give a hint to Damidov that his case is lost, or to his dissidents to act faster for his overthrow. It is decided to make a limited ground move, mainly to push back the Russian frontline force, some three to four KM back east. NATO hopes that with superior air power, this overnight operation will prove to the Russians that Damidov's leadership will cost them many lives if NATO wishes to overrun them to Vienna or Prague.

USAF aircraft are assigned to deal with the Russian armored divisions in the Burghausen area, providing CAS for NATO forces in a night mission to seize the Russians' front line attack posts.

Date   02 JUL 2005

Time   2100 HRS

Mission Type

Strike, CAS (Close Air Support)

Mission Description

Take control of the Russians' front posts facing the German border.

Situation

In order to force the Russian post-line one step back of the German border, USAF first have to achieve complete air superiority above NATO

forces.

Successful destruction of the SA-10 protection in the area triggers the beginning of the ground assault. After doing that, US Army ground forces will start advancing into Russian-occupied territory escorted by Army attack helicopters and USAF CAS.

On the other hand, the Russian front forces, with their fuselage artillery and helicopters, will try to stop NATO's move.

Weather

Clouds at 20000', visibility may be limited due to dawn smog

Intel

Targets

Austin target is an SA-10 site. The primary target in the battery is the radar.

SA-10 Site

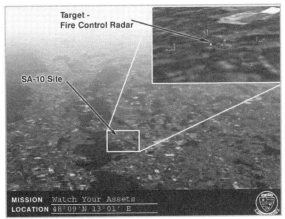

MISSION Watch Your Assets
LOCATION 48°09'N 13°01' E

Threats

Organic AAA with enemy's ground forces.

Primary Flights

Austin

Airframe 2 x F-15E
Task Strike
Target SA-10 site
Loadout AGM-130, AIM-120, AIM-9M, Mk 84

Buick

Airframe 4 x A-10A
Task CAS
Target N/A
Loadout AGM-65D, GBU-12, AIM-9M

Tasking

Austin

Start in a standoff strike, going after the SA-10 battery using AGM-130 missiles. The ground assault will not begin until this target is destroyed.

After destroying the SAM, hold CAP around the area and stay tuned for requests on the radio.

Buick

Hold position southeast of the border and provide CAS to any of our Army ground forces and helicopters who need assistance.

Mission Objectives

Austin

1. SA-10 radar must be destroyed.

In Addition

2. Any tasks assigned in the air must be carried out. They include destruction of an enemy command post, three Mi-24s, and two tanks.

Mission Tips

✦ Pay attention to the radio messages. All Buick's mission objectives will be assigned in the air.

✦ To operate the AGM-130 missile Press [↑]. This will toggle to the TV missile.

You will see the missile video source on your MFD (Multi-Function Display).

Switch your radar to A/G Map mode using [R] and [Q].

Lock onto the target and verify you are locking onto the right target using [F4].

Fly towards the target until you reach the DLZ (Dynamic Launch Zone). You can view this on the right side slide bar of the HUD (Head Up Display) — when the cursor is inside the marked limit, it's safe to launch the weapon.

After launch, turn back 90 degrees to keep a safe distance from the target, and engage the Autopilot by pressing [A] to prevent crashing while steering the missile.

Zoom in the picture using [+=] and [-].

Steer the missile to the target using [Ctrl] + [↑], [↓], [←], [→].

Flythrough

✦ Your bombing skills should be at an all-time high by now, so let's get in there and use them. First target is the SAM site, and you'll have to take this out fast or you'll spend most of this mission evading missiles. This target is Austin's responsibility and must be destroyed to pass this mission. After the SA-10 is taken out, look for air targets and send your wingman to take them out.

✦ Time to use that A-10 again. Switch to Buick and head to the target location to take out an enemy camp. It's dark, so use the nightvision you have ([Ctrl][N]) to make things easy.

✦ When you've found and destroyed the enemy camp, you now have a secondary mission, to support your ground forces nearby. You will get a radio call telling you to assist Tiger group. Tiger is nearby, so start cycling through the targets near you to find it.

✦ Once you've done this, you must get there and take out the opposing force. There will be several T-72s attacking your Tiger group; you need to take them out using any means.

✦ Next, look for two Mi-24s that are in the area — you need to kill these as well to finish the mission.

✦ You might want to stay around and finish the rest off, but don't. The next mission is going to take time to finish and is very challenging.

Commander's Summary

The nature of the ground battle is that the unexpected always occurs. That's why when things get complicated, the AF is the one who gets the job and not the ARMY CAS force.

Make no mistakes in identifying our forces from the enemy. Double-check before every pickle press. Get out there and do your best.

Assets & Opposition

Assets

2 X F-15E (Austin 1-2) PGU-28 (250), Chaff (120), Flare (60), AGM-130 (2), AIM-120 (6), AIM-9M (2), Mk 84 (1)

4 X A-10A (Buick 1-4) PGU-28 (270), Chaff (100), Flare (80), AGM-65D (8), AIM-9M (4), GBU-12 (7), LANTIRN Pod

4 X RAH-66 (Comanche 1-4) Chaff (30), Flare (30), Rocket (1)

Opposition Aircraft

3 X Mi-24 Rocket (20)

2 X Su-35 30mm (600), Chaff (90), Flare (90), AA-11 (6), AA-8 (4)

FINDERS KEEPERS

The continuing NATO strikes on valuable Russian assets, the deadlock on the German front and the growing shortage of food, medical supplies and fuel have all taken their toll. On the 5 August, 23:32 hours, NATO receives word from various sources that dissident Army generals have overthrown Sergei Damidov. These generals declared that they have taken control over the Russians army and civil centers, declared a state of emergency throughout Russia, and called all army units to join them. In addition, they have issued a message to NATO forces calling for an immediate cease-fire. NATO has been anticipating this overthrow, but demands that a cease-fire can only be agreed upon if Russia's new leaders accept conditions of defeat and withdraw from all territories taken by them prior to their invasion. Meanwhile, until the diplomats negotiate the terms of cease-fire, some NATO operations are continuing with zeal. One such operation is assigned to the USAF, that of hijacking the Russian Su-35 stealth fighter, which has taken an active and destructive part in the past weeks. An opportunity to study this fighter, and the technology it contains, will give the West an unprecedented advantage over Russia's technology for the next 50 years, experts claim. The daring plan relies on loose Russian watchfulness due to fatigue, the general disorder in the Russian army after the chaotic uprising, and general confusion of Russia's combat management.

The Su-35 stealth fighters are based at Salzburg Airfield. Navy SEALS have been called in for this mission, with the task of infiltrating Salzburg Airfield. Under the cover of darkness, two Jolly Green helicopters will bring in the team to the southern area of the airfield. The Navy Seals will make their way to the Su-35 hangars, and secure the area. Accompanying them is the USAF team, consisting of four ground personnel and two USAF pilots, specially briefed about the Russian fighter's technical details. These pilots will get the

plane into flight condition, and take off. The rest of the task force will then egress to the waiting Jolly Greens and fly back west.

A daring Secret Service operation to hijack a state-of-the-art Russian Su-35 before cease-fire is called.

Date 16 JUL 2005

Time 0506 HRS

Mission Type

Special Operation

Mission Description

A joint operation, aiming to hijack an Su-35 fighter equipped with a special ECM system, currently parked at Salzburg Airbase.

Situation

The war is about to end, and there is one very important asset that must be taken care of. An Su-35 parked at Salzburg has been reported to have a new ECM system, capable of jamming most modern radar systems. A few minutes before sunrise a Special Ops UH-60 helicopter, callsign Smokey 1, will fly to the airfield, which is still defended by SAMs and many of the last remaining Russian aircraft. Smokey 1 will be carrying an M-2 armored vehicle with a team of elite commandos and Major Ken Simmons, an experienced test pilot. Major Simmons will enter the Su-35 and take off to Erding.

Weather

30000' scattered, with unlimited visibility

Intel

Targets

Salzburg air defense has diminished, but an EWR (Early Warning Radar) site is located on a strategic hill not far from the airfield. This target must be destroyed prior to ingress, or the enemy defense system will awaken as soon as USAF aircraft arrive. This target will be destroyed by Austin F-117 flight. The target to destroy in the radar complex is the radome. See target photo below.

The second target will be an SA-10 site located on a lake west of the airfield. The target contains one radar, four launchers and a few command vehicles. The radar should be destroyed by Corvette.

The Su-35, which we are to hijack, is parked at runway 33 at Salzburg.

EWR Site

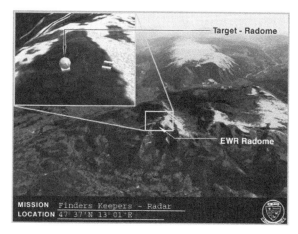

MISSION Finders Keepers - Radar
LOCATION 47° 37'N 13° 01'E

SA-10 Site

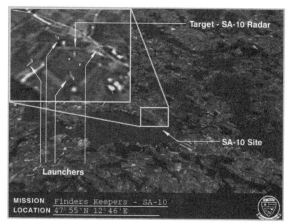

MISSION Finders Keepers - SA-10
LOCATION 47° 55'N 12° 46'E

Threats

The SA-10 battery may launch at any time, especially if the EWR site is not destroyed. A few Su-27s, Su-35s, and MiG-29s may scramble from Salzburg. Many armored vehicles such as T-72s and BMP-1s are present at Salzburg and may threaten Smokey or the Su-35 on the ground.

Primary Flights

Austin

Airframe	F-117A
Task	Strike
Target	EWR Site
Loadout	GBU-27

Buick

Airframe	2 x F-15C
Task	Escort
Target	N/A
Loadout	AIM-120, AIM-9M

Corvette

Airframe	2 x F-15E
Task	SAM Strike
Target	SA-10 Site
Loadout	AGM-88, AIM-9M, AIM-120, Mk 84

Dodge

Airframe	2 x A-10A
Task	CAS
Target	N/A
Loadout	AGM-65B, AIM-9M, CBU-87

Supporting Flights

Smokey

Airframe	UH-60
Task	Airlift
Target	N/A
Loadout	N/A

Flanker 1

Airframe	Su-35
Task	Special Ops
Target	N/A
Loadout	N/A

Big Bird

Airframe	E-3C AWACS
Task	AWACS
Target	N/A
Loadout	N/A

Tasking

Austin

You will lead the operation and under the cover of early morning darkness destroy the EWR site using laser bombs. Failing to destroy it will allow the enemy air defense system to send out SAMs and fighters, and to target USAF aircraft and helicopters.

Buick

Escort Smokey UH-60 chopper and destroy any air entities threatening it.

Corvette

Destroy the SA-10 radar. This radar is in close proximity to Flanker 1's route home and is a major threat to the hijacked fighter.

Dodge

Arrive at Salzburg after Smokey's landing, and provide CAS during Flanker 1's taxi and takeoff. Destroy any air and ground threats that try to stop Major Simmons.

Smokey

Smokey will land near the Salzburg flight line and drop the commando team and Major Simmons, our test pilot. Major Simmons will enter the Su-35 aircraft and take off ASAP, while Smokey evacuates the commando team.

Flanker 1

This will be Major Simmons' callsign as soon as he takes over the Su-35. The aircraft will take off and proceed to Erding AFB once all threats are cleared.

Mission Objectives

Austin

1. Destroy the EWR site.

Corvette

2. Destroy the SA-10 radar.

Buick

3. Smokey 1 must reach Salzburg, and drop its cargo. (In addition, it must survive to the end of the mission.)

Austin, Buick, Corvette and Dodge

4. Flanker 1 must take off safely and reach friendly territory.

Mission Tips

Flythrough

✦ Ok, time to separate the pilots from the non-pilots. This mission is going to take you to your limits as a pilot. Following this plan will be your best bet to finish this mission.

✦ Get into Austin and head to the target site. You're looking to take out the EWR; after you've done this you are clear to engage the rest of the flights.

✦ Switch to Buick and take out the Mi-24s that are targeting Smokey-1. Smokey-1 has the pilot that is going to take that new Su-35 plane that you want so bad.

✦ After you've taken out the Mi-24s, make sure to look around for air threats. If you find nothing around, you have a little time to take out the other Su-35s that are still sitting at the airfield, and some of the T-72s tanks as well. Only do this if you're confident of your piloting and bombing skills.

✦ After that, jump into Corvette and your target is the SA-10 radar. If you fail to take it out, Flanker-1 will not make it home.

✦ After you've done this, stay in Corvette and make sure to take out any and all air threats. If you run out of missiles, go on to Buick flight.

✦ If all your air targets are taken out, you can use Dodge to take the rest of the enemy airfield out. This mission is a tricky one and will be frustrating even for the most seasoned pilots. Take your time and work through it a few times.

Commander's Summary

We are not used to this kind of mission, but I'm counting on your common sense here. There may be all kinds of new air and ground threats. The two things you should remember are listen to your radio, and to think before you press the trigger. Good luck.

Assets & Opposition

Assets

F-117A (Austin 1) Chaff (80), Flare (60), GBU-27 (2)

2 X F-15C (Buick 1-2) PGU-28 (600), Chaff (60), Flare (60), AIM-120 (4), AIM-9M (4)

2 X F-15E (Corvette 1-2) PGU-28 (250), Chaff (120), Flare (60), AGM-88 (2), AIM-120 (4), AIM-9M (2), Fuel Tank, Mk 84 (2)

2 X A-10A (Dodge 1-2) PGU-14B (270), Chaff (100), Flare (80), AGM-65D (6), AIM-9M (4), CBU-87 (4)

UH-60 (Smokey)

Su-35 (Flanker 1) 2100lb (2), AA-11 (2), AA-8 (2), Mk 82 (2)

Opposition Aircraft

2 X MiG-29 30mm (600), Chaff (90), Flare (90), AA-10 (4), AA-8 (4)

6 X Su-35 2100lb (2), AA-11 (2), AA-8 (2)

2 X Mi-24 Flare (60), Rocket (1)

GERMANY SUPPLY MISSION

USAF aircraft escort cargo flight carrying a new loadout supply. You may fly this mission up to twice during the Sleeping Giant campaign.

MUNICH

Mission Type

Escort

Mission Description

Escort cargo flights carrying a new loadout supply into Erding AFB.

Situation

The continuing NATO campaign in Germany has drained USAF resources and the front headquarters have sent an urgent request for a special loadout supply task.

Two C-17s, loaded with weapons, spare parts and jet fuel, took off at dusk from England Alconbury AFB and are now making their way into Germany. They are scheduled to land at Erding AFB. Two USAF F-16Cs have been sent to escort them safely to base. Two F-15Es are on alert on the runway at Erding.

Weather

10000' cloudy, visibility 15 miles

Intel

Targets

N/A

Threats

Enemy forces are aware of this coming shipment and will do whatever they can to prevent it from landing. All enemy air forces are in high alert.

Primary Flights

Austin

Airframe	2 x F-16C
Task	Escort
Target	N/A
Loadout	AIM-9M, AIM-120

Buick

Airframe	2 x F-15E
Task	Alert
Target	N/A
Loadout	AIM-9M

Supporting Flights

Cargo

Airframe	2 x C-17A
Task	Supply
Target	N/A
Loadout	N/A

Tasking

Cargo

Cargo formation consisting of two USAF transports is making its way to Erding AFB from the north.

Austin

Greet the supply aircraft in the air, 10 minutes before landing, and escort them safely down.

Buick

You are on alert on the runway at Erding AFB.

Mission Objectives

Austin and Buick

1. Destroy all enemy fighters threatening the cargo planes. (They include three MiG-29s and four Su-27s.)

2. At least one of the transports must survive after all enemy aircraft are down.

   If the C-17As land safely, all your munitions are restored to 80% of their original quantities.

Mission Tips

✦ Keep your radar on TWS mode so you will be able to track incoming interceptors.

✦ Do not engage in unnecessary dogfights.

✦ Remember your number one task — intercept enemies attacking the cargo planes even if there are easier targets around.

✦ Cargo formation is flying at about 250K. You should fly pretty slow to escort it.

Commander's Summary

Bear in mind that this shipment is critical for the continuation of this campaign. Stay with them all the way until they land safely. Good luck.

Assets & Opposition

Assets

2 X F-16C (Austin 1-2) PGU-28 (510), Chaff (90), Flare (90), AIM-120 (2), AIM-9M (4)

2 X F-15E (Buick 1-2) PGU-28 (250), Chaff (120), Flare (60), AIM-9M (3)

2 X C-17A (Cargo 1-2)

Opposition Aircraft

MiG-29 GSh-301 (300), Chaff (60), Flare (60), AA-10 (1), AA-8 (4)

2 X MiG-29 GSh-301 (300), Chaff (60), Flare (60)

2 X Su-27 AA-8 (1)

2 X Su-27

DEPLOY TO LANDSBERG

A new batch of USAF aircraft is deployed to Landsberg AFB. You may fly this mission up to twice during the Sleeping Giant campaign.

Mission Type

CAP (Combat Air Patrol), Deployment

Mission Description

Protect an enforcement of three formations deploying to Landsberg airbase from enemy interceptors.

Situation

During the night three formations took off from friendly airbases in neighboring countries. All three formations are now approaching Landsberg airbase.

Weather

Clear, with unlimited visibility

Intel

Targets

N/A

Threats

The enemy is expected to try to intercept incoming formations using Su-25s and MiG-29s.

Primary Flights

Austin

Airframe	2 x F-15E
Task	CAP
Target	N/A
Loadout	AIM-9M, AIM-120

Buick

Airframe	4 x F-22A
Task	Deployment
Target	N/A
Loadout	AIM-120, AIM-9X

Corvette

Airframe	4 x F-16C
Task	Deployment
Target	N/A
Loadout	AIM-9M, AIM-120

Dodge

Airframe	4 x F-15E
Task	Deployment
Target	N/A
Loadout	AIM-9M, AIM-120

Tasking

Austin

This is the only flight with sufficient fuel to conduct long air combats, and therefore must be the main force to stop and shoot down enemy interceptors.

Buick, Corvette and Dodge

The main mission of these formations is to safely land at Landsberg. However, when threatened by enemy planes, self protection becomes first priority.

Mission Objectives

Austin

1. Destroy all enemy interceptors. (They include six MiG-29s and three Su-35s.)

Austin, Buick, Corvette and Dodge

2. Protect incoming flights.

   Those that land are added to your flight line. The pilots who flew them in are added to your roster. (Each F-15E has *two* crewmen.)

Mission Tips

✈ Buick is the closest flight to landing. Corvette is second and Dodge is third. Defend them in that order.

✈ Use Austin for intercepting enemy aircraft unless they were already encountered by another flight. The other formations are short on fuel.

✈ Don't waste all your long-range missiles at the start. Use your weapons smartly.

✈ Be sure to check your IFF before you launch.

Commander's Summary

With the number of aircraft we have left we will not be able to hold on much longer. The deploying aircraft are strategic assets and must be protected. Use your weapons and fuel wisely to achieve the best results.

Assets & Opposition

Assets

2 X F-15E (Austin 1-2)   PGU-28 (650), Chaff (120), Flare (60), AIM-120 (4), AIM-9M (3)

4 X F-22A (Buick 1-4)   PGU-28 (600), Chaff (40), Flare (50), AIM-120 (3), AIM-9X (2)

4 X F-16C (Corvette 1-4)   PGU-28 (510), Chaff (90), Flare (90), AIM-120 (2), AIM-9M (4)

4 X F-15E (Dodge 1-4)   PGU-28 (650), Chaff (120), Flare (60), AIM-120 (4), AIM-9M (3), Fuel Tank

Opposition Aircraft

MiG-29   30mm (500), Chaff (20), Flare (20), AA-6 (2), Mk 83 (6)

2 X MiG-29   GSh-301 (301), AA-8 (4)

3 X Su-35 30mm (600), Chaff (30), Flare (30), AA-10 (4), AA-8 (4)

444T

400

350

10

10

UNITED STATES AIR FORCE

3

AGM65B

AIM9M

20NT

3

GM65

IM9

AIM12

MK84

NT1

GUN 1000

4 X MRM

3 X SRM

UNITED STATES AIR FORCE

HQ USAF

(Air Reserve Components)

Air National Guard (ANG)

Air Force Reserve Command (AFRC)

(Direct Reporting Unit)

US Air Force Academy (USAFA)

(Field Operating Agency)

Air Force Flight Standards Agency (AFFSA)

(Major Commands)

Air Combat Command (ACC)

Air Force Materiel Command (AFMC)

Air Force Special Operations Command (AFSOC)

Pacific Air Forces (PACAF)

Air Education and Training Command (AETC)

Air Force Space Command (AFSPC)

Air Mobility Command (AMC)

United States Air Forces in Europe (USAFE)

> Note: The Air Force is constantly changing its allocation of assets, and no list of this sort can hope to stay current. All information here reflects the most recently available published material.

Organization of the USAF

HQ The Pentagon, Washington, DC 20330

Commander-in-Chief President Bill Clinton

USAF Chief of Staff General Michael Ryan

World War II had been over for two years and the Korean War lay three years ahead when the Air Force ended a 40-year association with the U.S. Army to become a separate service. The U.S. Air Force thus entered a new era in which airpower became firmly established as a major element of the nation's defense and one of its chief hopes for deterring war.

The Department of the Air Force was created when President Harry S Truman signed the National Security Act of 1947. It became effective Sept. 18, 1947, when Chief Justice Fred M. Vinson administered the oath of office to the first secretary of the Air Force, W. Stuart Symington, a position filled by presidential appointment.

Under the National Security Act, the functions assigned to the Army Air Force's commanding general transferred to the Department of the Air Force. The act provided for an orderly two-year transfer of these functions as well as property, personnel and records.

Later, under the Department of Defense Reorganization Act of 1958, the departments of Army, Navy and Air Force were eliminated from the chain of operational command. Commanders of unified and specified commands became responsible to the president and the secretary of defense through the Joint Chiefs of Staff. The act redefined the functions of the military departments to those of essentially organizing, training, equipping and supporting combat forces for the unified and specified commands. Each military department retained resource management of its service.

Currently, Air Force resources include eight major commands, 37 field operating agencies, three direct reporting units, 96 major installations in the United States and overseas, and more than three-quarters of a million active-duty, Air National Guard, Air Force Reserve and civilian personnel.

Air Force Vision

Air Force people building the world's most respected air and space force — global power and reach for America.

Air Force Mission

The mission of the U.S. Air Force is to defend the United States through control and exploitation of air and space. Teamed with the Army, Navy and Marine Corps, the Air Force is prepared to fight and win any war if deterrence fails. The Air Force is responsible for providing:

- aircraft and missile forces necessary to prevent or fight a general war.
- land-based air forces needed to establish air superiority, interdict the enemy and provide air support of ground forces in combat.
- the primary aerospace forces for the defense of the United States against air and missile attack.
- the primary airlift capability for use by all of the nation's military services.

- major space research and development support for the Department of Defense.
- assistance to the National Aeronautics and Space Administration to conduct the space program.

Air Force Management

The Department of the Air Force incorporates all elements of the U.S. Air Force. It is administered by a civilian secretary appointed by the president and is supervised by a military chief of staff. The Secretariat and Air Staff help the secretary and the chief of staff direct the Air Force mission.

To assure unit preparedness and overall effectiveness of the Air Force, the secretary of the Air Force is responsible for and has the authority to conduct all affairs of the Department of the Air Force. This includes training, operations, administration, logistical support and maintenance, and welfare of personnel. The secretary's responsibilities include research and development, and any other activity prescribed by the president or the secretary of defense.

The secretary of the Air Force exercises authority through civilian assistants and the chief of staff, but retains immediate supervision of activities that involve vital relationships with Congress, the secretary of defense, other governmental officials and the public.

Principal civilian assistants within the Secretariat are the under secretary of the Air Force, deputy under secretary for international affairs, assistant secretary for acquisition, assistant secretary for space, assistant secretary for manpower, reserve affairs, installations and environment, and assistant secretary for financial management and comptroller.

The Office of the Secretary of the Air Force includes a general counsel, auditor general, inspector general, administrative assistant, public affairs director, legislative liaison director, small and disadvantaged business utilization director and certain statutory boards and committees.

The Air Staff

The chief of staff, U.S. Air Force, is appointed by the president, with the consent of the Senate, from among Air Force general officers — normally for a four-year term. He serves as a member of the Joint Chiefs of Staff and the Armed Forces Policy Council. In the JCS capacity, he is one of the military advisers to the president, the National Security Council and the secretary of defense. Also, he is the principal adviser to the secretary of the Air Force on Air Force activities.

The chief of staff presides over the Air Staff, transmits Air Staff plans and recommendations to the secretary of the Air Force and acts as the secretary's agent in carrying them out. He is responsible for the efficiency of the Air Force and the preparation of its forces for military operations. He supervises the administration of Air Force personnel assigned to unified organizations and unified and specified commands. Also, he supervises support of these forces assigned by the Air Force as directed by the secretary of defense. In addition, the chief of staff has responsibility for activities assigned to the Air Force by the secretary of defense.

Other members of the Air Staff are the vice chief of staff, assistant vice chief of staff, chief master sergeant of the Air Force, deputy chief of staff for personnel, deputy chief of staff for plans and operations, deputy chief of staff for logistics, deputy chief of staff for command, control, communications and computers, assistant chief of staff for intelligence, civil engineer, chief of safety, chief of security police, Air Force historian, chief scientist, chief of the Air Force Reserve, chief of the National Guard Bureau, the U.S. Air Force Scientific Advisory Board, judge advocate general, director of test and evaluation, director of programs and evaluation, surgeon general, chief of chaplains, and director for services.

Field Organizations

The eight major commands, 37 field operating agencies, three direct reporting units and their subordinate elements constitute the field organization that carries out the Air Force mission. In addition, there are two reserve components, the Air Force Reserve and the Air National Guard.

Major commands are organized on a functional basis in the United States and a geographic basis overseas. They accomplish designated phases of Air Force worldwide activities. Also, they organize, administer, equip and train their subordinate elements for the accomplishment of assigned missions. Major commands generally are assigned specific responsibilities based on functions. In descending order of command, elements of major commands include numbered air forces, wings, groups, squadrons and flights.

The basic unit for generating and employing combat capability is the wing, which has always been the Air Forces prime war-fighting instrument. Composite wings operate more than one kind of aircraft, and may be configured as self-contained units designated for quick air intervention anywhere in the world. Other wings continue to operate a single aircraft type ready to join air campaigns anywhere they are needed. Air base and specialized mission wings such as training, intelligence and test also support the Air Force mission. Within the wing, operations, logistics and support groups are the cornerstones of the organization.

Field operating agencies and direct reporting units are other Air Force subdivisions and report directly to Headquarters U.S. Air Force. They are assigned a specialized mission that is restricted in scope when compared to the mission of a major command. Field operating agencies carry out field activities under the operational control of a Headquarters U.S. Air Force functional manager. Direct reporting units are not under the operational control of a Headquarters U.S. Air Force functional manager because of a unique mission, legal requirements or other factors.

Major Commands

- Air Combat Command, Langley AFB, VA
- Air Education and Training Command, Randolph AFB, TX
- Air Force Materiel Command, Wright-Patterson AFB, OH
- Air Force Space Command, Peterson AFB, CO
- Air Force Special Operations Command, Hurlburt Field, FL
- Air Mobility Command, Scott AFB, IL
- Pacific Air Forces, Hickam AFB, HI
- United States Air Forces in Europe, Ramstein AB, Germany

Field Operating Agencies

- Air Force Audit Agency, Washington, DC
- Air Force Base Conversion Agency, Arlington, VA
- Air Force Center for Environmental Excellence, Brooks AFB, TX
- Air Force Civil Engineer Support Agency, Tyndall AFB, FL
- Air Force Command, Control, Communications and Computer Agency, Scott AFB, IL
- Air Force Cost Analysis Agency, Arlington, VA
- Air Force Doctrine Center, Langley AFB, VA
- Air Force Flight Standards Agency, Andrews AFB, MD
- Air Force Frequency Management Agency, Arlington, VA
- Air Force Historical Research Agency, Maxwell AFB, AL
- Air Force History Support Office, Bolling AFB, DC
- Air Force Inspection Agency, Kirtland AFB, NM
- Air Force Legal Services Agency, Bolling AFB, DC
- Air Force Logistics Management Agency, Maxwell AFB, Gunter Annex, AL
- Air Force Management Engineering Agency, Randolph AFB, TX
- Air Force Medical Operations Agency, Bolling AFB, DC
- Air Force Medical Support Agency, Brooks AFB, TX
- Air Force News Agency, Kelly AFB, TX
- Air Force Office of Special Investigations, Bolling AFB, DC
- Air Force Operations Group, Washington, DC
- Air Force Pentagon Communications Agency, Washington, DC
- Air Force Personnel Center, Randolph AFB, TX
- Air Force Personnel Operations Agency, Washington, DC
- Air Force Program Executive Office, Washington, DC
- Air Force Real Estate Agency, Bolling AFB, DC
- Air Force Reserve, Robins AFB, GA
- Air Force Review Boards Agency, Washington, DC
- Air Force Safety Agency, Kirtland AFB, NM
- Air Force Security Police Agency, Kirtland AFB, NM
- Air Force Services Agency, Randolph AFB, TX
- Air Force Studies and Analyses Agency, Washington, DC
- Air Force Technical Applications Center, Patrick AFB, FL
- Air Intelligence Agency, Kelly AFB, TX
- Air National Guard Readiness Center, Andrews AFB, MD
- Air Reserve Personnel Center, Denver, CO
- Air Weather Service, Scott AFB, IL
- Joint Services Survival, Evasion, Resistance and Escape Agency, Fort Belvoir, VA

Direct Reporting Units

- 11th Wing, Bolling AFB, DC
- Air Force Operational Test and Evaluation Center, Kirtland AFB, NM
- United States Air Force Academy, Colorado Springs, CO

Order of Battle, USAF

Typical Unit Establishment (UE) levels for active duty forces:

Type of Aircraft	Number per Squadron *
A/OA-10A	6, 12 or 17
B-1B	6, 10, or 18
B-2A	8
B-52H	8 or 12
C-5A/B	16
C-9A	3 to 11
KC-10A	9 or 10
C-17A	12
C-130E/H	8, 10, 12, 13, 14 or 16
AC-130H/U	6 or 10
EC-130H	5
HC-130P/N	4 to 10
MC-130E/H	4 to 12
KC-135R/T	8 to 12
C-141B	14 or 16
E-3B/C	2 or 7
F-15C	18 or 24
F-15E	18 or 24
F-16C	18 or 24
F-117A	18
MH-53J	5 or 22
HH-60G	4, 5 or 8
MH-60G	8
LGM-30G	50
LGM-118A	50

* Comparable UE figures for Air National Guard and AFRC are generally lower than those detailed above, with transport and tanker units having about eight aircraft each. Continuing force reductions, particularly in area of combat squadrons, have resulted in Air National Guard and AFRC F-16 fighter squadrons now having UE of 15.

Order of Battle tables which follow are simplified by omission of intermediate command elements and all except the most significant non-flying units.

USAF Aircraft, Sorted by Role

Multirole Fighter

Boeing MD F-15E Strike Eagle
Lockheed Martin F-16A Fighting Falcon
Lockheed Martin F-16B Fighting Falcon
Lockheed Martin F-16C Fighting Falcon
Lockheed Martin F-16D Fighting Falcon

Air Superiority/Interceptor

Boeing MD F-15A Eagle
Boeing MD F-15B Eagle
Boeing MD F-15C Eagle
Boeing MD F-15D Eagle
Lockheed Martin F-22A Raptor

Airborne Early Warning and Control

Boeing E-3B/C Sentry

Airborne Laser Platform

Boeing AL-1A

Bomber

Boeing B-52H Stratofortress
Northrop Grumman B-2A Spirit
Rockwell B-1B Lancer

Command Post

Boeing C-135K Stratotanker
Boeing E-4B
Boeing EC-135N Stratotanker
Boeing EC-135Y Stratotanker
Lockheed Martin EC-130E Hercules

Communications
Beech C-12C/D King Air 200
Beech C-12J (Model 1900C)
Boeing C-22B
Boeing C-22C
Boeing C-32A
Boeing C-135B Stratotanker
Boeing C-135C Stratotanker
Boeing C-135E Stratotanker
Boeing C-137C
Boeing EC-137D
Fairchild C-26B Metro
Gulfstream Aerospace C-20A Gulfstream III
Gulfstream Aerospace C-20B Gulfstream III
Gulfstream Aerospace C-20C Gulfstream III
Gulfstream Aerospace C-20H Gulfstream IV
Gulfstream Aerospace C-37A Gulfstream V
IAI C-38A Astra SPX
Learjet Inc C-21A Learjet
McDonnell Douglas C-9C

Elint
Boeing RC-135S Stratotanker
Boeing RC-135U Stratotanker
Boeing RC-135V Stratotanker
Boeing RC-135W Stratotanker
Boeing RC-135X Stratotanker

Observation
Boeing OC-135W Stratotanker

Reconnaissance
Lockheed U-2S
Northrop Grumman E-8C Joint STARS

Tanker
Boeing KC-135D Stratotanker
Boeing KC-135E Stratotanker
Boeing KC-135R Stratotanker
Boeing KC-135T Stratotanker

Tanker-Transport
McDonnell Douglas KC-10A Extender

Transport
Boeing MD C-17A Globemaster III
Lockheed C-5A Galaxy
Lockheed C-5B Galaxy
Lockheed C-5C Galaxy
Lockheed C-141B Starlifter
Lockheed Martin C-130B Hercules
Lockheed Martin C-130E Hercules
Lockheed Martin C-130H Hercules
Lockheed Martin C-130J Hercules
McDonnell Douglas C-9A Nightingale

Utility
CASA C-212 Aviocar

Utility Helicopter
Bell UH-1N Iroquois
Sikorsky MH-53J
Sikorsky TH-53A
Sikorsky HH-60G
Sikorsky MH-60G

Combat Support
Bell Boeing CV-22 Osprey
Boeing WC-135W Stratotanker
Lockheed Martin EC-130E(CL) Hercules
Lockheed Martin EC-130E(RR) Hercules
Lockheed Martin EC-130H Hercules
Lockheed Martin EC-130J Hercules
Lockheed Martin HC-130H(N) Hercules
Lockheed Martin HC-130N Hercules
Lockheed Martin HC-130P Hercules
Lockheed Martin MC-130E Hercules
Lockheed Martin MC-130H Hercules
Lockheed Martin MC-130P Hercules

Drone Target
McDonnell Douglas QF-4 Phantom II

Experimental/Test
Boeing EC-18B
Boeing EC-18D
Boeing NKC-135B Stratotanker
Boeing NKC-135E Stratotanker
Boeing EC-135E Stratotanker
Boeing 707-320
Learjet Inc NC-21A Learjet
Lockheed Martin NC-130A Hercules
Lockheed Martin NC-130E Hercules
Lockheed Martin NC-130H Hercules
Lockheed Martin AFTI/F-16 Fighting Falcon
Lockheed Martin NF-16D Fighting Falcon
Lockheed Martin YF-117A Nighthawk
Rockwell NT-39A Sabreliner
Rockwell T-39B Sabreliner

Fighter-Bomber/Attack
Fairchild-Republic A/OA-10A Thunderbolt II
Lockheed Martin F-117A Nighthawk
Lockheed Martin AC-130H Hercules
Lockheed Martin AC-130U Hercules

Parachute Jump Platform
DHC UV-18B Twin Otter

Presidential Transport
Boeing VC-25A

Sailplane/Motor Glider
Schleicher TG-3A
Schleicher TG-9A
Schweizer TG-4A
Schweizer TG-7A
Stemme TG-11A
TG-10A

Telemetry Relay Platform
DHC E-9A Dash 8

Trainer
Cessna T-37B
Cessna T-41 Mescalero
Northrop T-38A Talon
Northrop AT-38B Talon
Lockheed TU-2S
Raytheon Beech T-6A Texan II
Slingsby T-3A Firefly

Crew Trainer
Beech T-1A Jayhawk
Boeing TC-18E
Boeing CT-43A
Boeing TC-135S Stratotanker
Boeing TC-135W Stratotanker

Weather Reconnaissance
Lockheed Martin WC-130H Hercules
Lockheed Martin WC-130J Hercules

Aircraft Sorted by Designation

Designation	Aircraft	Role
707-320	Boeing 707-320	Experimental/Test
A/OA-10A	Fairchild-Republic A/OA-10A Thunderbolt II	Fighter-Bomber/Attack
AC-130H	Lockheed Martin AC-130H Hercules	Fighter-Bomber/Attack
AC-130U	Lockheed Martin AC-130U Hercules	Fighter-Bomber/Attack
AFTI/F-16	Lockheed Martin AFTI/F-16 Fighting Falcon	Experimental/Test
AL-1A	Boeing AL-1A	Airborne Laser Platform
AT-38B	Northrop AT-38B Talon	Trainer
B-1B	Rockwell B-1B Lancer	Bomber
B-2A	Northrop Grumman B-2A Spirit	Bomber
B-52H	Boeing B-52H Stratofortress	Bomber
C-5A	Lockheed C-5A Galaxy	Transport
C-5B	Lockheed C-5B Galaxy	Transport
C-5C	Lockheed C-5C Galaxy	Transport
C-9A	McDonnell Douglas C-9A Nightingale	Transport
C-9C	McDonnell Douglas C-9C	Communications
C-12C/D	Beech C-12C/D King Air 200	Communications
C-12J	Beech C-12J (Model 1900C)	Communications
C-17A	Boeing MD C-17A Globemaster III	Transport
C-20A	Gulfstream Aerospace C-20A Gulfstream III	Communications
C-20B	Gulfstream Aerospace C-20B Gulfstream III	Communications
C-20C	Gulfstream Aerospace C-20C Gulfstream III	Communications
C-20H	Gulfstream Aerospace C-20H Gulfstream IV	Communications
C-21A	Learjet Inc C-21A Learjet	Communications
C-22B	Boeing C-22B	Communications
C-22C	Boeing C-22C	Communications
C-26B	Fairchild C-26B Metro	Communications
C-32A	Boeing C-32A	Communications
C-37A	Gulfstream Aerospace C-37A Gulfstream V	Communications
C-38A	IAI C-38A Astra SPX	Communications
C-130B	Lockheed Martin C-130B Hercules	Transport
C-130E	Lockheed Martin C-130E Hercules	Transport

Designation	Aircraft	Role
C-130H	Lockheed Martin C-130H Hercules	Transport
C-130J	Lockheed Martin C-130J Hercules	Transport
C-135B	Boeing C-135B Stratotanker	Communications
C-135C	Boeing C-135C Stratotanker	Communications
C-135E	Boeing C-135E Stratotanker	Communications
C-135K	Boeing C-135K Stratotanker	Command Post
C-137C	Boeing C-137C	Communications
C-141B	Lockheed C-141B Starlifter	Transport
CASA C-212	CASA C-212 Aviocar	Utility
CT-43A	Boeing CT-43A	Crew Trainer
CV-22	Bell Boeing CV-22 Osprey	Combat Support
E-3B/C	Boeing E-3B/C Sentry	Airborne Early Warning and Control
E-4B	Boeing E-4B	Command Post
E-8C	Northrop Grumman E-8C Joint STARS	Reconnaissance
E-9A	DHC E-9A Dash 8	Telemetry Relay Platform
EC-18B	Boeing EC-18B	Experimental/Test
EC-18D	Boeing EC-18D	Experimental/Test
EC-130E	Lockheed Martin EC-130E Hercules	Command Post
EC-130E(CL)	Lockheed Martin EC-130E(CL) Hercules	Combat Support
EC-130E(RR)	Lockheed Martin EC-130E(RR) Hercules	Combat Support
EC-130H	Lockheed Martin EC-130H Hercules	Combat Support
EC-130J	Lockheed Martin EC-130J Hercules	Combat Support
EC-135E	Boeing EC-135E Stratotanker	Experimental/Test
EC-135N	Boeing EC-135N Stratotanker	Command Post
EC-135Y	Boeing EC-135Y Stratotanker	Command Post
EC-137D	Boeing EC-137D	Communications
F-15A	Boeing MD F-15A Eagle	Air Superiority/Interceptor
F-15B	Boeing MD F-15B Eagle	Air Superiority/Interceptor
F-15C	Boeing MD F-15C Eagle	Air Superiority/Interceptor
F-15D	Boeing MD F-15D Eagle	Air Superiority/Interceptor

Designation	Aircraft	Role
F-15E	Boeing MD F-15E Strike Eagle	Multirole Fighter
F-16A	Lockheed Martin F-16A Fighting Falcon	Multirole Fighter
F-16B	Lockheed Martin F-16B Fighting Falcon	Multirole Fighter
F-16C	Lockheed Martin F-16C Fighting Falcon	Multirole Fighter
F-16D	Lockheed Martin F-16D Fighting Falcon	Multirole Fighter
F-22A	Lockheed Martin F-22A Raptor	Air Superiority/Interceptor
F-117A	Lockheed Martin F-117A Nighthawk	Fighter-Bomber/Attack
HC-130H(N)	Lockheed Martin HC-130H(N) Hercules	Combat Support
HC-130N	Lockheed Martin HC-130N Hercules	Combat Support
HC-130P	Lockheed Martin HC-130P Hercules	Combat Support
HH-60G	Sikorsky HH-60G	Utility Helicopter
KC-10A	McDonnell Douglas KC-10A Extender	Tanker-Transport
KC-135D	Boeing KC-135D Stratotanker	Tanker
KC-135E	Boeing KC-135E Stratotanker	Tanker
KC-135R	Boeing KC-135R Stratotanker	Tanker
KC-135T	Boeing KC-135T Stratotanker	Tanker
MC-130E	Lockheed Martin MC-130E Hercules	Combat Support
MC-130H	Lockheed Martin MC-130H Hercules	Combat Support
MC-130P	Lockheed Martin MC-130P Hercules	Combat Support
MH-53J	Sikorsky MH-53J	Utility Helicopter
MH-60G	Sikorsky MH-60G	Utility Helicopter
NC-130A	Lockheed Martin NC-130A Hercules	Experimental/Test
NC-130E	Lockheed Martin NC-130E Hercules	Experimental/Test
NC-21A	Learjet Inc NC-21A Learjet	Experimental/Test
NC-130H	Lockheed Martin NC-130H Hercules	Experimental/Test
NF-16D	Lockheed Martin NF-16D Fighting Falcon	Experimental/Test
NKC-135B	Boeing NKC-135B Stratotanker	Experimental/Test
NKC-135E	Boeing NKC-135E Stratotanker	Experimental/Test
NT-39A	Rockwell NT-39A Sabreliner	Experimental/Test
OC-135W	Boeing OC-135W Stratotanker	Observation
QF-4	McDonnell Douglas QF-4 Phantom II	Drone Target
RC-135S	Boeing RC-135S Stratotanker	Elint

Designation	Aircraft	Role
RC-135U	Boeing RC-135U Stratotanker	Elint
RC-135V	Boeing RC-135V Stratotanker	Elint
RC-135W	Boeing RC-135W Stratotanker	Elint
RC-135X	Boeing RC-135X Stratotanker	Elint
T-1A	Beech T-1A Jayhawk	Crew Trainer
T-3A	Slingsby T-3A Firefly	Trainer
T-6A	Raytheon Beech T-6A Texan II	Trainer
T-37B	Cessna T-37B	Trainer
T-38A	Northrop T-38A Talon	Trainer
T-39B	Rockwell T-39B Sabreliner	Experimental/Test
T-41	Cessna T-41 Mescalero	Trainer
TC-18E	Boeing TC-18E	Crew Trainer
TC-135S	Boeing TC-135S Stratotanker	Crew Trainer
TC-135W	Boeing TC-135W Stratotanker	Crew Trainer
TG-3A	Schleicher TG-3A	Sailplane/Motor Glider
TG-4A	Schweizer TG-4A	Sailplane/Motor Glider
TG-7A	Schweizer TG-7A	Sailplane/Motor Glider
TG-9A	Schleicher TG-9A	Sailplane/Motor Glider
TG-10A	TG-10A	Sailplane/Motor Glider
TG-11A	Stemme TG-11A	Sailplane/Motor Glider
TH-53A	Sikorsky TH-53A	Utility Helicopter
TU-2S	Lockheed TU-2S	Trainer
U-2S	Lockheed U-2S	Reconnaissance
UH-1N	Bell UH-1N Iroquois	Utility Helicopter
UV-18B	DHC UV-18B Twin Otter	Parachute Jump Platform
VC-25A	Boeing VC-25A	Presidential Transport
WC-130H	Lockheed Martin WC-130H Hercules	Weather Reconnaissance
WC-130J	Lockheed Martin WC-130J Hercules	Weather Reconnaissance
WC-135W	Boeing WC-135W Stratotanker	Combat Support
YF-117A	Lockheed Martin YF-117A Nighthawk	Experimental/Test

AIR COMBAT COMMAND

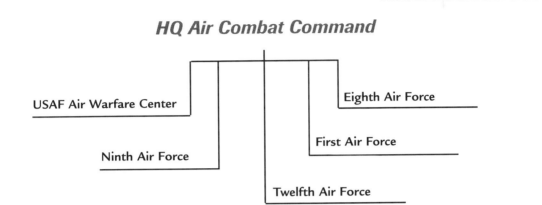

HQ Air Combat Command

USAF Air Warfare Center

Ninth Air Force

Eighth Air Force

First Air Force

Twelfth Air Force

Air Combat Command, with headquarters at Langley Air Force Base, Va., is a major command activated June 1, 1992. It is the primary provider of air combat forces to America's unified combatant commands.

Mission

Air Combat Command's operates fighters, bombers, reconnaissance, battle management, rescue and theater airlift aircraft, as well as command, control, communications and intelligence systems.

As a force provider, ACC organizes, trains, equips and maintains combat-ready forces for rapid deployment and employment while ensuring strategic air defense forces are ready to meet the challenges of peacetime air sovereignty and wartime air defense. ACC provides nuclear forces for U.S. Strategic Command, theater air forces for the five geographic unified commands (U.S. Atlantic Command, U.S. European Command, U.S. Pacific Command, U.S. Central Command and U.S. Southern Command). ACC also provides air defense forces to the North American Aerospace Defense Command (NORAD).

Personnel and Resources

More than 100,000 active-duty members and civilians make up ACC's work force (approximately 90,000 active-duty members and more than 11,000 civilians). When mobilized, more than 63,000 members of the Air National Guard and Air Force Reserve, along with about 760 aircraft, are assigned to ACC. In total, ACC and ACC-gained units consist of more than 1,700 aircraft.

Organization

ACC's forces are organized under four numbered air forces and two major direct reporting units. The ACC commander is also component commander of U.S. Air Forces Atlantic Command and U.S. Strategic Command. He also acts as executive agent for the Air Force chief of staff on search and rescue matters in the 48 contiguous states.

Numbered Air Forces

First Air Force, with headquarters at Tyndall Air Force Base, Fla., performs a daily operational mission as the continental U.S. NORAD Region. The First Air Force commander, as the region commander, reports directly to the commander in chief, NORAD. First Air Force includes three air defense sectors responsible for the air defense of their respective sectors of the continental U. S. using Air National Guard aircraft on around-the-clock alert.

First Air Force plays a key role in the nation's war on drugs by working closely with the U.S. Coast Guard and the U.S. Customs Service to monitor and intercept illegal drug traffic.

Eighth Air Force, with headquarters at Barksdale Air Force Base, La., is responsible for ACC forces in the central United States, and functions as the air planner under the commander in chief, U.S. Atlantic Command (USACOM) for the Atlantic area of responsibility, and commander, Task Force Bomber for U.S. Strategic Command.

Ninth Air Force, with headquarters at Shaw Air Force Base, S.C., is responsible for fighter, bomber, tanker, airlift and air control operations and training in the Eastern United States.

Ninth Air Force also is U.S. Central Command Air Forces, the Air Force component of U.S. Central Command. Operation Desert Shield deployed the USCENTAF staff to the Southwest Asia theater, operationally controlling joint and coalition air forces. To prepare for this type mission, USCENTAF active and reserve forces train regularly with Army, Navy and Marine Corps units.

Twelfth Air Force, with headquarters at Davis-Monthan AFB, Ariz., operates combat-ready forces and equipment in the Western and Midwestern United States and Panama. In addition, 12th Air Force is the Air Force component of the U.S. Southern Command. The command's units perform fighter and bomber operations, training, reconnaissance, air control and a wide range of electronic combat tasks.

Direct Reporting Units

U.S. Air Force Air Warfare Center, at Nellis Air Force Base, Nev., manages advanced pilot training and integrates many of the Air Force's test and evaluation requirements. The 53rd Wing at Eglin AFB, Fla. is assigned to the Air Warfare Center.

Aerospace Command and Control, Intelligence, Surveillance and Reconnaissance Center, at Langley AFB, Va., serves as the lead organization to integrate and influence command and control (C2) and intelligence, surveillance and reconnaissance (ISR) for the Air Force. Its primary task is to merge air and space C2 and ISR operational and delegated systems architectures, requirements and standards in a continuing drive toward commonality. Other tasks are to build aerospace C2 and ISR modernization strategies, integrated mission area investment plans and divestment strategies, appropriate C4I Support Plans and associated programming documents, and ensure they are linked to current Air Force Modernization Planning Process, Air Force Strategic Plan and Thrust Area Transformation Plans; work with appropriate Air Force agencies and major commands to ensure training programs are developed for emerging, current and future C2 and ISR systems and concepts; and serve as the Air Force interface for establishment of all C2 and ISR related joint tactics, techniques and procedures.

USAF Air Warfare Center
HQ Nellis Air Force Base, NV

53 Wing, Eglin Air Force Base, FL

85 Test & Evaluation Squadron	F-15A/B/C/D/E, F-16B/C/D	R&D, Test & Evaluation

57 Test Group, Nellis Air Force Base, NV

422 Test & Evaluation Squadron	A-10A, F-15C/D/E, F-16C/D, HH-60G	R&D, Test & Evaluation
422 Test & Evaluation Squad. Det 1	F-117A	R&D, Test & Evaluation [1]

475 Weapons Evaluation Group, Tyndall Air Force Base, FL

82 Aerial Target Squadron	QF-4	Unmanned Aerial Vehicle Targets
	E-9A	Telemetry Relay
82 Aerial Target Squadron Det 1	QF-4	Unmanned Aerial Vehicle Targets[1]
475 Test Support Squadron	QF-4	Unmanned Aerial Vehicle Targets

57 Wing, Nellis Air Force Base, NV

USAF Weapons School	A-10A, F-15C/D/E F-16C/D	Tactics Training
Combat Rescue School	HH-60G	Combat SAR Training
Air Demo Squadron	F-16C/D	'Thunderbirds' Display Team

57 Operations Group

11 Reconnaissance Squadron	RQ-1A	Reconnaissance Unmanned Aerial Vehicle [2]
15 Reconnaissance Squadron	RQ-1A [3]	Reconnaissance Unmanned Aerial Vehicle [2]
66 Rescue Squadron	HH-60G	Combat SAR
414 Combat Training Squadron	F-16C/D	Aggressor Training/'Red Flag' Support

[1] At Holloman Air Force Base, NM.

[2] At Indian Springs Air Force Auxiliary Field, NV.

[3] Currently forming but will not be equipped until late 1998.

First Air Force

HQ Tyndall Air Force Base, FL

No dedicated resources assigned; directs Air National Guard air defense assets and had transferred to Air National Guard control in entirety by mid-1997. Subordinate echelons comprise the Southeast Air Defense Sector at Tyndall; the Northeast Air Defense Sector at Rome, NY; and the Western Air Defense Sector at McChord Air Force Base, WA.

Eighth Air Force

HQ Barksdale Air Force Base, LA

2 Bomb Wing, Barksdale Air Force Base, LA

11 Bomb Squadron	B-52H	Bomber Training
20 Bomb Squadron	B-52H	Bomber
96 Bomb Squadron	B-52H	Bomber

5 Bomb Wing, Minot Air Force Base, ND

23 Bomb Squadron	B-52H	Bomber

7 Bomb Wing, Dyess Air Force Base, TX

9 Bomb Squadron	B-1B	Bomber
13 Bomb Squadron	B-1B	Bomber
28 Bomb Squadron	B-1B	Bomber

27 Fighter Wing, Cannon Air Force Base, NM

428 Fighter Squadron	F-16C	Strike/Attack Training *
522 Fighter Squadron	F-16C/D	Strike/Attack
523 Fighter Squadron	F-16C/D	Strike/Attack
524 Fighter Squadron	F-16C/D	Strike/Attack

* Singapore Air Force Training Squadron

28 Bomb Wing, Ellsworth Air Force Base, SD

37 Bomb Squadron	B-1B	Bomber
77 Bomb Squadron	B-1B	Bomber

85 Group, Keflavik Naval Air Station, Iceland

Detachment	F-15 or F-16	Air Defense *
56 Rescue Squadron	HH-60G	Combat SAR

* Limited air defense capability maintained by five F-15 Eagles or F-16 Fighting Falcons deployed from Air National Guard and Air Combat Command units in USA on rotational basis.

509 Bomb Wing, Whiteman Air Force Base, MO

325 Bomb Squadron	B-2A	Bomber
393 Bomb Squadron	B-2A	Bomber
394 Combat Training Squadron	T-38A	Training *

* Also uses B-2A on loan from other squadrons as and when required.

Ninth Air Force

HQ Shaw Air Force Base, SC

1 Fighter Wing, Langley Air Force Base, VA

27 Fighter Squadron	F-15C/D	Air Superiority
71 Fighter Squadron	F-15C/D	Air Superiority
94 Fighter Squadron	F-15C/D	Air Superiority

4 Fighter Wing, Seymour Johnson Air Force Base, NC

333 Fighter Squadron	F-15E	Strike/Attack
334 Fighter Squadron	F-15E	Strike/Attack
335 Fighter Squadron	F-15E	Strike/Attack
336 Fighter Squadron	F-15E	Strike/Attack

20 Fighter Wing, Shaw Air Force Base, SC

77 Fighter Squadron	F-16C/D	Multirole Fighter
78 Fighter Squadron	F-16C/D	Multirole Fighter
79 Fighter Squadron	F-16C/D	Multirole Fighter

23 Fighter Group, Pope Air Force Base, NC

| 74 Fighter Squadron | A/OA-10A | Attack/Forward Air Control |
| 75 Fighter Squadron | A/OA-10A | Attack/Forward Air Control |

Reports to 347 Wing

33 Fighter Wing, Eglin Air Force Base, FL

| 58 Fighter Squadron | F-15C/D | Air Superiority |
| 60 Fighter Squadron | F-15C/D | Air Superiority |

93 Air Control Wing, Robins Air Force Base, GA

| 12 Airborne Command & Control Squadron | E-8C | Surveillance * |

* Other elements to be activated in due course.

347 Wing, Moody Air Force Base, GA

41 Rescue Squadron	HH-60G	Combat SAR
68 Fighter Squadron	F-16C/D	Multirole Fighter
69 Fighter Squadron	F-16C/D	Multirole Fighter
70 Fighter Squadron *	A/OA-10A	Attack/Forward Air Control
71 Rescue Squadron	HC-130P	Combat SAR

* To lose 12 aircraft in FY99 and 12 in FY00 before inactivating.

Twelfth Air Force

HQ Davis-Monthan Air Force Base, AZ

9 Reconnaissance Wing, Beale Air Force Base, CA

1 Reconnaissance Squadron	U-2S	Reconnaissance
	TU-2S, T-38A	Training
5 Reconnaissance Squadron	U-2S	Reconnaissance [1]
99 Reconnaissance Squadron	U-2S	Reconnaissance
Det 1	U-2S	Reconnaissance [2]
OL-CH	U-2S	Reconnaissance [3]
OL-FR	U-2S	Reconnaissance [4]

[1] *At Osan AB, South Korea*

[2] *At Royal Air Force Akrotiri, Cyprus*

[3] *Operating Location-Camel Hump; at Taif AB, Saudi Arabia; also known as 4402 RS (Provisional)*

[4] *Operating Location-France; at Istres-Le Tube, France; also known as 99 Expeditionary Reconnaissance Squadron*

24 Wing, Howard Air Force Base, Panama

310 Airlift Squadron	C-21A, C-130H, CT-43A	Transport

49 Fighter Wing, Holloman Air Force Base, NM

7 Fighter Squadron2	F-117A	Strike/Attack
	AT-38B	Training
8 Fighter Squadron	F-117A	Strike/Attack
9 Fighter Squadron	F-117A	Strike/Attack
20 Fighter Squadron [1]	F-4F	Training
48 Rescue Squadron [2]	HH-60G	Combat SAR

[1] *German Air Force Training Squadron.*

[2] *To inactivate in FY99.*

55 Wing, Offutt Air Force Base, NB

1 Airborne Command & Control Squadron	E-4B	Command Post
38 Reconnaissance Squadron	RC-135U/V/W	Electronic Recce
	TC-135W	Training/Support
45 Reconnaissance Squadron	RC-135S	Electronic Recce
	OC-135W	Surveillance
	TC-135S, WC-135W	Training/Support
82 Reconnaissance Squadron	RC-135U/V/W	Electronic Recce [1]
95 Reconnaissance Squadron	RC-135U/V/W	Electronic Recce [2]
343 Reconnaissance Squadron	RC-135S/U/V/W	Electronic Recce [3]

[1] *At Kadena AB, Japan; aircraft assigned on Temporary Duty basis.*

[2] *At Royal Air Force Mildenhall, England; aircraft assigned on Temporary Duty basis.*

[3] *Provides sensor operators for RC-135 aircraft.*

355 Wing, Davis-Monthan Air Force Base, AZ

41 Electronic Combat Squadron	EC-130H	Electronic Combat
42 Airborne Command & Control Squadron	EC-130E	Command Post
	C-130H	Training/Support
43 Electronic Combat Squadron	EC-130H	Electronic Combat
354 Fighter Squadron	A/OA-10A	Attack/Forward Air Control
357 Fighter Squadron	A/OA-10A	Attack/Forward Air Control
358 Fighter Squadron	A/OA-10A	Attack/Forward Air Control

366 Wing, Mountain Home Air Force Base, ID

22 Air Refueling Squadron	KC-135R	Tanker
34 Bomb Squadron	B-1B	Bomber
389 Fighter Squadron	F-16C/D	Multirole Fighter
390 Fighter Squadron	F-15C/D	Air Superiority
391 Fighter Squadron	F-15E	Strike/Attack

366 Wing exercises administrative control of joint USAF/USN EA-6B Prowler squadrons via Detachment One of 366th Operations Group at Whidbey Island, WA.

388 Fighter Wing, Hill Air Force Base, UT

4 Fighter Squadron	F-16C/D	Multirole Fighter
34 Fighter Squadron	F-16C/D	Multirole Fighter
421 Fighter Squadron	F-16C/D	Multirole Fighter

Detachment One controls Utah Test and Training Range.

552 Airborne Control Wing, Tinker Air Force Base, OK

963 Airborne Control Squadron	E-3B/C	Airborne Air Control
964 Airborne Control Squadron	E-3B/C	Airborne Air Control
965 Airborne Control Squadron	E-3B/C	Airborne Air Control
966 Airborne Control Training Squadron	E-3B/C	Airborne Air Control
	TC-18E	Training

E-3 aircraft from this unit manned by crews from 513 Airborne Control Group (AFRC) under associate programme.

AIR MOBILITY COMMAND

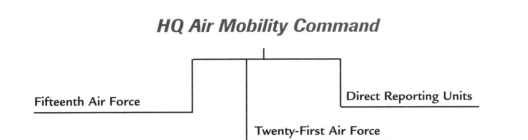

Mission

Air Mobility Command, a major command with headquarters at Scott Air Force Base, Ill., was created June 1, 1992. AMC provides America's Global Reach. This rapid, flexible and responsive air mobility promotes stability in regions by keeping America's capability and character highly visible.

Mission

Air Mobility Command's primary mission is rapid, global mobility and sustainment for America's armed forces. The command also plays a crucial role in providing humanitarian support at home and around the world. The men and women of the Air Mobility Command — active, Air National Guard, Air Force Reserve and civilians — provide tactical and strategic airlift and aerial refueling for all of America's armed forces. Many special duty and operational support aircraft and stateside aeromedical evacuation missions are also assigned to AMC. On Apr. 1, 1997, stateside-based C-130E/H's and C-21s returned to AMC's stewardship.

Global Capabilities

U.S. forces must be able to provide a rapid, tailored response with a capability to intervene against a well-equipped foe, hit hard, and terminate quickly. Rapid global mobility lies at the heart of U.S. strategy in this environment — without the capability to project forces, there is no conventional deterrent. As U.S. forces stationed overseas continue to decline, global interests remain, making the unique capabilities only AMC can provide even more in demand.

As the air component of the United States Transportation Command, AMC serves many customers and, as the single manager for air mobility, AMC's customers have only one number to call for Global Reach.

Airlift aircraft provide the capability to deploy our armed forces anywhere in the world and help sustain them in a conflict. Air refueling aircraft are the lifeline of Global Reach, increasing range, payloads and flexibility. Since Air Force tankers can also refuel Navy, Marine and many allied aircraft, they leverage all service capabilities on land, sea and in the air. Refuelers also have an inherent cargo-carrying capability — maximizing AMC's lift options.

Personnel

AMC's mission encompasses more than 142,000 active-duty and Air Reserve component military and civilian personnel. They include approximately 52,990 active duty, 9,240 civilians, 45,260 Air Force Reserve and 35,420 Air National Guard.

Resources

AMC's strategic mobility aircraft include the C-5 Galaxy, C-9A Nightingale, C-17 Globemaster III, C-141 Starlifter, KC-10 Extender and KC-135 Stratotanker. The stateside based C-130 Hercules is AMC's tactical airlifter. Operational support aircraft are the VC-9, VC-25 (Air Force One), C-137, C-20, C-21 and UH-1.

Organization

AMC is headquartered at Scott AFB, Ill., along with its agency for centralized command and control, the Tanker Airlift Control Center. The TACC schedules and tracks strategic tanker and airlift resources worldwide. The TACC also has the responsibility for AMC's in-place peacetime en route structure. Air Force and Department of Defense support taskings are channeled through this state-of-the-art hub of mobility control.

The command also has the Air Mobility Warfare Center located at Fort Dix, N.J., adjacent to McGuire AFB, N.J. One of the responsibilities of the center is the Global Reach Laydown Packages system for contingency or war.

The command assigns its active-duty resources to two numbered air forces, the 15th Air Force at Travis AFB, Calif.; and the 21st Air Force at McGuire. AMC bases are: Andrews AFB, Md.; Charleston AFB, S.C.; Dover AFB, Del.; Fairchild AFB, Wash.; Grand Forks AFB, N.D.; MacDill AFB, Fla.; McChord AFB, Wash.; McConnell AFB, Kan.; McGuire AFB, N.J.; Pope AFB, N.C.; Scott AFB, Ill.; and Travis AFB, Calif.

In mobilization, AMC gains 71 Air Reserve flying units at group level or above.

Fifteenth Air Force
HQ Travis Air Force Base, CA

22 Air Refueling Wing, McConnell Air Force Base, KS

344 Air Refueling Squadron	KC-135R/T	Tanker
349 Air Refueling Squadron	KC-135R/T	Tanker
350 Air Refueling Squadron	KC-135R/T	Tanker
384 Air Refueling Squadron	KC-135R/T	Tanker

KC-135 aircraft from this unit also manned by crews from 931 Air Refueling Wing (AFRC) under associate programme.

60 Air Mobility Wing, Travis Air Force Base, CA

6 Air Refueling Squadron	KC-10A	Tanker/Transport
9 Air Refueling Squadron	KC-10A	Tanker/Transport
21 Airlift Squadron	C-5A/B/C	Transport
22 Airlift Squadron	C-5A/B/C	Transport

C-5 and KC-10 aircraft from this unit also manned by crews from 349 Air Mobility Wing (AFRC) under associate programme.

62 Airlift Wing, McChord Air Force Base, WA

4 Airlift Squadron	C-141B	Transport
7 Airlift Squadron	C-141B	Transport
8 Airlift Squadron	C-141B	Transport

C-141 aircraft from this unit also manned by crews from 446 Airlift Wing (AFRC) under associate programme; to re-equip with C-17A beginning in FY99.

92 Air Refueling Wing, Fairchild Air Force Base, WA

43 Air Refueling Squadron	KC-135R/T	Tanker
92 Air Refueling Squadron	KC-135R/T	Tanker
96 Air Refueling Squadron	KC-135R/T	Tanker
97 Air Refueling Squadron	KC-135R/T	Tanker
98 Air Refueling Squadron	KC-135R/T	Tanker

317 Airlift Group, Dyess Air Force Base, TX

39 Airlift Squadron	C-130H	Transport
40 Airlift Squadron	C-130H	Transport

319 Air Refueling Wing, Grand Forks Air Force Base, ND

905 Air Refueling Squadron	KC-135R/T	Tanker
906 Air Refueling Squadron	KC-135R/T	Tanker
911 Air Refueling Squadron	KC-135R/T	Tanker
912 Air Refueling Squadron	KC-135R/T	Tanker

375 Airlift Wing, Scott Air Force Base, IL

11 Airlift Squadron	C-9A	Medical Airlift [1]
457 Airlift Squadron	C-21A	Communications [2]
12 Airlift Flight	C-21A	Communications [3]
47 Airlift Flight	C-21A	Communications [4]
54 Airlift Flight	C-21A	Communications [5]
458 Airlift Squadron	C-21A	Communications
84 Airlift Flight	C-21A	Communications [6]
311 Airlift Flight	C-21A	Communications [7]
332 Airlift Flight	C-21A	Communications [8]

[1] *C-9 aircraft from this unit also manned by crews from 932 Airlift Wing (AFRC) under associate programme.*

[2] *At Andrews Air Force Base, MD.*

[3] *At Langley Air Force Base, VA.*

[4] *At Wright-Patterson Air Force Base, OH.*

[5] *At Maxwell Air Force Base, AL.*

[6] *At Peterson Air Force Base, CO.*

[7] *At Offutt Air Force Base, NB.*

[8] *At Randolph Air Force Base, TX.*

Twenty-First Air Force

HQ McGuire Air Force Base, NJ

V6 Air Refueling Wing, MacDill Air Force Base, FL

91 Air Refueling Squadron	KC-135R	Tanker

Also manages Central Command EC-135N/Y and EC-137D command post aircraft and CT-43A of US Southern Command.

19 Air Refueling Group, Robins Air Force Base, GA

99 Air Refueling Squadron	KC-135R	Tanker

43 Airlift Wing, Pope Air Force Base, NC

2 Airlift Squadron	C-130E	Transport
41 Airlift Squadron	C-130E	Transport

89 Airlift Wing, Andrews Air Force Base, MD

Executive Flight	VC-25A	Presidential Transport
1 Airlift Squadron	C-137C, C-135E , C-32A, C-12C	VIP Transport
1 Helicopter Squadron	UH-1N	Communications
99 Airlift Squadron	VC-9C, C-20B/C/H, C-37A	VIP Transport

305 Air Mobility Wing, McGuire Air Force Base, NJ

2 Air Refueling Squadron	KC-10A	Tanker/Transport
6 Airlift Squadron	C-141B	Transport
13 Airlift Squadron	C-141B	Transport
32 Air Refueling Squadron	KC-10A	Tanker/Transport

KC-10 and C-141 aircraft from this unit also manned by crews from 514 Air Mobility Wing (AFRC) under associate programme.

436 Airlift Wing, Dover Air Force Base, DE

3 Airlift Squadron	C-5A/B	Transport
9 Airlift Squadron	C-5A/B	Transport

C-5 aircraft from this unit also manned by crews from 512 Airlift Wing (AFRC) under associate programme.

437 Airlift Wing, Charleston Air Force Base, SC

14 Airlift Squadron	C-17A	Transport
15 Airlift Squadron	C-141B	Transport
16 Airlift Squadron	C-141B	Transport
17 Airlift Squadron	C-17A	Transport

C-17 and C-141 aircraft from this unit also manned by crews from 315 Airlift Wing (AFRC) under associate programme; C-17A transition continuing.

463 Airlift Group, Little Rock Air Force Base, AR

50 Airlift Squadron	C-130E/H	Transport
61 Airlift Squadron	C-130E/H	Transport

Direct Reporting Units

US Military Training Mission, Dhahran AB, Saudi Arabia

Base and Country	Aircraft Type
Support Flight	C-12C

US Embassy Flights *	Aircraft Type	US Embassy Flights	Aircraft Type
Abidjan, Ivory Coast	C-12C/D	Canberra, Australia	C-12C
Ankara, Turkey	C-12C	Djakarta, Indonesia	C-12C
Athens, Greece	C-12C	Islamabad, Pakistan	C-12C
Bangkok, Thailand	C-12C	Kinshasa, Zaire	C-12C
Brasilia, Brazil	C-12C	La Paz, Bolivia	C-12D
Buenos Aires, Argentina	C-12D	Manila, Philippines	C-12C
Bogotá, Colombia	C-12C	Mexico City, Mexico	C-12D
Budapest, Hungary	C-12D	Riyadh, Saudi Arabia	C-12C
Cairo, Egypt	C-12C	Tegucigalpa, Honduras	C-12C

* Embassy Flights equipped with C-12 for use on liaison and communications duties by air attaché and Military Assistance Advisory Group (MAAG) personnel; single example usually assigned, although some have two or three aircraft, with Turkey having four.

AIR FORCE MATERIEL COMMAND

Air Force Materiel Command, with headquarters at Wright-Patterson Air Force Base, Ohio, was created July 1, 1992. The command was formed through the reorganization of Air Force Logistics Command and Air Force Systems Command.

Mission

AFMC's mission is to develop, deliver and sustain the best products for the world's best Air Force. It is the Air Force's largest command in terms of employees and funding. AFMC supports other U.S. military forces and allies and handles major aerospace responsibilities for the Department of Defense. This includes research, development, testing, and evaluation of satellites, boosters, space probes and associated systems needed to support specific National Aeronautics and Space Administration projects.

AFMC researches, develops, tests, acquires, delivers and logistically supports every Air Force weapon system as well as other military non-weapon systems. AFMC works closely with its customers — the operational commands — to ensure each has the most capable aircraft, missiles and support equipment possible. AFMC uses five goals to help build a better Air Force:

- Satisfies its customers' needs in war and peace
- Enables its people to excel
- Sustains technological superiority
- Enhances the excellence of its business practices
- Operates quality installations

Personnel and Resources

AFMC employs a highly professional and skilled command work force of about 108,000 military and civilian employees. It is the Air Force's largest command in terms of employees and funding, as it manages 57 percent of the total Air Force budget. The command's work force operates major product centers throughout the United States.

AFMC fulfills its mission of equipping the Air Force with the best weapons systems through a series of facilities that foster "cradle-to-grave" oversight for aircraft, missiles, munitions and the people who operate them. Weapon systems, such as aircraft and missiles, are developed and acquired through four product centers, using science and technology from the research sites that make up the Air Force Research Laboratory. The systems are tested in AFMC's three test centers, then are serviced and receive major repairs over their lifetime at the command's five air logistics centers. The command's specialized centers perform many other development and logistics functions. Eventually, aircraft and missiles are "retired" to AFMC's Arizona desert facility.

Product Centers

Aeronautical Systems Center, at Wright-Patterson AFB, Ohio, is responsible for research, development, test, evaluation and initial acquisition of aeronautical systems and related equipment for the Air Force. Its major active programs are the B-2 and B-1B bombers, C-17 airlifter, F-22 fighter and continuing work on the F-117A fighter, F-15 Eagle and F-16 Fighting Falcon.

Electronic Systems Center, at Hanscom AFB, Mass., develops and acquires command, control, communications, computer and intelligence systems. Among the systems developed by the center are mission planning systems, the Airborne

Warning and Control System, the Ballistic Missile Early Warning System, the Joint Surveillance Target Attack Radar System and the North American Aerospace Defense Command Center in Cheyenne Mountain, Colo.

Space and Missile Systems Center, at Los Angeles AFB, Calif., designs and acquires all Air Force and most DOD space systems. It oversees launches, completes on-orbit checkouts, then turns systems over to user agencies. It supports the Program Executive Office for Space on the Navstar Global Positioning, Defense Satellite Communications and Milstar systems. SMSC also supports the Titan IV, Defense Meteorological Satellite and Defense Support programs, and Follow-on Early Warning System. In addition, it supports development and acquisition of land-based intercontinental ballistic missiles for the Air Force Program Executive Office - Strategic Systems.

Human Systems Center, at Brooks AFB, Texas, has the role of integrating and maintaining people in Air Force systems and operations. The center concentrates on crew-system integration, crew protection, environmental protection and force readiness (human resources and aerospace medicine). It develops and acquires systems such as life support, chemical warfare defense, air base support and aeromedical casualty.

Air Force Research Laboratory

The Air Force Research Laboratory's mission is to identify and provide advanced, affordable, integrated technologies to keep the U.S. Air Force the best in the world. As a full-spectrum laboratory, it is responsible for planning and executing the Air Force's entire science and technology budget. The headquarters, located at Wright-Patterson AFB, directs the activities of research facilities across the nation.

Test Centers

Arnold Engineering Development Center, at Arnold AFB, Tenn., has the nation's most advanced and largest complex of flight simulation test facilities. The center has more than 50 aerodynamic and propulsion wind tunnels, rocket and turbine engine test cells, space environmental chambers, arc heaters, ballistics ranges and other units. The center tests aircraft, missiles and space systems and subsystems at flight conditions they will experience during a mission.

Air Force Development Test Center, at Eglin AFB, Fla., tests and evaluates non-nuclear munitions, electronic combat systems, and navigation and guidance systems. The center's test wing manages all of the large test ranges on the 724-square-mile Eglin complex, as well as 97,963 square miles of water ranges in the adjacent Gulf of Mexico. Major tests include aircraft systems and subsystems, missiles, guns, bombs, rockets, targets and drones, high-powered radar and airborne electronic countermeasures equipment.

Air Force Flight Test Center, at Edwards AFB, Calif., covers 301,000 acres on the western edge of the Mojave Desert. It has tested all the aircraft in the Air Force inventory. The nation's first jet- and rocket-powered aircraft completed their first flights at Edwards. The center is where piloted aircraft first exceeded Mach 1 through 6. It is also the site of lifting-body research flights, critical to the design and development of the space shuttle.

Air Logistics Centers

Ogden Air Logistics Center, at Hill AFB, Utah, provides logistics support for the entire Air Force inventory of intercontinental ballistic missiles, as well as depot-level maintenance for F/RF-4, F-16 and C-130 aircraft. Other responsibilities include management of the Maverick air-to-ground missile, GBU-15 and laser-guided bombs and the Emergency Rocket Communications Systems. The center is the logistics manager for all landing gear, air munitions, solid propellants and explosive devices used by the Air Force.

Oklahoma City Air Logistics Center, at Tinker AFB, Okla., provides worldwide logistics support and depot-level maintenance for a variety of weapons systems, including the B-1B, B-52, multipurpose 135-series aircraft, the E-3, E-4 and management of the B-2 bomber. It supports the short-range attack missile and the air-launched cruise missile. The center also manages a large variety of aircraft engines.

Sacramento Air Logistics Center, at McClellan AFB, Calif., provides worldwide logistics management and depot-level maintenance for a number of aircraft, including the F-111, A-10, C-12, C-21, T-39 and F-117A. It has worldwide responsibility for ground communications electronics, which includes several space-support programs and major ground-communications electronics system networks. The center will support the F-22 air superiority fighter

San Antonio Air Logistics Center, at Kelly AFB, Texas, provides worldwide logistics support for such weapon systems as the C-17, T-37 and T-38 aircraft. The center manages the Air Force's nuclear ordnance and fuels, liquid propellants and lubricants used by the Air Force, NASA and other agencies.

Warner Robins Air Logistics Center, at Robins AFB, Ga., provides worldwide logistics management and depot-level maintenance for the C-5, C-141, C-130 and F-15 aircraft. In addition, the ALC has worldwide management responsibilities for the U-2, all Air Force helicopters, all special operations aircraft and their avionics systems. Also, the center provides logistics support for all Air Force missiles, vehicles, general purpose computers and many avionics and electronic warfare systems used on most Air Force aircraft.

Major Specialized Centers

Aerospace Maintenance and Regeneration Center, at Davis-Monthan AFB, Ariz., is the site for storing surplus aircraft and for aircraft regeneration. The center stores preserved aircraft indefinitely with minimum deterioration and corrosion because of the meager rainfall, low humidity and alkaline soil in the Tucson area. It presently stores more than 3,600 aircraft from all the services. When production of older aircraft ceases, the center sometimes is the sole source for parts. Reclamation projects have become a major part of the center's work load.

Air Force Security Assistance Center, at Wright-Patterson AFB, Ohio, integrates and coordinates the security assistance activities of Air Force Materiel Command. The center ensures fulfillment of Air Force commitments for goods and services to its foreign customers - more than 80 foreign governments, allies and international organizations. The center is responsible for information systems and process management that support the logistics and financial management of security-assistance programs.

Joint Logistics System Center, at Wright-Patterson AFB, Ohio, equips forces with improved, standardized and interoperable logistics processes, systems and information. The center's item entry control process compares and technically assesses the form, fit, function and safety requirements of new items against currently cataloged items. This prevents duplicating in the inventory. Its logistics data management division develops, monitors and updates logistics data on all supply items used by the Air Force. A customer support division provides users with information on stock and part numbers and the interchangeability of spare parts.

History

AFMC traces its heritage to 1917 when the Equipment Division of the U.S. Army Signal Corps established a headquarters for its new Airplane Engineering Department at McCook Field, Dayton, Ohio, a World War I experimental engineering facility.

Functionally divided during World War II, research and development, and logistics were reunited for several years as Air Materiel Command during the late 1940s. In 1950, the Air Research and Development Command became a separate organization devoted strictly to research and development.

In 1961, Air Materiel Command was redesignated Air Force Logistics Command while Air Research and Development Command, gaining responsibility for weapon system acquisition, was redesignated Air Force Systems Command. The two commands were integrated to form Air Force Materiel Command July 1, 1992.

HQ Wright-Patterson Air Force Base, OH

Air Force Flight Test Center, Edwards Air Force Base, CA

412 Test Wing, Edwards Air Force Base, CA

412 Operations Group

410 Flight Test Squadron	F-117A	R&D, Test & Evaluation [1]
411 Flight Test Squadron	F-22A	R&D, Test & Evaluation
415 Flight Test Squadron	F-15	R&D, Test & Evaluation
416 Flight Test Squadron	F-16	R&D, Test & Evaluation
417 Flight Test Squadron	C-17A	R&D, Test & Evaluation
418 Flight Test Squadron	–	R&D, Test & Evaluation
419 Flight Test Squadron	B-52H, B-1B, B-2A	R&D, Test & Evaluation
445 Flight Test Squadron	T-38A, UH-1N	Test Pilot Training [2]
452 Flight Test Squadron	EC-18, C-135 , NC-141	R&D, Test & Evaluation
453 Flight Test Squadron	T/NT-39	R&D, Test & Evaluation

[1] At Air Force Plant 42, Palmdale, CA.

[2] USAF Test Pilots' School.

Air Armament Center, Eglin Air Force Base, FL

46 Test Wing, Eglin Air Force Base, FL

46 Operations Group		
39 Flight Test Squadron	F-16A/B/C/D, UH-1N	R&D, Test & Evaluation
40 Flight Test Squadron	F-15A/B/C/D/E UH-1N, NC-130A	R&D, Test & Evaluation

46 Test Group, Holloman Air Force Base, NM

586 Test Support Squadron	AT-38B	R&D, Test & Evaluation

Aeronautical Systems Center, Wright-Patterson Air Force Base, OH

88 Air Base Wing	Boeing 707, C-22C	R&D, Test & Evaluation Support

311 Human Systems Wing, Brooks Air Force Base, TX

Aerospace Guidance and Metrology Center, Newark Air Force Base, OH

Aerospace Maintenance and Regeneration Center, Davis-Monthan Air Force Base, AZ

(nil flying a/c) — Storage Site

Arnold Engineering Development Center, Arnold Air Force Base, TN

Electronic Systems Center, Hanscom Air Force Base, MA

Space and Missile Systems Center, Los Angeles Air Force Base, CA

USAF Museum, Wright-Patterson Air Force Base, OH

(Operational Support Elements) [1]

Ogden Air Logistics Center,
Hill Air Force Base, UT (75 Air Base Wing)

15 Flight Test Squadron	F-16A/B	Test Tasks
514 Flight Test Squadron	NC-130H, HH-10	Drone Operations

Oklahoma City Air Logistics Center,
Tinker Air Force Base, OK (72 Air Base Wing)

10 Flight Test Squadron	-	Test Tasks [2]

[1] *Air Logistics Centers responsible for overhaul of USAF aircraft.*

[2] *Nil aircraft permanently assigned; unit conducts pre-delivery test flights.*

Sacramento Air Logistics Center,
McClellan Air Force Base, CA (77 Air Base Wing)

San Antonio Air Logistics Center,
Kelly Air Force Base, TX (76 Air Base Wing)

313 Flight Test Squadron	-	Test Tasks [2]

Warner Robins Air Logistics Center,
Robins Air Force Base, GA (78 Air Base Wing)

339 Flight Test Squadron	F-15A/E	Test Tasks

[1] *Air Logistics Centers responsible for overhaul of USAF aircraft.*

[2] *Nil aircraft permanently assigned; unit conducts pre-delivery test flights.*

AIR FORCE
SPECIAL OPERATIONS COMMAND

HQ Hurlburt Field, FL

Air Force Special Operations Command (AFSOC), with headquarters at Hurlburt Field, Fla., was established May 22, 1990. AFSOC is a major command and the Air Force component of U.S. Special Operations Command, a unified command.

Mission

AFSOC is America's specialized air power. It is a step ahead in a changing world, delivering special operations combat power anytime, anywhere.

The command is committed to continual improvement to provide Air Force special operations forces for worldwide deployment and assignment to regional unified commands to conduct: unconventional warfare; direct action; special reconnaissance; counter-proliferation; foreign internal defense; information and psychological operations; personnel recovery and counter-terrorism operations.

Personnel and Resources

AFSOC has approximately 12,500 active, reserve and national guard personnel, 20 percent of whom are stationed overseas. The command's three active duty flying units epitomize the composite wing/group concept. They are composed of over 100 fixed and rotary-wing aircraft.

Organization

The 16th Special Operations Wing, at Hurlburt Field, is the oldest and most seasoned unit in AFSOC. It includes the 6th Special Operations Squadron, which is the wing's combat aviation advisory unit; the 4th SOS, which flies the AC-130U gunship; the 8th SOS, which flies the MC-130E Combat Talon I; the 15th SOS, which flies the MC-130H Combat Talon II; the 16th SOS, which flies the AC-130H Spectre gunship; the 20th SOS, which flies the MH-53J Pave Low III helicopter; and the 55th SOS, which flies the MH-60G Pave Hawk helicopter. One squadron, the 9th SOS, is located on nearby Eglin Air Force Base, Fla. and flies the MC-130P Combat Shadow.

The 352nd Special Operations Group, at RAF Mildenhall, England, is the designated Air Force component for Special Operations Command Europe. Its squadrons are the 7th SOS, which flies the MC-130H; the 21st SOS, equipped with the MH-53J; the 67th SOS, with the MC-130P; and the 321st Special Tactics Squadron.

The 353rd Special Operations Group, at Kadena Air Base, Japan, is the Air Force component for Special Operations Command Pacific. The squadrons are the 1st SOS, which flies the MC-130E Combat Talon II; the 17th SOS, with the MC-130P Combat Shadow; the 31st SOS at Osan Air Base, Korea, which flies the MH-53J Pave Low helicopter; and the 320th STS.

The 720th Special Tactics Group, with headquarters at Hurlburt Field has special operations combat controllers and pararescuemen who work jointly in special tactics teams. Its squadrons include the 21st STS and 24th STS at Pope AFB, N.C; the 22nd STS at McChord AFB, Wash.; and the 23rd STS and the 10th Combat Weather Squadron at Hurlburt Field. Their missions include: air traffic control for establishing air assault landing zones, close air support for strike aircraft and gunship missions, establishing casualty collection stations, providing trauma care for injured personnel and tactical meteorological forecasting for Army Special Operations Command (USASOC).

The U.S. Air Force Special Operations School at Hurlburt Field, provides special operations-related education to Department of Defense personnel, government agencies and allied nations. Subjects covered in its 17 courses range from regional affairs and cross-cultural communications to antiterrorism awareness, revolutionary warfare and psychological operations.

The 18th Flight Test Squadron, with headquarters at Hurlburt Field, provides expertise to improve the capabilities of special operations forces worldwide. The center conducts operational and maintenance suitability tests and evaluations for equipment, concepts, tactics and procedures for employment of special operations forces. Many of these tests are joint command and joint service projects.

Air Reserve Components

AFSOC gains some air reserve component units when the organizations are mobilized. One is the 919th Special Operations Wing (AFRC) at Duke Field, Fla. Its 711th SOS flies the MC-130E Combat Talon, while its 5th SOS flies the MC-130P Combat Shadow. Air National Guard units include the 193rd Special Operations Wing, Harrisburg International Airport, Pa., the 123rd Special Tactics Flight, Standiford Field, Ky.; the 107th Air Weather Flight, Selfridge ANGB, Mich.; the 146th AWF, Pittsburgh, Pa.; and the 181st AWF, Dallas, Texas.

Air Support Operations Squadron, Fort Bragg, NC

Nil aircraft assigned.

16 Special Operations Wing, Hurlburt Field, FL

4 Special Operations Squadron	AC-130U	Gunship
6 Special Operations Squadron	UH-1N, CASA C-212	Training
8 Special Operations Squadron	MC-130E	Special Operations
9 Special Operations Squadron	MC-130P	Combat SAR [1]
15 Special Operations Squadron	MC-130H	Special Operations
16 Special Operations Squadron	AC-130H	Gunship
19 Special Operations Squadron	AC-130H/U	Training [2]
20 Special Operations Squadron	MH-53J	Special Operations/Combat SAR
	NCH-53A	Training/Trials
55 Special Operations Squadron	MH-60G	Special Operations/Combat SAR

[1] *At Eglin Air Force Base, FL.*

[2] *Uses aircraft of 4 Special Operations Squadron and 16 Special Operations Squadron when necessary.*

18 Flight Test Squadron, Hurlburt Field, FL

Nil aircraft assigned; uses assets loaned from 16 Special Operations Wing.

352 Special Operations Group, Royal Air Force Mildenhall, England

7 Special Operations Squadron	MC-130H	Special Operations
21 Special Operations Squadron	MH-53J	Special Operations/Combat SAR
67 Special Operations Squadron	MC-130P	Combat SAR
	C-130E	Training/Support Tasks

353 Special Operations Group, Kadena AB, Japan

1 Special Operations Squadron	MC-130H	Special Operations
	C-130E	Training/Support Tasks
17 Special Operations Squadron	MC-130P	Combat SAR
31 Special Operations Squadron	MH-53J	Special Operations/Combat SAR *

* *At Osan AB, South Korea.*

427 Special Operations Squadron, Pope Air Force Base, NC

	CASA C-212	Special Operations

AIR FORCE SPACE COMMAND

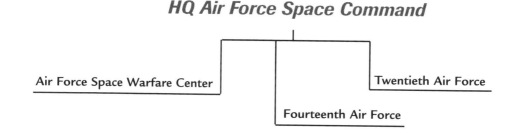

HQ Air Force Space Command

Air Force Space Warfare Center

Fourteenth Air Force

Twentieth Air Force

Air Force Space Command (AFSPC), created Sept. 1, 1982, is one of nine Air Force major commands, and is headquartered at Peterson Air Force Base, Colo. AFSPC defends America through its space and intercontinental ballistic missile (ICBM) operations, vital force elements in projecting global reach and global power. AFSPC is a key factor in implementing the expeditionary aerospace force organizational structure.

Mission

Air Force Space Command brings space to the warfighter by continuously improving the command's ability to provide and support combat forces — assuring their access to space. In addition, the command's ICBM forces deter any adversary contemplating the use of weapons of mass destruction. AFSPC has four primary mission areas:

Space forces support involves launching satellites and other high-value payloads into space using a variety of expendable launch vehicles and operating those satellites once in the medium of space.

Space control ensures friendly use of space through the conduct of counterspace operations encompassing surveillance, negation and protection.

Force enhancement provides weather, communications, intelligence, missile warning and navigation.

Force application involves maintaining and operating a rapid response land-based ICBM force as part of the nation's strategic nuclear triad.

Personnel

Approximately 37,200 people, including 25,800 active-duty military and civilians, and 11,360 contractor employees, combine to perform AFSPC missions.

Organization

Air Force Space Command has two numbered air forces. **Fourteenth Air Force** provides space warfighting forces to U.S. Space Command, and is located at Vandenberg AFB, Calif. Fourteenth Air Force manages the generation and employment of space forces to support U.S. Space Command and North American Aerospace Defense Command (NORAD) operational plans and missions. **Twentieth Air Force**, located at F.E. Warren AFB, Wyo., operates and maintains AFSPC's ICBM weapon systems in support of U.S. Strategic Command war plans.

The Space Warfare Center at Schriever AFB, Colo. is also part of the command. The center plays a major role in fully integrating space systems into the operational Air Force. Its force enhancement mission looks at ways to use space systems to support warfighters in the areas of navigation, weather, intelligence, communications and theater ballistic missile warning, and how these apply to theater operations. The center is also home to the Space Battlelab.

AFSPC is the major command providing space forces for the U.S. Space Command and trained ICBM forces for U.S. Strategic Command. AFSPC also supports NORAD with ballistic missile warning information, operates the Space Warfare Center to develop space applications for direct warfighter support, and is responsible for the Department of Defense's ICBM follow-on operational test and evaluation program.

AFSPC bases and stations include: Cheyenne Mountain Air Station, Schriever and Peterson AFBs and Buckley Air National Guard Base, Colo.; Onizuka AS and Vandenberg AFB, Calif.; Cape Canaveral AS and Patrick AFB, Fla.; Cavalier AS, N.D.; F.E. Warren AFB, Wyo.; Malmstrom AFB, Mont.; Clear AS, Alaska; Thule AB, Greenland; and Woomera AS, Australia. AFSPC units are located around the world, including Japan, the United Kingdom and Germany.

Space Capabilities

Spacelift operations at the East and West Coast launch bases provide services, facilities and range safety control for the conduct of DOD, National Aeronautics and Space Administration (NASA) and commercial launches. Through the command and control of all DOD satellites, satellite operators provide force-multiplying effects — continuous global coverage, low vulnerability and autonomous operations. Satellites provide essential in-theater secure communications, weather and navigational data for ground, air and fleet operations, and threat warning. Ground-based radar and Defense Support Program satellites monitor ballistic missile launches around the world to guard against a surprise attack on North America. Space surveillance radars provide vital information on the location of satellites and space debris for the nation and the world. With a readiness rate above 99 percent, America's ICBM team plays a critical role in maintaining world peace and ensuring the nation's safety and security.

Resources

AFSPC operates and supports the Global Positioning System, Defense Satellite Communications Systems Phase II and III, Defense Support Program, NATO III and IV communications and Fleet Satellite Communications System UHF follow-on and MILSTAR satellites. AFSPC currently operates the Atlas II, Delta II, Titan II and Titan IV launch vehicles. This includes all of the nation's primary boosters from the Eastern and Western ranges and range support for the space shuttle. AFSPC also operates the nation's primary source of continuous, real-time solar flare warnings. The command also operates a worldwide network of satellite tracking stations to provide communications links to satellites — a system called the Air Force Satellite Control Network.

Ground-based radars used primarily for ballistic missile warning include the Ballistic Missile Early Warning System, PAVE PAWS and PARCS radars. The Ground-based Electro-Optical Deep Space Surveillance System, Passive Space Surveillance System, phased-array and mechanical radars provide primary space surveillance coverage.

The ICBM force consists of Minuteman III and Peacekeeper missiles that provide the critical component of America's on-alert strategic forces. As the nation's "silent sentinels," ICBMs, and the people who operate them, have remained on continuous around-the-clock alert since 1959 — longer than any other U.S. strategic force. Five hundred Minuteman III and 50 Peacekeeper ICBMs are currently on alert in reinforced concrete launch facilities beneath the Great Plains.

AFSPC is the Air Force's largest operator of UH-1N Huey helicopters, responsible for missile operations support and security.

History

Missile warning and space operations were combined to form Air Force Space Command in 1982, the same year NASA launched the first space shuttle. During the Cold War, space operations focused on missile warning, and command and control for national leadership. In 1991, Operation Desert Storm provided emphasis for the command's new focus on support to the warfighter. ICBM forces were merged into AFSPC in 1993.

Air Force Space Warfare Center, Schriever Air Force Base, CO

Nil combat assets assigned.

Fourteenth Air Force

HQ Vandenberg Air Force Base, CA

30 Space Wing, Vandenberg Air Force Base, CA

76 Helicopter Flight	UH-1N	Utility/SAR
576 Flight Test Squadron	LGM-30G, LGM-118A	ICBM Testing/Training

Twentieth Air Force

HQ Francis E. Warren Air Force Base, WY

90 Space Wing, Francis E. Warren Air Force Base, WY

319 Missile Squadron	LGM-30G	ICBM
320 Missile Squadron	LGM-30G	ICBM
321 Missile Squadron	LGM-30G	ICBM
400 Missile Squadron	LGM-118A	ICBM
37 Helicopter Flight	UH-1N	Utility/SAR

91 Space Wing, Minot Air Force Base, ND

740 Missile Squadron	LGM-30G	ICBM
741 Missile Squadron	LGM-30G	ICBM
742 Missile Squadron	LGM-30G	ICBM
54 Helicopter Flight	UH-1N	Utility/SAR

341 Space Wing, Malmstrom Air Force Base, MT

10 Missile Squadron	LGM-30G	ICBM
12 Missile Squadron	LGM-30G	ICBM
490 Missile Squadron	LGM-30G	ICBM
564 Missile Squadron	LGM-30G	ICBM
40 Helicopter Flight	UH-1N	Utility/SAR

PACIFIC AIR FORCES

HQ Pacific Air Forces

Fifth Air Force

Thirteenth Air Force

Eleventh Air Force

Seventh Air Force

15 Air Base Wing

Pacific Air Forces, headquartered at Hickam Air Force Base, Hawaii, is one of nine major commands of the U.S. Air Force and is the air component of the U.S. Pacific Command.

Mission

PACAF's primary mission is to provide ready air and space power to promote U.S. interests in the Asia-Pacific region during peacetime, through crisis and in war.

The command's vision is to be the most respected air warrior team employing the full spectrum of air and space power, with our Asia-Pacific partners, to ensure peace and advance freedom.

PACAF's area of responsibility extends from the west coast of the United States to the east coast of Africa and from the Arctic to the Antarctic, more than 100 million square miles. The area is home to nearly two billion people who live in 44 countries. PACAF maintains a forward presence to help ensure stability in the region.

Personnel and Resources

The command has approximately 45,000 military and civilian personnel serving in nine major locations and numerous smaller facilities, primarily in Hawaii, Alaska, Japan, Guam and South Korea. Approximately 300 fighter and attack aircraft are assigned to the command.

Organization

PACAF's major units are 5th Air Force, Yokota Air Base, Japan; 7th Air Force, Osan AB, South Korea; 11th Air Force, Elmendorf AFB, Alaska; and 13th Air Force, Andersen AFB, Guam.

Major units also include 3rd Wing, Elmendorf AFB; 8th Fighter Wing, Kunsan AB, South Korea; 15th Air Base Wing, Hickam AFB; 18th Wing, Kadena AB, Japan (Okinawa); 51st Wing, Osan AB; 343rd Wing, Eielson AFB, Alaska; 35th Fighter Wing, Misawa AB, Japan; 374th Airlift Wing, Yokota AB; and the 36th Air Base Wing, Andersen AFB.

History

PACAF traces its roots to the activation of Far East Air Forces, Aug. 3, 1944, at Brisbane, Queensland, Australia. FEAF was subordinate to the U.S. Army Forces Far East and served as the headquarters of Allied Air Forces Southwest Pacific Area. By 1945, three numbered air forces — 5th, 7th and 13th — were supporting operations in the Pacific. At that time, the Army Air Forces in the Pacific became part of the largest and most powerful military organization ever fielded by any country in the world.

After World II, FEAF and 5th Air Force remained in Japan, while 7th Air Force operated from Hawaii, and 13th Air Force from the Philippines. In the post-war years, FEAF was designated the theater air force for the Far East Command. All air forces in the Far East and Southwest Pacific were placed under one Air Force commander for the first time.

When the North Koreans crossed the 38th parallel June 25, 1950, FEAF consisted of 5th Air Force, 13th Air Force, 20th Air Force and the Far East Materiel Command. Four years after the Korean War armistice, FEAF was redesignated Pacific Air Forces and transferred its headquarters to Hickam.

By 1960, PACAF maintained a combat-ready deterrent force of some 35 squadrons, operating from 10 major bases in a half-dozen countries. In the early 1960s communist military strength and firepower in Vietnam increased. As a result, PACAF began a buildup in the area with the addition of troops and better arms and equipment.

Combat aircraft of PACAF flew their last strikes in Cambodia Aug. 15, 1973, writing the final chapter to the long history of active American participation in the Indochina War. The post-Vietnam era found the command focusing on improving its readiness.

PACAF's organizational structure saw a marked period of rapid and extensive changes. Andersen was reassigned from Strategic Air Command in 1989, and 11th Air Force became a part of the command in late 1990. Following the volcanic eruption of Mount Pinatubo, Clark AB, the Philippines, was closed and 13th Air Force relocated to Andersen in 1991.

In 1992, changes took place in force structure within PACAF as the command assumed control of theater-based tactical airlift wings, theater C-130 aircraft and crews, and associated theater C-130 support. PACAF also gained control of all operational support aircraft and all aeromedical airlift assets in the Pacific.

Throughout its history PACAF has played a vital role in world events. In addition to its key combat role in World War II, Korea and Vietnam, PACAF units fought in Desert Storm in 1991, and they continue to deploy to Saudi Arabia, Turkey and Italy for peacekeeping operations.

Since 1944, the command has participated in more than 140 humanitarian operations within its area of responsibility and beyond. In these operations PACAF people quickly and efficiently airlifted food, medicine and other supplies to areas devastated by storms, floods, earthquakes, volcanoes and other natural disasters.

The command supported three of the largest evacuations ever undertaken by the Air Force: the Newlife evacuation of Vietnamese in 1975, the Fiery Vigil evacuation of Clark AB after the eruption of Mount Pinatubo, and the Pacific Haven operation to support and resettle Kurdish evacuees in 1997.

For more than five decades PACAF has served in defense of the nation. The command continually prepares to bring air power quickly and decisively to the far reaches of the Pacific.

15 Air Base Wing

HQ Hickam Air Force Base, HI

65 Airlift Squadron	C-135E/K, KC-135E	Pacific Air Forces Support Tasks

Fifth Air Force

HQ Yokota AB, Japan

18 Wing, Kadena AB, Japan

12 Fighter Squadron	F-15C/D	Air Superiority
33 Rescue Squadron	HH-60G	Combat SAR
44 Fighter Squadron	F-15C/D	Air Superiority
67 Fighter Squadron	F-15C/D	Air Superiority
909 Air Refueling Squadron	KC-135R	Tanker
961 Airborne Control Squadron	E-3B/C	Airborne Air Control

35 Fighter Wing, Misawa AB, Japan

13 Fighter Squadron	F-16C/D	Multirole Fighter
14 Fighter Squadron	F-16C/D	Multirole Fighter
33 Rescue Squadron Det 2	HH-60G	Combat SAR

374 Airlift Wing, Yokota AB, Japan

30 Airlift Squadron	C-9A	Medical Airlift
36 Airlift Squadron	C-130E/H	Transport
459 Airlift Squadron	C-21A, UH-1N	Communications

Seventh Air Force

HQ Osan AB, South Korea

8 Fighter Wing, Kunsan AB, South Korea

35 Fighter Squadron	F-16C/D	Multirole Fighter
80 Fighter Squadron	F-16C/D	Multirole Fighter

51 Fighter Wing, Osan AB, South Korea

Unit	Aircraft	Role
25 Fighter Squadron	OA-10A	Attack/Forward Air Control
36 Fighter Squadron	F-16C/D	Multirole Fighter
33 Rescue Squadron Det 1	HH-60G	Combat SAR
55 Airlift Flight	C-12J	Communications

Eleventh Air Force
HQ Elmendorf Air Force Base, AK

3 Wing, Elmendorf Air Force Base, AK

Unit	Aircraft	Role
19 Fighter Squadron	F-15C/D	Air Superiority
54 Fighter Squadron	F-15C/D	Air Superiority
90 Fighter Squadron	F-15E	Strike/Attack
517 Airlift Squadron	C-130H	Transport
	C-12J	Communications
962 Airborne Control Squadron	E-3B/C	Airborne Air Control

354 Fighter Wing, Eielson Air Force Base, AK

Unit	Aircraft	Role
18 Fighter Squadron	F-16C/D	Multirole Fighter
353 Combat Training Squadron	–	Training Support *
355 Fighter Squadron	A/OA-10A	Attack/Forward Air Control

* Nil aircraft assigned; organizes 'Cope Thunder' tactical exercises.

Thirteenth Air Force
HQ Andersen Air Force Base, Guam

36 Air Base Wing, Andersen Air Force Base, Guam
– Support Functions

497 Combat Training Squadron, Paya Lebar, Singapore
– Training Support

U.S. AIR FORCES IN EUROPE

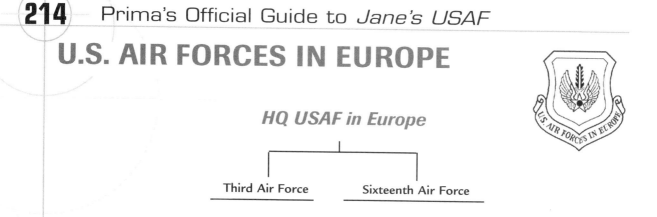

U.S. Air Forces in Europe, headquartered at Ramstein Air Base, Germany, is a major command of the U.S. Air Force. It is also the air component of the U.S. European Command, a Department of Defense unified command and the U.S. component of the North Atlantic Treaty Organization.

Mission

As the face of Europe has changed since the fall of the Berlin Wall, USAFE has changed as well. USAFE has transitioned from a fight-in-place fighter force postured for a large-scale conflict, to a mobile and deployable mixed force that can simultaneously operate in multiple locations. Since the end of the Cold War, USAFE's role in Europe has also expanded from tasks associated with warfighting to a mission that includes supporting humanitarian and peacekeeping operations, and other non-traditional tasks.

In peacetime, USAFE trains and equips U.S. Air Force units pledged to NATO. USAFE plans, conducts, controls, coordinates and supports air and space operations to achieve U.S. national and NATO objectives based on taskings by the commander in chief, United States European Command. Under wartime conditions USAFE assets, augmented by people, aircraft and equipment from other major commands and the Air National Guard and Air Force Reserve, come under the operational command of NATO. The command's inventory of aircraft is ready to perform close air support, air interdiction, air defense, in-flight refueling, long range transport and support of maritime operations.

In fulfilling its NATO responsibilities, the command maintains combat-ready wings dispersed from Great Britain to Turkey. USAFE supports U.S. military plans and operations in Europe, the Mediterranean, the Middle East and parts of Africa. USAFE remains a formidable force in Europe despite a rapid drawdown that saw its main operating bases cut by 67 percent following the end of the Cold War. As witnessed in the command's support of contingency and humanitarian operations throughout Europe and parts of Africa, USAFE remains a highly responsive combat command with a strong, capable force.

Personnel & Resources

More than 32,000 active-duty, reserve and civilian employees are assigned to USAFE. Equipment assets include about 230 fighter, attack, tanker and transport aircraft, and a full complement of conventional weapons.

Organization

USAFE is organized geographically through two numbered air forces: the 3rd Air Force, headquartered at RAF Mildenhall, England, and the 16th Air Force, headquartered at Aviano Air Base, Italy.

History

USAFE originated as the 8th Air Force in 1942 and flew heavy bombardment missions over the European continent during World War II. In August 1945, the command was given its current name, U.S. Air Forces in Europe.

During the Berlin Airlift, USAFE airlifted more than 2.3 million tons of food, fuel and medical supplies with the aid of the U.S. Navy and the British Royal Air Force. With the formation of NATO in 1949, the United States was committed to help defend Western Europe and USAFE again strengthened its airpower.

By the end of 1951, the command's responsibilities had expanded in Europe and eventually to French Morocco, Libya, Saudi Arabia, Greece, Turkey, Italy and Spain. The increased responsibilities led to far reaching changes, including a major reorganization in 1967 when France withdrew from the NATO military command structure, forcing all foreign troops to leave.

In March 1973, Headquarters USAFE transferred from Lindsey Air Station, Wiesbaden, West Germany, to Ramstein Air Base. NATO's Allied Air Forces Central Europe was then established at Ramstein in June 1974, and the USAFE commander took command of Allied Air Forces Central Europe in addition to commanding U.S. Air Force units in Europe.

The Intermediate Range Nuclear Forces Treaty, ratified in 1988, mandated the first ever elimination of an entire class of weapons from U.S. and Soviet inventories. USAFE completed removal of its ground launched cruise missiles and other weaponry in March 1991, when the last 16 missiles were removed from Comiso Air Station, Italy.

USAFE mobilized and moved more than 180 aircraft and 5,400 people to the Persian Gulf area in support of Operations Desert Shield and Desert Storm. In addition, 100 aircraft and 2,600 personnel were deployed to Turkey for Operation Proven Force, which denied the Iraqis a safe haven for their military forces in northern Iraq. USAFE also activated aeromedical staging facilities and contingency hospitals. More than 9,000 patients, mostly suffering from noncombat-related illnesses and injuries, were evacuated to Europe and more than 3,000 were treated at USAFE medical facilities.

After Desert Storm, USAFE provided immediate emergency relief to Kurdish refugees fleeing Iraqi forces by implementing Operation Provide Comfort, a no-fly zone enforcement over northern Iraq. As the initial Operation Provide Comfort drew to a close, Kurdish leaders asked for continued protection. Operation Provide Comfort continues today with USAFE maintaining a deterrent presence in Turkey.

Since the Gulf War, USAFE has been operating at a double-time pace to save lives and meet the demands of real-world contingencies at hot spots throughout the European theater. This frequently puts the command's troops on the road supporting critical operations in northern and southern Iraq, the former Yugoslavia, Somalia, Rwanda and a host of other locations.

USAFE has participated in several major humanitarian efforts, including Provide Hope I and II, which airlifted food and medical supplies to the people of the former Soviet Union, and Provide Promise, the airlifting of supplies into a war-torn Yugoslavia from July 1992 until December 1995.

Following 16 years of civil war in Angola, USAFE provided airmen and C-130 aircraft for Operation Provide Transition, which relocated government and rebel soldiers within the country in a United Nations effort to support democratic elections. USAFE also provided air protection over the skies of Bosnia-Herzegovina in Operation Deny Flight. Along with allies from NATO countries, USAFE aircrews applied airpower in Operation Deliberate Force, the bombing campaign that paved the way for the Dayton Peace Agreement. USAFE's application of its diverse air assets delivered peace Implementation Force people and equipment for Operation Joint Endeavor and maintained sustaining airlift for the operation.

USAFE airmen today are engaged in a wide range of active U.S. military efforts in Europe, including realistic U.S. and NATO exercises and real-world contingencies. The command also plays a major role in furthering democracy in the former Eastern Bloc, as USAFE people take part in Partnership for Peace exercises and Military-to-Military contact programs.

Third Air Force

HQ Royal Air Force Mildenhall, England

48 Fighter Wing, RAF Lakenheath, England

492 Fighter Squadron	F-15E	Strike/Attack
493 Fighter Squadron	F-15C/D	Air Superiority
494 Fighter Squadron	F-15E	Strike/Attack

52 Fighter Wing, Spangdahlem AB, Germany

22 Fighter Squadron	F-16C/D	Multirole Fighter
23 Fighter Squadron	F-16C/D	Multirole Fighter
53 Fighter Squadron	F-15C/D	Air Superiority
81 Fighter Squadron	A/OA-10A	Attack/Forward Air Control

86 Airlift Wing, Ramstein AB, Germany

37 Airlift Squadron	C-130E	Transport
75 Airlift Squadron	C-9A	Medical Airlift
75 AS Det 1	C-9A	Communications *
76 Airlift Squadron	C-20A, C-21A	Communications

* Based at Chievres, Belgium.

100 Air Refueling Wing, Royal Air Force Mildenhall, England

351 Air Refueling Squadron	KC-135R	Tanker

Sixteenth Air Force

HQ Aviano AB, Italy

Headquarters to move to Naples, Italy, by 2000.

31 Fighter Wing, Aviano AB, Italy

510 Fighter Squadron	F-16C/D	Multirole Fighter
555 Fighter Squadron	F-16C/D	Multirole Fighter

39 Wing, Incirlik AB, Turkey

Supports rotational elements from other US AIR FORCES IN EUROPE units.

AIR EDUCATION AND TRAINING COMMAND

HQ Air Education & Training Command

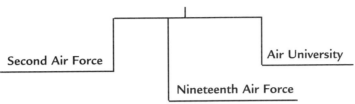

Air University no longer has aircraft assigned.

Air Education and Training Command, with headquarters at Randolph Air Force Base near San Antonio, Texas, was established July 1, 1993, with the realignment of Air Training Command and Air University.

Mission

AETC recruits new people into the U.S. Air Force and provides them with military, technical and flying training; and precommissioning, professional military and continuing education. After receiving basic training and prior to placement in Air Force jobs, enlisted people are trained in a technical skill. More than 1,350 active technical courses offer a wide variety of job skills for today's young adults. During their careers in the Air Force, every officer and enlisted person receives education and training administered by the command.

Personnel and Resources

The command includes two numbered air forces, the Air University, Air Force Recruiting Service and Wilford Hall Medical Center. More than 43,000 active-duty members and 13,400 civilian personnel make up AETC. The command has responsibility for approximately 1,600 aircraft.

Organization

Air University

Air University, headquartered at Maxwell AFB, Ala., is responsible for precommissioning education and training, professional military education, professional continuing education, degree granting education, and citizenship education and training.

AU students are primarily Air Force officers, airmen and selected Air Force civilians. A number of personnel from other services and Department of Defense activities also attend AU schools. In addition, international officers from more than 100 countries have studied in AU schools.

Air Force Officer Accession and Training Schools. These schools provides coordinated leadership and policy direction for the Air Force's officer recruiting, training and commissioning programs at Officer Training School and Air Force Reserve Officer Training Corps detachments. The organization's staff manages support and develops curriculum to train tomorrow's Air Force officers. AFOATS also directs the Air Force's high school citizenship training program — Air Force Junior ROTC. Over the years, OTS has functioned as a flexible commissioning program to meet the constantly changing manning requirements of the Air Force. Additionally, OTS formally trains medical service officers, chaplains and lawyers.

AFROTC, operating in partnership with more than 140 colleges and universities, educates, trains and commissions qualified students in a diversified college and university environment.

Professional Military Education. The PME schools of AU - Air War College, Air Command and Staff College, Squadron Officer School and the College for Enlisted Professional Military Education - prepare senior, midcareer and junior commissioned and noncommissioned officers and civilians for more responsible positions throughout the Air Force.

Professional Continuing Education. Several AU organizations provide continuing education to meet Air Force needs. The College of Aerospace Doctrine, Research and Education assists in the development of Air Force doctrine and military strategy, conducts operational and educational wargames, and conducts warplanning and warfighting courses. The Ira C. Eaker College for Professional Development provides continuing education through the U.S. Air Force Chaplain Service Institute, U.S. Air Force First Sergeant Academy, Air Force Human Resource Management School, Air Force Judge Advocate General School, Commanders' Professional Development School and Professional Military Comptroller School. The Air Force Institute of Technology (AFIT), located at Wright-Patterson Air Force Base, Ohio, meets continuing education needs through its School of Systems and Logistics and the School of Civil Engineering.

Degree Granting Education. AU awards both associate degrees and graduate degrees. The Community College of the Air Force develops and administers education programs leading to an associate degree in applied science for Air Force active duty, Reserve and Air National Guard enlisted personnel. The School for Advanced Airpower Studies awards master's degrees to future airpower strategists. At AFIT, masters degrees are awarded through the School of Logistics and Acquisitions Management. Both master's and doctorate degrees are awarded through AFIT's

School of Engineering. AFIT also manages Air Force graduate and undergraduate degree programs and continuing education programs at civilian institutions as well as Air Force health care education programs and Education with Industry.

Citizenship. Citizenship is enhanced through AU oversight of the Civil Air Patrol and its cadet program, and through the Air Force Junior ROTC program that reaches into more than 600 high schools across the U.S.

Academic Support. Air University's Office of Academic Support (OAS) directs organizations which enhance the ability of AU's major schools to accomplish their missions. The AU Library provides educational and research library services and cartographic support to the headquarters, schools, colleges and tenant units. The Academic Instructor School prepares AU and other Air Force instructors for both resident and distance learning education. The International Officer School prepares international students to enter AU schools and courses. Other organizations under the OAS include: Air University Television, which supports resident and distance learning instruction; the Extension Course Institute, which publishes approximately 330 correspondence courses in specialized, career development and PME; Air University Press, which acquires, edits and publishes books, monographs, and journals on airpower topics; and Educational Technology.

Second Air Force

The 2nd Air Force, headquartered at Keesler AFB, Miss., was activated July 1, 1993, and manages all operational aspects of basic and technical training for AETC. Four training wings, including nine technical training groups and basic military training, report to 2nd AF. Geographically separated units are located at Vandenberg and Edwards Air Force bases in California.

Basic Military Training. A basic military training course for all new enlistees in the regular Air Force, Air Force Reserve and Air National Guard is conducted at Lackland AFB, Texas. Training starts on a Monday, with graduation on Friday six weeks later, followed by travel to technical training. In addition to processing and counseling, courses emphasize discipline, professional courtesy, physical fitness, teamwork and academic instruction in Air Force organization, history, human relations and quality Air Force principles.

Technical Training. Technical training in more than 250 technical specialties is provided to men and women in all branches of service throughout their careers. Technical training courses, many accredited through the Community College of the Air Force, provide job qualification and advanced training to Air Force people in support of their primary missions. Each year more than 175,000 students graduate from AETC formal training courses.

Resident courses are conducted at Keesler AFB; Lackland, Sheppard, and Goodfellow Air Force bases in Texas; and Vandenberg AFB, Calif.

Keesler AFB is host to 2nd Air Force's only flying mission. The 45th Airlift Squadron conducts initial and upgrade training for C-12 and C-21 aircrews. The graduates are assigned to provide operational support airlift for a variety of missions around the world.

Defense Language Institute English Language Center. International military members and some civilians attend full-time English language training at the Defense Language Institute English Language Center at Lackland AFB. The center is a Department of Defense agency that reports to AETC.

Inter-American Air Forces Academy. The Inter-American Air Forces Academy provides Spanish-language technical and management training to military forces and governmental agencies of Latin America and the Caribbean. The school at Lackland AFB provides training in 70 different courses for both officer and enlisted personnel.

Nineteenth Air Force

The 19th Air Force, headquartered at Randolph AFB, was activated July 1, 1993, and exercises operational control over 11 active duty units and has operational oversight of three Air National Guard units. AETC provides undergraduate and specialized pilot and navigator training, initial fighter fundamental training, specific initial skills training, upgrade and requalification aircraft training for combat crews and advanced training for helicopter pilots.

Flying Training. AETC conducts primary and advanced flight training for pilots, navigators and enlisted crew members. Command training programs produce mission-ready crew members. Pilot training begins with the flight screening program conducted in the T-3 aircraft by the 3rd Flying Training Squadron in Hondo, Texas, and the 557th Flying Training Squadron at the U.S. Air Force Academy. Pilot training continues with an undergraduate pilot training program and ends with combat crew training in specific major weapons systems.

Specialized undergraduate pilot training (SUPT) begins in either the Air Force's T-37 or the Navy's T-34 if an Air Force pilot is initially trained by the Navy. SUPT advanced training may occur in one of four aircraft. Students designated for a bomber or fighter aircraft receive advanced training in the T-38. Airlift and tanker pilots train in the T-1A, and helicopter pilots train in the UH-1 in a joint training environment at Fort Rucker, Ala. Air Force C-130-bound students train in the T-44 with the

Navy at Naval Air Station Corpus Christi, Texas. Total SUPT training includes between 193 flying hours for the airlift/tanker track to 208 for the bomber/fighter track.

Euro-NATO Joint Jet Pilot Training is an international effort conducted by the U.S. Air Force and its North Atlantic Treaty Organization (NATO) allies. This program at Sheppard AFB, Texas, trains pilots from NATO countries as well as some U.S. Air Force pilots. Primary training is conducted in the T-37 and advanced training in the T-38. ENJJPT instructor pilots are also trained at Sheppard AFB.

Students electing to fly fighters are given an introductory course in fighter fundamentals. This training is conducted at Randolph, Columbus and Sheppard Air Force bases. After this training, students bound for training in the F-15 aircraft are trained at Tyndall AFB, Fla. At Tyndall, different courses are offered for pilots who have never flown a fighter aircraft, experienced pilots converting to or requalifying in the F-15, and pilots selected to become F-15 instructor pilots. Similar training is conducted at Luke AFB, Ariz., for F-16 pilots.

Airlift training for C-5, C-17, C-141 and KC-135 pilots and enlisted aircrew members is conducted at Altus AFB, Okla. For C-130 aircrew members, training is conducted at Little Rock AFB, Ark.

Special operations training for pilots and enlisted aircrew members in the MC-130 aircraft, and the MH-53J and HH-60G helicopter, is conducted along with UH-1 training at Kirtland AFB, N.M.

Navigator Training. Joint undergraduate navigator training (JUNT) begins at Naval Air Station Pensacola, Fla., with a six-week Aviation Preflight Indoctrination course. This course consists of aviation fundamentals such as meteorology, aerodynamics, air navigation and aircraft systems; physical fitness training; and water and land survival regimen. All students then enter Primary Navigator/Naval Flight Officer flight training at NAS Pensacola. Primary training is accomplished in the T-34, a tandem, two-seat turboprop aircraft, and lasts 14 weeks. Follow-on training is in four main tracks: airlift/tanker/maritime, strike/bomber, strike/fighter and heavy electronic warfare officer. Approximately half of the students from primary go to the airlift/tanker/maritime track at Randolph AFB. This is a 24-week program training in the T-43 jet aircraft (a modified B-737) with three to five weeks of follow-on training in theater operations. Students selected for the strike/bomber, strike/fighter and heavy EWO tracks proceed from primary into intermediate training and remain at NAS Pensacola for the remainder of their training. Intermediate is a 14-week course flying T-34 and T-1 aircraft. Strike/bomber track students move on to a 12-week course flying the T-39 and T-2 aircraft. Heavy EWO track students graduate from intermediate and attend 13 weeks of academic and simulator electronic warfare training at Corry Station, adjacent to NAS Pensacola.

Other Training. AETC also conducts the Air Force combat survival course at Fairchild AFB, Wash., where more than 4,000 aircrew members receive training annually. Specialized courses are provided at NAS Pensacola for water survival; and Eielson AFB, Alaska, for arctic survival. Training for enlisted combat controllers and pararescuemen is conducted at Kirtland AFB.

Other Major Units

Air Force Recruiting Service. AETC is responsible for all personnel accessions with the exception of the U.S. Air Force Academy, lawyers and chaplains. Its mission is to recruit a high-quality volunteer force reflective of a cross-section of America. It manages this through the Air Force Recruiting Service, also headquartered at Randolph AFB. Recruiting Service is divided into four recruiting groups with 28 squadrons and about 3,000 highly motivated recruiters. The recruiting mission is accomplished from more than 900 offices worldwide. Air Force personnel requirements are given to Recruiting Service in the form of program goals for non-prior service enlistees, line officers (Officer Training School), health care professionals (physicians, nurses, etc.), applicants for Air Force Reserve Officer Training Corps scholarships, and others as required.

Wilford Hall Medical Center. Wilford Hall Medical Center, located at Lackland AFB, is one of America's national medical resources and home of the 59th Medical Wing. The medical center's staff totals more than 4,900 personnel, officers, enlisted and civilians, a number which includes almost 500 students. The 500-bed medical center serves as Lackland's hospital, a specialized treatment center for the southern United States and a referral center for patients evacuated from around the world. The Wilford Hall commander also serves as lead agent for DOD TRICARE Region VI, encompassing Arkansas, Oklahoma and most of Louisiana and Texas. Wilford Hall admits almost 25,000 patients per year, sees more than one million outpatients and serves an additional 12,000 patients per year from worldwide locations. Wilford Hall provides unique services as the DOD center for allogeneic bone marrow transplantation and liver transplantation and the Air Force-HIV evaluation and treatment center. Wilford Hall's medical outreach initiatives include training and fielding teams that perform forward surgery with the equipment in their rucksacks, the only Extracorporeal Membrane Oxygenator (heart lung machine for babies) capable of providing care to a patient in-flight, and the Critical Care Aeromedical Transport Teams which provide in-flight medical care to patients during air transport. The medical center has extensive education and research programs, and operates the only certified Level-I trauma center in the defense establishment.

Air Force Security Assistance Training Squadron. The Air Force Security Assistance Training Squadron, Randolph AFB, is the executive agent for all USAF-sponsored international training. It develops, integrates and manages international training in support of U.S. national security objectives. Nearly 5,000 students from 148 friendly and allied countries are trained annually under USAF sponsorship.

History

AETC's predecessor, Air Training Command, was formed in 1942 and trained more than 13 million people. ATC installations between 1942 and 1993 ranged from a peak of more than 600 installations during World War II, to a low of 13 when it was redesignated July 1, 1993. Command headquarters was located in Fort Worth, Texas, and Barksdale AFB, La., during the mid- and late-1940s. It was relocated to Scott AFB, Ill., in 1949, and moved to Randolph AFB in 1957.

Second Air Force

HQ Keesler Air Force Base, MS

17 Training Wing, Goodfellow Air Force Base, TX

	–	Technical Training

37 Training Wing, Lackland Air Force Base, TX

	–	Technical Training

81 Training Wing, Keesler Air Force Base, MS

45 Airlift Squadron	C-12C	Training
	C-21A	

82 Training Wing, Sheppard Air Force Base, TX

	–	Technical Training

Non-flying airframes used for instructional purposes.

381 Space & Missile Training Group, Vandenberg Air Force Base, CA

	–	ICBM Training

Nineteenth Air Force

HQ Randolph Air Force Base, TX

Nineteenth Air Force is to establish a new training unit at Moody Air Force Base, GA, in FY00; this will take over responsibility for fighter fundamentals task training now accomplished at Randolph and Columbus.

12 Flying Training Wing, Randolph Air Force Base, TX

3 Flying Training Squadron	T-3A	Training [1]
99 Flying Training Squadron	T-1A	Training
435 Flying Training Squadron	AT-38B	Weapons Training
557 Flying Training Squadron	T-3A	Training [2]
559 Flying Training Squadron	T-37B	Training
560 Flying Training Squadron	T-38A	Training
562 Flying Training Squadron	CT-43A	Navigation Training

[1] *At Hondo Municipal Airport, TX.*

[2] *At US Air Force Academy, Colorado Springs, CO.*

14 Flying Training Wing, Columbus Air Force Base, MS

37 Flying Training Squadron	T-37B	Training
41 Flying Training Squadron	T-37B	Training
48 Flying Training Squadron	T-1A	Training
49 Flying Training Squadron	AT-38B	Weapons Training
50 Flying Training Squadron	T-38A	Training

Aircraft from this unit flown by personnel from 340 Flying Training Group (AFRC) under associate programme.

47 Flying Training Wing, Laughlin Air Force Base, TX

84 Flying Training Squadron	T-37B	Training
85 Flying Training Squadron	T-37B	Training
86 Flying Training Squadron	T-1A	Training
87 Flying Training Squadron	T-38A	Training

Aircraft from this unit flown by personnel from 340 Flying Training Group (AFRC) under associate programme.

56 Fighter Wing, Luke Air Force Base, AZ

21 Fighter Squadron	F-16A/B	Fighter Training [1]
61 Fighter Squadron	F-16C/D	Fighter Training
62 Fighter Squadron	F-16C/D	Fighter Training
63 Fighter Squadron	F-16C/D	Fighter Training
308 Fighter Squadron	F-16C/D	Fighter Training
309 Fighter Squadron	F-16C/D	Fighter Training
310 Fighter Squadron	F-16C/D	Fighter Training
425 Fighter Squadron	F-16C/D	Fighter Training [2]

[1] *Taiwan Air Force Training Squadron.*

[2] *Singapore Air Force Training Squadron.*

58 Special Operations Wing, Kirtland Air Force Base, NM

512 Special Operations Squadron	HH-60G, UH-1N	Combat SAR Training
550 Special Operations Squadron	MC-130P	Combat SAR Training
	MC-130H	Special Ops Training
551 Special Operations Squadron	MH-53J	Special Ops Training
	TH-53A	

To move to Holloman Air Force Base, NM, on unspecified date with constituent squadrons.

71 Flying Training Wing, Vance Air Force Base, OK

8 Flying Training Squadron	T-37B	Training
25 Flying Training Squadron	T-38A	Training
32 Flying Training Squadron	T-1A	Training
33 Flying Training Squadron	T-37B	Training

Aircraft from this unit flown by personnel from 340 Flying Training Group (AFRC) under associate programme.

80 Flying Training Wing, Sheppard Air Force Base, TX

88 Flying Training Squadron	AT-38B	Weapons Training
89 Flying Training Squadron	T-37B	Training
90 Flying Training Squadron	T-38A	Training

Aircraft from this unit flown by personnel from 340 Flying Training Group (AFRC) under associate programme.

97 Air Mobility Wing, Altus Air Force Base, OK

55 Air Refueling Squadron	KC-135R	Tanker Training
56 Airlift Squadron	C-5A	Transport Training
57 Airlift Squadron	C-141B	Transport Training
58 Airlift Squadron	C-17A	Transport Training

314 Airlift Wing, Little Rock Air Force Base, AR

53 Airlift Squadron	C-130E	Transport Training
62 Airlift Squadron	C-130E	Transport Training
314 Logistics Support Squadron	GC-130E	Ground Instruction

325 Fighter Wing, Tyndall Air Force Base, FL

1 Fighter Squadron	F-15C/D	Fighter Training
2 Fighter Squadron	F-15C/D	Fighter Training
95 Fighter Squadron	F-15C/D	Fighter Training

336 Training Group, Fairchild Air Force Base, WA

36 Rescue Flight	UH-1N	Aircrew Survival Training

AIR FORCE RESERVE COMMAND

HQ Air Force Reserve Command

The Air Force Reserve Command, with headquarters at Robins Air Force Base, Ga., became a major command of the Air Force on Feb. 17, 1997, as a result of Title XII, Reserve Forces Revitalization, in Public Law 104-201. Previously, the Air Force Reserve was a field operating agency established April 14, 1948.

Mission

The Air Force Reserve Command (AFRC) supports the Air Force mission to defend the United States through control and exploitation of air and space by providing global reach and global power. The AFRC plays an integral role in the day-to-day Air Force mission and is not a force held in reserve for possible war or contingency operations.

Resources

AFRC has 37 flying wings equipped with their own aircraft and seven associate units that share aircraft with an active-duty unit. Two space operations squadrons share satellite control mission with the active force. There also are more than 620 mission support units in the AFRC, equipped and trained to provide a wide range of services, including medical and aeromedical evacuation, aerial port, civil engineer, security police, intelligence, communications, mobility support, logistics and transportation operations, among others.

AFRC has more than 440 aircraft assigned to it. The inventory includes the latest, most capable models of the F-16, O/A-10, C-5, C-141, C-130, MC-130, MC-130P, KC-135, B-52 and MH-60. On any given day, 99 percent of these aircraft are mission-ready and able to deploy within 72 hours. Air Combat Command, Air Mobility Command and Air Force Special Operations Command would gain these aircraft and support personnel if mobilized. These aircraft and their crews are immediately deployable without need for additional training.

Organization

Office of the Air Force Reserve. The Office of Air Force Reserve, located in the Pentagon, Washington, D.C., is headed by the chief of Air Force Reserve, a Reserve major general, who is the principal adviser to the Air Force chief of staff for all Reserve matters. Consistent with Air Force policy, the chief of Air Force Reserve establishes Reserve policy and initiates plans and programs. In addition to being a senior member of the Air Staff, he is also commander of AFRC.

Headquarters Air Force Reserve Command. Headquarters AFRC supervises the unit training program, provides logistics support, reviews unit training and ensures combat readiness. Within the headquarters element are divisions for operations, logistics, comptroller, administration and personnel support.

Fourth Air Force at March Air Reserve Base, Calif.; 10th Air Force at Naval Air Station Joint Reserve Base, Fort Worth, Texas, and 22nd Air Force at Dobbins Air Reserve Base, Ga., report to Headquarters AFRC. They act as operational headquarters for their subordinate units, providing operational, logistical and safety support, and regional support for geographically separated units.

Air Reserve Personnel Center. Air Reserve Personnel Center, a field operating agency located in Denver, Colo., provides personnel services to all members of the AFRC and Air National Guard. Services include assignments, promotions, career counseling and development, and separation actions. The center also manages individual programs for the Ready Reserve, and maintains master personnel records for all Guard and Reserve members not on extended active duty. In times of national need, the center would mobilize individual reservists and certain categories of Air Force retirees.

Reserve Categories

Ready Reserve. The Ready Reserve is made up of about 132,574 trained reservists who may be recalled to active duty to augment active forces in time of war or national emergency. Of this number, 70,118 reservists are members of the Selected Reserve who train regularly and are paid for their participation in unit or individual programs. These reservists are combat ready and can deploy to anywhere in the world in 72 hours. Additionally, 62,456 are part of the Individual Ready Reserve. Members of the IRR continue to have a service obligation, but do not train and are not paid. They are subject to recall if needed.

The president may recall Ready Reserve personnel from all Department of Defense components for up to 270 days if necessary. Some 24,000 Air Force reservists from 220 units were called to active duty during the Persian Gulf War to work side-by-side with the active-duty counterparts.

Standby Reserve. The Standby Reserve includes reservists whose civilian jobs are considered key to national defense, or who have temporary disability or personal hardship. Most Standby reservists do not train and are not assigned to units. There are about 14,425 reservists in this category.

Retired Reserve. The Retired Reserve is made up of officers and enlisted personnel who receive pay after retiring from active duty or from the Reserve, or are reservists awaiting retirement pay at age 60. There are nearly 665,665 members in the Retired Reserve.

Training

Reserve training often is scheduled to coincide with Air Force mission support needs. Since most AFRC skills are the same needed in peace or war, training often results in the accomplishment of real-world mission requirements. This mission support is referred to as a by-product of training and benefits both the AFRC and the active force.

Unit Training Program. About 60,000 reservists are assigned to specific Reserve units. These are the people who are obligated to report for duty one weekend each month and 15 additional days a year. Most work many more days than that. Reserve aircrews, for example, average more than 100 duty days a year, often flying in support of national objectives at home and around the world.

Air reserve technicians are a special group of reservists who work as civil service employees during the week in the same jobs they hold as reservists on drill weekends. ARTs are the full-time backbone of the unit training program, providing day-to-day leadership, administrative and logistical support, and operational continuity for their units.

Individual Training Program. The individual training program is made up of more than 12,000 individual mobilization augmentees. IMAs are assigned to active-duty units in specific wartime positions and train on an individual basis. Their mission is to augment active-duty manning by filling wartime surge requirements. IMAs were used extensively during Operation Desert Storm and can be found in nearly every career field.

Reserve Associate Program

The AFRC Associate Program provides trained crews and maintenance personnel for active-duty owned aircraft and space operations. This unique program pairs a Reserve unit with an active-duty unit to share a single set of aircraft. The result is a more cost-effective way to meet increasing mission requirements. Associate aircrews fly C-5, C-141, C-17, C-9, KC-10, KC-135 and E-3 aircraft.

Exercises and Deployments

Realistic exercises and deployments are an essential element in maintaining combat readiness. AFRC units participate in dozens of exercises each year and deploy to locations around the world. Exercises and deployments help reservists hone skills needed when responding to a variety of possible contingencies anywhere in the world.

Real-World Missions

Air Force reservists are on duty today around the world carrying out the Air Force vision of global engagement. A proven and respected combat force, the AFRC also is quick to lend a helping hand. Humanitarian relief missions may involve anything from repairing roads and schools in a small village in Central America, to airlifting badly needed supplies into a war-torn city, to rescuing the victims of nature's worst disasters.

At the request of local, state or federal agencies, the AFRC conducts aerial spray missions using specially equipped C-130s. With the only fixed-wing capability in the Department of Defense, these missions range from spraying pesticides to control insects to spraying compounds used in the control of oil spills. Other specially equipped C-130s check the spread of forest fires by dropping fire retardant chemicals. Real-world missions also include weather reconnaissance, rescue, international missions in support of U.S. Southern Command and aeromedical evacuation.

AFRC also takes an active role in the nation's counternarcotics effort. Reservists offer a cost-effective way to provide specialized training, airlift, analysis , and other unique capabilities to local, state and federal law enforcement officials.

Fourth Air Force

HQ March Air Reserve Base, CA

Any or all Fourth Air Force units would be 'gained' by Air Mobility Command in event of being called to active duty.

349 Air Mobility Wing, Travis Air Force Base, CA

70 Air Refueling Squadron	KC-10A	Tanker/Transport
79 Air Refueling Squadron	KC-10A	Tanker/Transport
301 Airlift Squadron	C-5A/B/C	Transport
312 Airlift Squadron	C-5A/B/C	Transport

Personnel assigned to 349 Air Mobility Wing fly aircraft provided by Air Mobility Command's 60 Air Mobility Wing at same base.

433 Airlift Wing, Kelly Air Force Base, TX

68 Airlift Squadron	C-5A	Transport

434 Air Refueling Wing, Grissom Air Reserve Base, IN

72 Air Refueling Squadron	KC-135R	Tanker
74 Air Refueling Squadron	KC-135R	Tanker

445 Airlift Wing, Wright-Patterson Air Force Base, OH

89 Airlift Squadron	C-141B *	Transport
356 Airlift Squadron	C-141B *	Transport

* To be replaced by upgraded C-141C version by 1999.

446 Airlift Wing, McChord Air Force Base, WA

97 Airlift Squadron	C-141B	Transport
313 Airlift Squadron	C-141B	Transport
728 Airlift Squadron	C-141B	Transport

Personnel assigned to 446 AW fly aircraft provided by Air Mobility Command's 62 AW at same base.

452 Air Mobility Wing, March Air Reserve Base, CA

336 Air Refueling Squadron	KC-135R	Tanker
729 Airlift Squadron	C-141B/C *	Transport
730 Airlift Squadron	C-141B/C *	Transport

* Converting from C-141B to upgraded C-141C version.

507 Air Refueling Wing, Tinker Air Force Base, OK
507 Operations Group, Tinker Air Force Base, OK

465 Air Refueling Squadron	KC-135R	Tanker

916 Air Refueling Wing, Seymour Johnson Air Force Base, NC

77 Air Refueling Squadron	KC-135R	Tanker

927 Air Refueling Wing, Selfridge Air National Guard Base, MI

63 Air Refueling Squadron	KC-135E	Tanker

931 Air Refueling Group, McConnell Air Force Base, KS

18 Air Refueling Squadron	KC-135R	Tanker

Personnel assigned to 931 Air Refueling Group fly aircraft provided by Air Mobility Command's 22 Air Refueling Wing at same base.

932 Airlift Wing, Scott Air Force Base, IL

73 Airlift Squadron	C-9A	Medical Airlift

Personnel assigned to 932 Airlift Wing fly aircraft provided by Air Mobility Command's 375 Airlift Wing at same base.

940 Air Refueling Wing, Beale Air Force Base, CA

314 Air Refueling Squadron	KC-135E	Tanker

Tenth Air Force

HQ Naval Air Station Fort Worth JRB, TX

Any or all Tenth Air Force units would be 'gained' by Air Combat Command in event of being called to active duty, with the exception of the 340 FTG elements which are 'gained' by Air Education and Training Command.

301 Fighter Wing, Naval Air Station Fort Worth JRB, TX

457 Fighter Squadron	F-16C/D	Multirole Fighter

340 Flying Training Group, Randolph Air Force Base, TX

5 Flying Training Squadron [1]	(various)	Training
43 Flying Training Squadron [2]	(various)	Training
96 Flying Training Squadron [3]	(various)	Training
97 Flying Training Squadron [4]	(various)	Training

[1] *At Vance Air Force Base, OK; personnel fly aircraft provided by Air Education and Training Command's 71 Flying Training Wing at same base.*

[2] *At Columbus Air Force Base, MS; personnel fly aircraft provided by Air Education and Training Command's 14 Flying Training Wing at same base.*

[3] *At Laughlin Air Force Base, TX; personnel fly aircraft provided by Air Education and Training Command's 47 Flying Training Wing at same base.*

[4] *At Sheppard Air Force Base, TX; personnel fly aircraft provided by Air Education and Training Command's 80 Flying Training Wing at same base.*

419 Fighter Wing, Hill Air Force Base, UT

466 Fighter Squadron	F-16C/D	Multirole Fighter

442 Fighter Wing, Whiteman Air Force Base, MO

303 Fighter Squadron	A/OA-10A	Attack/Forward Air Control

482 Fighter Wing, Homestead Air Reserve Station, FL

93 Fighter Squadron	F-16C/D	Multirole Fighter

513 Airborne Control Group, Tinker Air Force Base, OK

970 Airborne Control Squadron	E-3B/C	Airborne Air Control

Personnel assigned to 513 Airborne Control Group fly aircraft provided by Air Combat Command's 552 ACW at same base; note also that the 513 Airborne Control Group reports to the 507 Air Refueling Wing (see Fourth Air Force/AFRC) for administrative control.

917 Wing, Barksdale Air Force Base, LA

47 Fighter Squadron	A/OA-10A	Attack/Forward Air Control Training
93 Bomb Squadron	B-52H	Bomber

919 Special Operations Wing, Duke Field, FL

5 Special Operations Squadron	MC-130P	Combat SAR
711 Special Operations Squadron	MC-130E	Special Operations

926 Fighter Wing, Naval Air Station New Orleans JRB, LA

706 Fighter Squadron	A/OA-10A	Attack/Forward Air Control

939 Rescue Wing, Portland IAP, OR

303 Rescue Squadron	HC-130P	Combat SAR
304 Rescue Squadron	HH-60G	Combat SAR
305 Rescue Squadron	HH-60G	Combat SAR *

* At Davis-Monthan Air Force Base, AZ.

920 Rescue Group, Patrick Air Force Base, FL

39 Rescue Squadron	HC-130N/P	Combat SAR
301 Rescue Squadron	HH-60G	Combat SAR

944 Fighter Wing, Luke Air Force Base, AZ

302 Fighter Squadron	F-16C/D	Multirole Fighter

Twenty-Second Air Force

HQ Dobbins Air Reserve Base, GA

Any or all Twenty-Second Air Force units would be 'gained' by Air Mobility Command in event of being called to active duty.

94 Airlift Wing, Dobbins Air Reserve Base, GA

700 Airlift Squadron	C-130H	Transport

302 Airlift Wing, Peterson Air Force Base, CO

731 Airlift Squadron	C-130H	Transport

315 Airlift Wing, Charleston Air Force Base, SC

300 Airlift Squadron	C-17A	Transport
317 Airlift Squadron	C-17A	Transport
701 Airlift Squadron	C-141B	Transport
707 Airlift Squadron	C-141B	Transport

Personnel assigned to 315 Airlift Wing fly aircraft provided by Air Mobility Command's 437 AW at same base.

403 Wing, Keesler Air Force Base, MS

53 Weather Reconnaissance Squadron	WC-130H	Weather Reconnaissance *
815 Airlift Squadron	C-130E	Transport

* To convert to WC-130J in 1998-99.

439 Airlift Wing, Westover Air Reserve Base, MA

337 Airlift Squadron	C-5A	Transport

440 Airlift Wing, Gen. Mitchell IAP-Air Reserve Station, WI

95 Airlift Squadron	C-130H	Transport

459 Airlift Wing, Andrews Air Force Base, MD

756 Airlift Squadron	C-141B *	Transport

* To be replaced by upgraded C-141C version by 1999.

512 Airlift Wing, Dover Air Force Base, DE

326 Airlift Squadron	C-5A/B	Transport
709 Airlift Squadron	C-5A/B	Transport

Personnel assigned to 512 Airlift Wing fly aircraft provided by Air Mobility Command's 436 Airlift Wing at same base.

514 Air Mobility Wing, McGuire Air Force Base, NJ

76 Air Refueling Squadron	KC-10A	Tanker/Transport
78 Air Refueling Squadron	KC-10A	Tanker/Transport
335 Airlift Squadron	C-141B	Transport
702 Airlift Squadron	C-141B	Transport

Personnel assigned to 514 Air Mobility Wing fly aircraft provided by Air Mobility Command's 305 Air Mobility Wing at same base.

908 Airlift Wing, Maxwell Air Force Base, AL

357 Airlift Squadron	C-130H	Transport

910 Airlift Wing, Youngstown-Warren Regional Airport-Air Reserve Station, OH

757 Airlift Squadron	C-130H	Transport
773 Airlift Squadron	C-130H	Transport

911 Airlift Wing, Pittsburgh IAP-Air Reserve Station, PA

758 Airlift Squadron	C-130H	Transport

To inactivate on unspecified date.

913 Airlift Wing, Willow Grove Air Reserve Station, PA

327 Airlift Squadron	C-130E	Transport

914 Airlift Wing, Niagara Falls IAP-Air Reserve Station, NY

328 Airlift Squadron	C-130H	Transport

934 Airlift Wing, Minneapolis-St. Paul IAP-Air Reserve Station, MN

96 Airlift Squadron	C-130E	Transport

Air National Guard

HQ Washington, DC

Following unit details presented by 'gaining' Command that would assume jurisdiction in event of mobilization for active duty service.

The Air National Guard is administered by the National Guard Bureau, a joint bureau of the departments of the Army and Air Force, located in the Pentagon, Washington, D.C.

Mission

The ANG's state and federal mission is to provide trained, well-equipped men and women who can augment the active force during national emergencies or war, and provide assistance during natural disasters and civil disturbances.

When Guard units are in a non-mobilized status they are commanded by the governor of their respective state, Puerto Rico, Guam, Virgin Islands and the commanding general of the District of Columbia National Guard. The governors (except in the District of Columbia) are represented in the chain of command by the adjutant general of the state or territory.

State Mission

The ANG, under order of state authorities, provides protection of life and property, and preserves peace, order and public safety. State missions, which are funded by the individual states, include disaster relief in times of earthquakes, hurricanes, floods and forest fires; search and rescue; protection of vital public services; and support to civil defense.

Federal Mission

As part of the total Air Force, the ANG provides operationally ready combat units and combat support units and qualified personnel for active duty in the Air Force to fulfill war and contingency commitments. ANG units are assigned to most major commands during peacetime to accomplish this mission. The major commands establish training standards, provide advisory assistance and evaluate ANG units for unit training, readiness and safety programs.

Personnel and Resources

The primary means of providing full-time support for ANG units is through use of dual-status military technicians, plus guardsmen on active duty. These full-time support personnel perform day-to-day management, administration and maintenance. By law, dual-status military technicians are civil service employees of the federal government who must be military members of the unit in which they are employed. They participate in training activities and are mobilized with the unit when it is ordered to active duty. Active duty members serve under the command authority of their respective state and territorial governors until mobilized, and are not a part of the worldwide pool of Air Force manpower until that time.

The ANG has more than 109,000 officers and enlisted personnel who serve in 89 flying units and 242 mission support units.

Flying Units

The ANG provides 100 percent of the Air Force's air defense interceptor force, 33 percent of the general purpose fighter force, 45 percent of the tactical airlift and 6 percent of the special operations capability. In addition, the ANG provides 43 percent of the air refueling KC-135 tankers, 28 percent of the rescue and recovery capability, 23 percent of tactical air support forces, 10 percent of the bomber force and 8 percent of the strategic airlift forces.

Airlift squadrons, flying C-130 Hercules aircraft, transport personnel, equipment and supplies. Eleven aeromedical evacuation units and 23 aerial port units augment the Air Force. The ANG's airlift capability includes one C-5 Galaxy and two C-141 Starlifter units. Air refueling units, flying KC-135 Stratotankers, provide air-to-air refueling for strategic and tactical missions. The ANG has one special operations unit flying EC-130 aircraft.

Rescue units, flying HH-60 helicopters and HC-130 aircraft, provide a lifesaving capability to military and civilian agencies. The ANG has three rescue and recovery squadrons.

The first heavy bomber unit was activated in 1994. Flying B-1 bomber aircraft, the unit provides strategic strike and deterrence capabilities. Air support units, flying OA-10s, provide forward air control support for close air support missions. The general-purpose fighter force is equipped with F-15, F-16, A-10 and F-4G Wild Weasel aircraft.

Support Units

Support units are essential to the Air Force mission. In the ANG they include: air control units; combat communications squadrons; civil engineering, engineering installation and civil engineering heavy repair squadrons; and communication flights and squadrons. Support units also include weather flights, aircraft control and warning squadrons, a range control squadron and an electronic security unit.

ANG men and women provide 80 percent of the Air Force's combat communication units and 74 percent of the engineering installation capability. Other mission support units contribute 49 percent of the total Air Force civil engineering forces, 68 percent of air control, and 100 percent of the aircraft control and warning forces.

ANG weather flights provide weather support to Air Force as well as Army National Guard and Army Reserve divisions and brigades. The gaining command for the weather flights is Air Combat Command, except for one unit gained by Pacific Air Forces.

Civil engineering squadrons provide engineer and firefighter forces trained and equipped to deploy on short notice. Other civil engineering squadrons provide self-sufficient, deployable civil engineering teams to perform heavy repair and maintenance on air bases and remote sites.

Medical units, located with parent flying organizations, provide day-to-day health care for flying and non-flying personnel during their two-week annual training period or during monthly two-day unit training assemblies.

Training and Education

Training in the ANG is categorized into two general areas for officers and enlisted personnel — technical skills training and professional military education. ANG officers and airmen have opportunities to participate in the same professional military education as their active-duty Air Force counterparts. Professional military education also is available through correspondence courses, on-base seminars and video teleconferencing.

To Air Combat Command

102 Fighter Wing, Otis Air National Guard Base, MA

101 Fighter Squadron	F-15A/B	Air Superiority

103 Fighter Wing, Bradley IAP, CT

118 Fighter Squadron	A/OA-10A	Attack

104 Fighter Wing, Barnes Municipal Airport, MA

131 Fighter Squadron	A/OA-10A	Attack

106 Rescue Wing, Francis Gabreski IAP, NY

102 Rescue Squadron	HC-130H	Combat SAR
	HH-60G	

110 Fighter Wing, Kellogg Airport, MI

172 Fighter Squadron	A/OA-10A	Attack

111 Fighter Wing, Willow Grove Air Reserve Station, PA

103 Fighter Squadron	A/OA-10A	Attack/Forward Air Control

113 Wing, Andrews Air Force Base, MD

121 Fighter Squadron	F-16C/D	Multirole Fighter
201 Airlift Squadron	C-38A, C-22B/C	Communications

114 Fighter Wing, Joe Foss Field, SD

175 Fighter Squadron	F-16C/D	Multirole Fighter

115 Fighter Wing, Truax Field, WI

176 Fighter Squadron	F-16C/D	Multirole Fighter

116 Bomb Wing, Robins Air Force Base, GA

128 Bomb Squadron	B-1B	Bomber

119 Fighter Wing, Hector IAP, Fargo, ND

178 Fighter Squadron	F-16A/B(ADF)	Air Defense

120 Fighter Wing, Great Falls IAP, MT

186 Fighter Squadron	F-16A/B (ADF)	Air Defense

122 Fighter Wing, Fort Wayne IAP, IN

163 Fighter Squadron	F-16C/D	Multirole Fighter

124 Wing, Boise Air Terminal, ID

189 Airlift Squadron	C-130E	Transport/Firefighting
190 Fighter Squadron	A/OA-10A	Attack

125 Fighter Wing, Jacksonville IAP, FL

159 Fighter Squadron	F-15A/B	Air Superiority

127 Wing, Selfridge Air National Guard Base, MI

107 Fighter Squadron	F-16C/D	Multirole Fighter
171 Airlift Squadron	C-130E	Transport

129 Rescue Wing, Moffett Federal Airfield, CA

129 Rescue Squadron	HC-130P **HH-60G**	Combat SAR

To move to McClellan Air Force Base, Ca on unspecified date.

131 Fighter Wing, Lambert-St Louis IAP, MO

110 Fighter Squadron	F-15A/B	Air Superiority

132 Fighter Wing, Des Moines IAP, IA

124 Fighter Squadron	F-16C/D	Multirole Fighter

138 Fighter Wing, Tulsa IAP, OK

125 Fighter Squadron	F-16C/D	Multirole Fighter

140 Wing, Buckley Air National Guard Base, CO

120 Fighter Squadron	F-16C/D	Multirole Fighter
200 Airlift Squadron	CT-43A *	Communications

* To be retired in FY98.

142 Fighter Wing, Portland IAP, OR

123 Fighter Squadron	F-15A/B	Air Superiority

144 Fighter Wing, Fresno Air Terminal, CA

194 Fighter Squadron	F-16C/D	Air Defense

147 Fighter Wing, Ellington Field, TX

111 Fighter Squadron	F-16C/D	Multirole Fighter

148 Fighter Wing, Duluth IAP, MN

179 Fighter Squadron	F-16A/B (ADF)	Air Defense

149 Fighter Wing, Kelly Air Force Base, TX

182 Fighter Squadron	F-16C/D	Multirole Fighter

150 Fighter Wing, Kirtland Air Force Base, NM

150 Defense Systems Evaluation	F-16C/D	Multirole Fighter
188 Fighter Squadron	F-16C/D	Multirole Fighter

158 Fighter Wing, Burlington IAP, VT

134 Fighter Squadron	F-16C/D	Multirole Fighter

159 Fighter Wing, Naval Air Station New Orleans JRB, LA

122 Fighter Squadron	F-15A/B	Air Superiority

169 Fighter Wing, McEntire Air National Guard Base, SC

157 Fighter Squadron	F-16C/D	Multirole Fighter

174 Fighter Wing, Syracuse Hancock IAP, NY

138 Fighter Squadron	F-16C/D	Multirole Fighter

175 Wing, Glenn Martin Airport, Baltimore, MD

104 Fighter Squadron	A/OA-10A	Attack
135 Airlift Squadron	C-130E *	Transport

* To receive C-130J beginning in FY99.

177 Fighter Wing, Atlantic City Airport, NJ

119 Fighter Squadron	F-16C/D	Multirole Fighter

178 Fighter Wing, Springfield-Beckley Municipal Airport, OH

162 Fighter Squadron	F-16C/D	Multirole Fighter

To move on unspecified date to Wright-Patterson Air Force Base, OH.

180 Fighter Wing, Toledo Express Airport, OH

112 Fighter Squadron	F-16C/D	Multirole Fighter

181 Fighter Wing, Hulman Regional Airport, Terre Haute, IN

113 Fighter Squadron	F-16C/D	Multirole Fighter

183 Fighter Wing, Capital Municipal Airport, Springfield, IL

170 Fighter Squadron	F-16C/D	Multirole Fighter

184 BW, McConnell Air Force Base, KS

127 Bomb Squadron	B-1B	Bomber

185 Fighter Wing, Sioux City Municipal Airport, IA

174 Fighter Squadron	F-16C/D	Multirole Fighter

187 Fighter Wing, Dannelly Field, Montgomery, AL

160 Fighter Squadron	F-16C/D	Multirole Fighter

188 Fighter Wing, Fort Smith Municipal Airport, AR

184 Fighter Squadron	F-16A/B	Multirole Fighter

192 Fighter Wing, Byrd Field, Richmond, VA

149 Fighter Squadron	F-16C/D	Multirole Fighter

To Air Education and Training Command

162 Fighter Wing, Tucson IAP, AZ

148 Fighter Squadron	F-16A/B	Fighter Training
152 Fighter Squadron	F-16C/D	Fighter Training
195 Fighter Squadron	F-16A/B	Fighter Training
Air National Guard/AFRC Test Center	F-16C/D	Research, Development, Test & Evaluation

173 Fighter Wing, Klamath Falls IAP (Kingsley Field), OR

114 Fighter Squadron	F-15C/D	Fighter Training

To Air Force Special Operations Command

193 Special Operations Wing, Harrisburg IAP, PA

193 Special Operations Squadron	EC-130E(CL/RR)	Special Operations

To Air Mobility Command

101 Air Refueling Wing, Bangor IAP, ME

132 Air Refueling Squadron	KC-135E	Tanker

105 Airlift Wing, Stewart IAP, NY

137 Airlift Squadron	C-5A	Transport

107 Air Refueling Wing, Niagara Falls IAP/Air Reserve Station, NY

136 Air Refueling Squadron	KC-135R	Tanker

108 Air Refueling Wing, McGuire Air Force Base, NJ

141 Air Refueling Squadron	KC-135E	Tanker
150 Air Refueling Squadron	KC-135E	Tanker

109 Airlift Wing, Schenectady Airport, NY

139 Airlift Squadron	C/LC-130H	Transport

117 Air Refueling Wing, Birmingham Airport, AL

106 Air Refueling Squadron	KC-135R	Tanker

118 Airlift Wing, Nashville Metropolitan Airport, TN

105 Airlift Squadron	C-130H	Transport

121 Air Refueling Wing, Rickenbacker IAP, OH

145 Air Refueling Squadron	KC-135R	Tanker
166 Air Refueling Squadron	KC-135R	Tanker

123 Airlift Wing, Standiford Field, Louisville, KY

165 Airlift Squadron	C-130H	Transport

126 Air Refueling Wing, Chicago-O'Hare IAP/Air Reserve Station, IL

108 Air Refueling Squadron	KC-135E	Tanker

128 Air Refueling Wing, General Mitchell IAP/Air Reserve Station, WI

126 Air Refueling Squadron	KC-135R	Tanker

130 Airlift Wing, Yeager Airport, WV

130 Airlift Squadron	C-130H	Transport

133 Airlift Wing, Minneapolis-St Paul IAP/Air Reserve Station, MN

109 Airlift Squadron	C-130H	Transport

134 Air Refueling Wing, McGhee Tyson Airport, TN

151 Air Refueling Squadron	KC-135E	Tanker

136 Airlift Wing, Naval Air Station Dallas, TX

181 Airlift Squadron	C-130H	Transport

137 Airlift Wing, Will Rogers World Airport, OK

185 Airlift Squadron	C-130H	Transport

139 Airlift Wing, Rosecrans Memorial Airport, MO

180 Airlift Squadron	C-130H	Transport

141 Air Refueling Wing, Fairchild Air Force Base, WA

116 Air Refueling Squadron	KC-135E	Tanker

143 Airlift Wing, Quonset State Airport, RI

143 Airlift Squadron	C-130E	Transport

145 Airlift Wing, Charlotte/Douglas IAP, NC

156 Airlift Squadron	C-130H	Transport

146 Airlift Wing, Channel Islands Air National Guard Base, Naval Air Station Point Mugu, CA

115 Airlift Squadron	C-130E	Transport

151 Air Refueling Wing, Salt Lake City IAP, UT

191 Air Refueling Squadron	KC-135E	Tanker

152 Airlift Wing, Reno-Tahoe IAP, NV

192 Airlift Squadron	C-130E	Transport

153 Airlift Wing, Cheyenne Municipal Airport, WY

187 Airlift Squadron	C-130H	Transport

155 Air Refueling Wing, Lincoln Municipal Airport, NB

173 Air Refueling Squadron	KC-135R	Tanker

156 Airlift Wing, Luis Muniz Marin IAP, PR

198 Airlift Squadron	C-130E	Transport

157 Air Refueling Wing, Pease Air National Guard Base, NH

133 Air Refueling Squadron	KC-135R	Tanker

161 Air Refueling Wing, Sky Harbor IAP, Phoenix, AZ

197 Air Refueling Squadron	KC-135E	Tanker

163 Air Refueling Wing, March Air Reserve Base, CA

196 Air Refueling Squadron	KC-135R	Tanker

164 Airlift Wing, Memphis IAP, TN

155 Airlift Squadron	C-141B *	Transport

* To be replaced by upgraded C-141C version by 1999.

165 Airlift Wing, Savannah IAP, GA

158 Airlift Squadron	C-130H	Transport

166 Airlift Wing, New Castle County Airport, Wilmington, DE

142 Airlift Squadron	C-130H	Transport

167 Airlift Wing, Eastern West Virginia Regional Airport, Martinsburg, WV

167 Airlift Squadron	C-130H	Transport

171 Air Refueling Wing, Pittsburgh IAP/Air Reserve Station, PA

146 Air Refueling Squadron	KC-135E	Tanker
147 Air Refueling Squadron	KC-135E	Tanker

172 Airlift Wing, Allen C. Thompson Field, Jackson, MS

183 Airlift Squadron	C-141B *	Transport

* To be replaced by upgraded C-141C version by 1999.

179 Airlift Wing, Mansfield Lahm Airport, OH

164 Airlift Squadron	C-130H	Transport

182 Airlift Wing, Greater Peoria Airport, IL

169 Airlift Squadron	C-130E	Transport

186 Air Refueling Wing, Key Field, Meridian, MS

153 Air Refueling Squadron	KC-135R	Tanker

189 Airlift Wing, Little Rock Air Force Base, AR

154 Training Squadron	C-130E	Transport Training

190 Air Refueling Wing, Forbes Field, Topeka, KS

117 Air Refueling Squadron	KC-135D/E	Tanker

To Pacific Air Forces

154 Wing, Hickam Air Force Base, HI

199 Fighter Squadron	F-15A/B	Air Superiority
203 Air Refueling Squadron	KC-135R	Tanker
204 Airlift Squadron	C-130H	Transport

168 Air Refueling Wing, Eielson Air Force Base, AK

168 Air Refueling Squadron	KC-135R	Tanker

176 Wing, Kulis Air National Guard Base, AK

144 Airlift Squadron	C-130H	Transport
210 Rescue Squadron	HC-130H HH-60G	Combat SAR

Some Air National Guard units also possess one Fairchild C-26B Metro Operational Support Aircraft although it appears these are progressively being disposed of. These aircraft are employed on routine communications tasks and are assigned to the parent Wing organization. Units believed to still utilize the C-26B are the 109 Airlift Wing, 115 Fighter Wing, 125 Fighter Wing, 131 Fighter Wing, 140 Wing, 141 Air Refueling Wing, 144 Fighter Wing, 147 Fighter Wing, 150 Fighter Wing, 162 Fighter Wing, 186 Air Refueling Wing and 187 Fighter Wing.

AIR FORCE FLIGHT STANDARDS AGENCY

HQ Andrews Air Force Base, MD

Support Flight (Andrews)	C-21A, NC-21A	Communications

United States Air Force Academy

HQ Colorado Springs, CO

The United States Air Force Academy offers a four-year program of instruction and experience designed to provide cadets the knowledge and character essential for leadership, and the motivation to serve as Air Force career officers. Each cadet graduates with a bachelor of science degree and a commission as a second lieutenant in the Air Force.

Course of Study

Cadets are exposed to a balanced curriculum that provides a general and professional foundation essential to a career Air Force officer. Special needs of future Air Force officers are met by professionally oriented courses, including human physiology, computer science, economics, military history, astronautics, law and political science.

The core curriculum includes courses in science, engineering, social sciences and humanities. Cadets take additional elective courses to complete requirements for one of 25 major areas of study. About 60 percent of the cadets complete majors in science and engineering; the other 40 percent graduate in the social sciences and humanities. Some of the most popular majors include management, astronautical engineering, international affairs and political science, history, behavioral science, civil engineering, aeronautical engineering, electrical engineering and engineering mechanics.

Nominations

Nominations to the academy may be obtained through a congressional sponsor or by meeting eligibility criteria in other categories of competition established by law. For information on admission procedures, write to HQ USAFA/RRS; 2304 Cadet Drive, Suite 200; USAF Academy, CO 80840-5025.

History

In 1948 a board of leading civilian and military educators was appointed to plan the curriculum for an academy that would meet the needs of the newly established Air Force. The board determined that Air Force requirements could not be met by expanding the other service academies and recommended an Air Force academy be established without delay.

In 1949, then Secretary of the Air Force W. Stuart Symington appointed a commission to assist in selecting a site and on April 1, 1954, President Dwight D. Eisenhower authorized creation of the United States Air Force Academy. After considering 580 sites in 45 states, the commission narrowed the choice to three locations. The summer of 1954, Secretary of the Air Force Harold Talbott selected a site near Colorado Springs, Colo. Colorado contributed $1 million toward purchase of the property.

In July 1955, the first academy class entered interim facilities at Lowry Air Force Base, Denver, while construction began. It was sufficiently completed for occupancy by the cadet wing in late August 1958. Initial construction cost was $142 million.

Women entered the academy on June 28, 1976, as members of the class of 1980.

Athletic Program

The academy's athletic program is designed to improve physical fitness, teach athletic skills and develop leadership qualities. To achieve its goals, the academy offers some of the most extensive physical education, intramural sports and intercollegiate athletic programs in the nation. Cadets take at least three different physical education courses each year.

Faculty Composition

The majority of the academy's nearly 600 faculty members are Air Force officers. They are selected primarily from career-officer volunteers who have established outstanding records of performance and dedication. Each has at least a master's degree and more than 35 percent have doctorates.

In addition to imparting knowledge, each faculty member must assist with the development of character and qualities of leadership essential to future Air Force career officers and the motivation of service to country. To provide greater contributions by a diverse faculty, the academy has several distinguished civilian professors and associate professors who serve one or more years. Officers from other services are members of the faculty as well, and a small number of officers from allied countries teach in the foreign language, history and political science departments. Distinguished civilian and military lecturers also share their expertise with the cadets during the academic year.

Military Education and Training

An aerospace-oriented military education, training and leadership program begins with basic cadet training and continues throughout the four years. Seniors are responsible for the leadership of the cadet wing, while juniors and sophomores perform lower-level leadership and instructional tasks. Cadets are projected into as many active leadership roles as possible to prepare them to be effective Air Force officers.

Fundamental concepts of military organization — drill, ethics, honor, Air Force heritage and physical training — are emphasized the first summer during basic cadet training. Freshmen then study the military role in U.S. society as well as the mission and organization of the Air Force. Sophomores receive instruction in communicative skills, and juniors study the combat and operational aspects of the Air Force. Military studies for the senior class focus on military thought.

The academy offers courses in flying, navigation, soaring and parachuting, building from basic skills to instructor duties. Cadets may fly light aircraft with the cadet aviation club. Those not qualified for flight training must enroll in a basic aviation course. Astronomy and advanced navigation courses also are available. Students bound for pilot training enroll in the pilot indoctrination course and fly the T-3 Firefly.

Summer training for cadets is divided into three, three-week training periods. There are a variety of programs available, and each cadet is required to complete two training periods each summer with leave during the other period. All new cadets take six weeks of basic cadet training in the first summer.

Combat survival training is a required three-week program during cadets' second summer. For the other second-summer training period, cadets can with young airmen in an operational unit at an Air Force installation, airborne training, soaring or basic free-fall parachute training.

During their last two summers, all cadets are offered leadership training as supervisors or instructors in summer programs, such as basic cadet training, survival training and soaring.

Extracurricular activities also are an integral part of the education program. The cadet ski club, drum and bugle corps, cadet chorale and forensics are a few of the programs available.

US AIR FORCE ACADEMY, Colorado Springs, CO

50 Airmanship Training Squadron	-	Navigation Training *
94 Airmanship Training Squadron	T-3A	Training
	UV-18B	Parachuting Platform
	various gliders	Sport Flying

* Employs Colorado Air National Guard T-43A as training platform.

USER MISSION EDITOR

AGM65B

AIM9M

20NT

GUN 1000

4 X MRM

3 X SRM

USER MISSION EDITOR (UME) MANUAL

With *Jane's USAF* User Mission Editor (referred to as the UME in this manual), you can create complex missions, save them, send them to other *Jane's USAF* players. You can also load them from the *Single Mission* screen (under the *My Mission* tab) in order to fly them.

If you've dreamed up a great scenario, and want to design it quickly so you can get in and try it out, wizards can speed up the mission-making process. However, if you want to get your hands dirty, event scripting lets you get as customized and complex as you'd like.

You can't modify any existing game missions through the UME.

How to Use This Manual

The following sections provide an overview of the User Mission Editor features:

Getting Started   Explains different ways you can use the UME program.

UME Screen Elements (p. 250)   Describes the menu options, tabs, and buttons in the *UME* screen.

Using the Mission Wizard (p. 277)   Describes the mission creation wizard and takes you through the creation of a tutorial mission.

Advanced UME Features (p. 284)   Describes more complex features of the UME.

Getting Started

The *Jane's USAF* User Mission Editor (UME), is not a part of the *Jane's USAF* game, but a separate executable. To open the UME, go to the *Windows 95/98* desktop, and click **Start > Programs > Jane's Combat Simulations > USAF > User Mission Editor**.

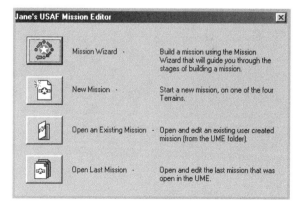

When you first open the User Mission Editor, a pop-up window appears (shown on the previous page). From this window, you can choose how you want to begin or resume creating a mission. Click one of the four buttons:

Mission Wizard	Create a new mission with the Mission Wizard. See **Using the Mission Wizard**, p. 277, for an intro and walkthrough of a sample mission.
New Mission	Create a new mission from scratch. Type in a mission name (up to 64 characters) and select a terrain (GERMANY / IRAQ / LAS VEGAS / VIETNAM) and you're off and running.
Open an Existing Mission	Open a mission to edit it. The mission map, object icons and all information about the mission objects load into the *User Mission Editor* screen. You can open missions you've already created and saved with the UME.
Open Last Mission	Open the last mission you opened in the User Mission Editor.
Close	Close the mission you currently have open.

Saving Missions

To save a mission, left-click the **Save** icon (the one that looks like a floppy disk), or left-click **File > Save** to save the file. Please note that this overwrites the current file with the same name.

- ✪ You can change any of the mission information at any time. Just open the file, select the appropriate tab and edit the information displayed.

- ✪ If you want to fly your mission and test it, left-click the **Run** icon on the toolbar. The game automatically opens and launches your mission.

- ✪ All missions you create and save are then available from the *Single Mission* screen from within the game (under the *My Missions* tab).

UME SCREEN ELEMENTS

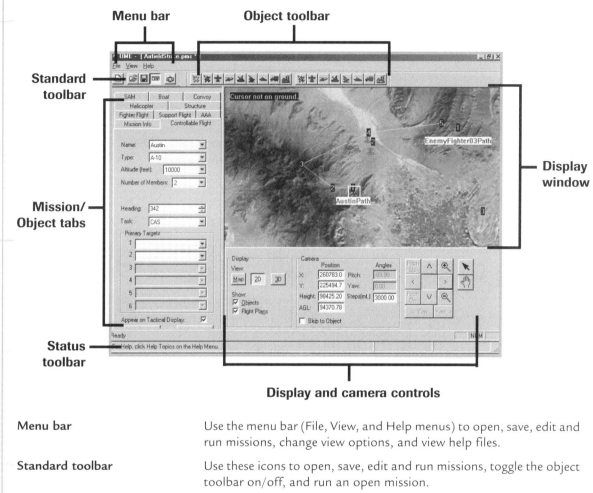

Menu bar

Object toolbar

Standard toolbar

Mission/ Object tabs

Status toolbar

Display window

Display and camera controls

Menu bar	Use the menu bar (File, View, and Help menus) to open, save, edit and run missions, change view options, and view help files.
Standard toolbar	Use these icons to open, save, edit and run missions, toggle the object toolbar on/off, and run an open mission.
Status toolbar	When you move your cursor over a button, tool, or tab, a definition of the item appears in the status bar at the bottom of the screen. You can hide this bar if you want to – see **View Menu Options**, p. 252.
Object toolbar	Use the Object toolbar to add new objects to the map.
Mission/Object tabs	Use the tabs to view and input information about the mission and different mission elements, such as flights, AAA, SAMs, etc.
Display window	The display window shows mission objects on a terrain map. You can create icons and place them on the map using the Object toolbar. You can change the map view using the Display and camera control buttons.
Display and camera controls	These buttons at the bottom of the screen control the map and views, and let you select and move objects on the map.

Menu Bar

With the menu bar (and toolbar), you can open, edit, save and run files, control view options and view help files.

File menu   **View menu**   **Help menu**

File Menu Options

New	Create a new mission. Choose a map (or use the Mission Wizard) from the submenu. The mission map determines where your mission takes place and what terrain you fly over. Type in a mission name.
LAS VEGAS	Set your mission around Nellis AFB.
GERMANY	Set your mission over southern Germany.
IRAQ	Set your mission in Iraq.
VIETNAM	Set your mission in Vietnam.
Wizard	Begin the Mission Wizard.
Open	Open an existing mission. Double-click on a mission name in the pop-up window that appears and click **OK**.
Save	Save the mission you are currently working on. (You cannot change the filename or folder.)
Run	Start *Jane's USAF* and load the current mission.
	If you have made any unsaved changes to the mission, a window opens, prompting you to save it. Click **OK** to save your changes and continue, or **Cancel** to return to the User Mission Editor without saving the changes.
	You must have at least one controllable flight defined in a mission in order to run it.
Exit	Quit the User Mission Editor and return to the *Windows 95/98* desktop.

View Menu Options

The options below determine what toolbars are displayed on screen. Highlight an option to select or deselect it. Selected options have a check mark beside them and are displayed onscreen. Deselected options have no check mark and are hidden.

Standard Toolbar	Display/hide the Standard toolbar. (This toolbar shows icons for file options at the top of the screen.).
Status Bar	Display/hide the Status bar. (The Status bar is the bar at the bottom of the screen. It displays information about tabs, buttons, etc., as you move your cursor over them.)
Objects Bar	Display/hide the Object toolbar. (This toolbar shows objects that you can place on the map.)

Help Menu Options

User's Mission Editor Help	Launches the electronic version of this manual in your default browser.
About User's Mission Editor	Lists copyright info and version number for the User Mission Editor.

Toolbars

The UME has three toolbars – Standard (displays button icons), Status (displays rollover information for different buttons) and Object (displays objects and lets you place them on the map).

Standard toolbar

Object toolbar

Ready   NUM

Status toolbar

Standard Toolbar

The Standard toolbar has button icons you click to open, edit, save and run files. It also has a button that toggles the **Object toolbar** on/off.

Each button works as follows:

Create a new mission. Choose the map where the mission takes place (Germany / Iraq / Las Vegas / Vietnam) from the pop-up window that appears and click **OK**.

Open a pre-existing mission. The mission map, object icons and information about mission objects loads into the *User Mission Editor* screen.

You can open missions you've already created and saved with the UME, but you can't open missions that shipped with the game.

Save the mission you are currently working on. All files are saved in the Resource/UME folder.

Toggle the **Object toolbar** on/off.

Start *Jane's USAF* and load the current mission.

If you have made any unsaved changes to the mission, a window opens, prompting you to save it. Click **OK** to save your changes and continue, or **Cancel** to return to the User Mission Editor without saving the changes.

You must have at least one **controllable flight** defined in a mission in order to run it.

Status Toolbar

The Status toolbar is the long gray strip along the bottom of the UME screen. When this is active and you move the mouse cursor over an icon, this toolbar describes its function. (This does not work for text fields or drop-down menus, however.)

Object Toolbar

When active, the Object toolbar displays button icons for different objects in the game – fighter flights, heavy flights, AAA and SAM sites, boats, convoys, helicopters and structures. Blue icons on this toolbar represent friendly objects, while red icons represent enemy objects.

Using the Objects Toolbar, p. 257, describes the function of each button on this toolbar.

Using Display and Camera Controls

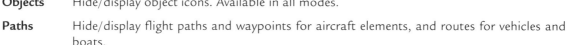

With the display and camera controls, you choose how to view the mission area and whether to display objects and icons. You can also scroll and zoom the view, move the camera (in 3-D view), and select and drag object icons and waypoints.

Display Mode Options

The following buttons control how the mission area is displayed in the Display Window. (Only one of these options can be active at a time.) Click a button to choose an option.

Map   Display a map of the mission area. This shows the map that appears in the Tactical Display screen in the game.

2D   Display a 2-D view of the mission area. This view is similar to an overhead photograph.

3D   Display a 3-D view of mission area terrain. This lets you view the area as if you were standing on the terrain map.

The following checkboxes toggle display features on and off.

Objects   Hide/display object icons. Available in all modes.

Paths   Hide/display flight paths and waypoints for aircraft elements, and routes for vehicles and boats.

Camera Data Options

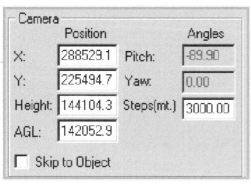

The camera data options let you change the current position, angle and height of the camera. This affects the viewing area of the map above the display and camera controls. By adjusting the camera position, angle and zoom, you effectively change the map display.

As you move the camera with the camera control buttons listed below, the numbers displayed in this window change. You can also edit the data in any of these fields by placing the cursor in the fields and typing.

Position	Displays the camera's **X** and **Y** coordinates, **Height** and **AGL (above ground level).**
	X and Y control the camera's horizontal coordinates on the map, measured in meters. X moves the camera East-West, while Y moves it North-South.
	Moving the camera position East and North increases coordinates, while moving it West and South decreases coordinates.
	Height and **AGL** control the zoom level of the map. **Height** is the object's height above sea level, and **AGL** is the object's height above ground level. Both are given in feet.
Angles	Displays the camera's current **Pitch** (vertical) and **Yaw** (horizontal) angles.
	The **Steps** field defines how many meters the camera moves each time you click the camera control buttons (see below).
Skip to Object	When this box is checked, the camera automatically centers the view on an object when you place it on the map.

Camera Controls

These buttons control the camera's movement over the mission area. Current data on the camera's position and view angle is visible in the Camera Data Options area.

Zoom Buttons

Click the following buttons to zoom the display. Zooming is available for all display modes (2D, 3D and Map). When you're in 2D mode, the camera is pointed straight down at the ground and changes altitude when zoomed. In 3D mode, the camera zooms in/out along its line of sight.

 Zoom the camera view out.

The camera's current **Height** and **AGL** is displayed in the **Position** field of the **Camera Data Options** area.

 Zoom the camera view in.

The camera's current **Height AGL** is displayed in the **Position** field of the **Camera Data Options** area.

Scroll Buttons

Click the buttons marked with arrows to move the display camera. You can also use Numpad 2, 4, 6, and 8. The scroll buttons act differently, depending on whether you're in Map/2D or 3D camera mode. These controls are available in all **display mode options** (3D, 2D and Map).

(2D/Map) Pan the camera left/right (West-East). The camera remains at a fixed altitude.

(3D) Same, except that the camera also moves along the current pitch angle. (It can change altitude as well as X coordinates.)

The camera's current X coordinate appears in the **Position** field of the **Camera Data Options** area.

(2D/Map) Pan the camera up/down (North-South) at a fixed altitude.

(3D) Same, except that the camera also moves along the current pitch angle. (It can change altitude as well as Y coordinates.)

The camera's current **Y** coordinate appears in the **Position** field of the **Camera Data Options** area.

Pitch/Yaw Buttons

These controls are only available in **3D display mode**. Click the following buttons to swivel the display camera. Its X and Y coordinates remain fixed, while the buttons control its pitch and yaw angles.

Yaw the camera view left / right.

The camera's current yaw angle appears in the **Angles** field of the **Camera Data Options** area.

Pitch the camera view up / down.

The camera's current pitch angle appears in the **Angles** field of the **Camera Data Options** area.

Cursor Controls

(2D/Map only) Change the cursor to a hand. Use the hand cursor to click and drag the map. This moves the current view around.

Change cursor back to an arrow. Use the arrow cursor to select objects (by clicking on them) and move them (by clicking on them and dragging them.)

Click-and-hold over a location on the map, then drag the cursor to a second location. A line is drawn between the two points, and the distance between the two points appears in both nautical miles and meters.

Using the Objects Toolbar

Click on the icons on the Object toolbar to add objects and groups of objects to the mission. (You can toggle the Object toolbar on/off by clicking the Object toolbar icon on the Standard toolbar.) Whenever you add an object, a pop-up window appears in which you can define properties for that object.

Refer to the sections below to view information about a particular type of object.

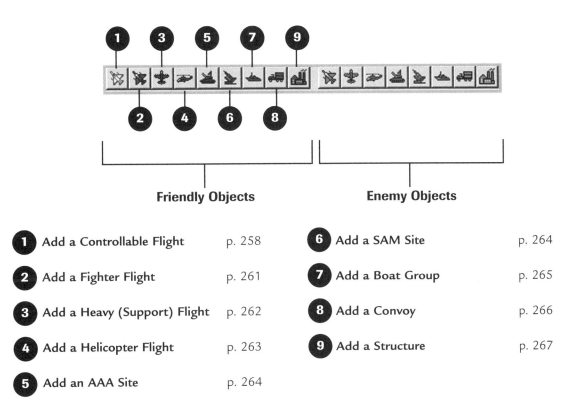

Friendly Objects   **Enemy Objects**

1 Add a Controllable Flight   p. 258

2 Add a Fighter Flight   p. 261

3 Add a Heavy (Support) Flight   p. 262

4 Add a Helicopter Flight   p. 263

5 Add an AAA Site   p. 264

6 Add a SAM Site   p. 264

7 Add a Boat Group   p. 265

8 Add a Convoy   p. 266

9 Add a Structure   p. 267

- Onscreen, blue icons represent friendly objects, while red ones represent enemy objects.

- To add an object, click on its icon. (The cursor changes to match the object you select.) Then, click anywhere on the map to place that object.

- Each time you add an object, a pop-up window appears where you can set basic information about that object. Options vary somewhat according to which icon you choose.

The rest of this section discusses the available options for each individual icon on the Object toolbar.

Add a Friendly Controllable Flight

The mission must contain at least one player-controllable flight before you can run it in *Jane's USAF*. You can add up to four friendly, player-controllable flights to a mission. If no player is available to control a player-controlled flight, the computer controls it. However, the player can jump in and take over in mid-flight. (See **Interface: Switching Aircraft/Flights**, p. 1.21, in the printed manual.)

 Add a friendly, player-controlled flight to the mission.

Controllable Flight Pop-Up Window Options

For each parameter, choose an option from the pull-down menu.

Name	Select the flight's name – AUSTIN / BUICK / CORVETTE / DODGE (Flights 1-4, respectively).
Type	Select an aircraft type – A-10 / F-105 / F-117 / F-15C / F-15E / F-16C / F-22 / F-4E.
Number of Members	Select the number of aircraft in the flight – 1 / 2 / 3 / 4.

Add Waypoints

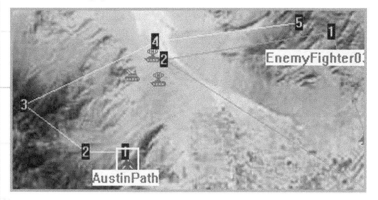

Once you add a controllable flight to the map, a numbered waypoint appears next to it. The position of the object icon marks its starting point. You can adjust the initial position using the mouse, as well as move, add and delete waypoints. The paths connecting waypoints marks the flight route, the route that the flight travels in the mission. You must designate a flight path for every flight you place on the map.

- ○ **Left-click-and-drag** a waypoint to move it around.

- ○ **Left-click, then right-click** on a waypoint to add a waypoint before it, add a waypoint after it, or delete the waypoint. (Choose any of these options from the pop-up menu that appears.)

- ○ **Left-click, then right-click** on a waypoint and choose **Properties** to assign waypoint parameters.

Change Waypoint Parameters

You use this window to set specific parameters for each waypoint. Parameters in grayed-out boxes are automatically adjusted by the UME.

Name	Type in a name for the waypoint (up to 64 characters long).
Flight Stage	Click the drop-down menu to select an objective for this leg of the flight.

Waypoint Parameters dialog box fields shown:

- Name: Ingress
- Flight Stage: Attack
- Speed (MPH): 369
- ETA (hh:mm:ss): 0:01:39
- Altitude (feet): 5000
- Heading: 88

OK / Cancel

ALERT	Orbit the previous waypoint and attack enemies.
ATTACK	Attack a target object. For controllable flights, this causes this waypoint to appear as a "T" on the HUD and as a triangle on the Tactical Display.
GENERAL	No specific action is assigned.
IP	Make an approach toward the attack waypoint.
LANDING	For aircraft; make an approach for a landing at the nearest base.
REFUELING	For aircraft; rendezvous with a refueling tanker.
TAKEOFF	For aircraft; take off from home base. (If the aircraft starts out on the ground, this flight stage is automatically attached to the first waypoint.)

Speed (MPH)	Recommended speed in miles per hour. Click the arrows to increase/decrease speed in increments of 10 mph. Or, type a number into the text field.
	During flight, the speed you select here appears as a caret on the airspeed ladder.
	For aircraft, changing this value affects the ETA to the next waypoint. You can set individual speeds for each leg of the flight.
	For ground vehicles, speed remains constant throughout the mission. If you change the speed for one leg, it affects speed and ETA for all other waypoints.
ETA (hh:mm:ss)	Estimated time-to-arrival, in minutes and seconds, to the currently selected waypoint. This value is automatically calculated according to the distance to the waypoint and the recommended speed you set along that leg of the journey.
	(1st waypoint only) When you place a plane on an airfield, the ETA to the first waypoint can serve as the taxi and takeoff time. (This does not apply to a player-controlled aircraft — it only works with AI-controlled aircraft.)
	After this length of time has passed, the aircraft will taxi to the runway and take off. Use this function to control takeoff timing — such as when you're scrambling enemy aircraft at a certain time.

Altitude (feet)	Recommended altitude in feet. Click the pulldown menu to select a different altitude. Or, type a number into the text field.
	During flight, the altitude you select here appears as a caret on the altitude ladder.
Heading	This field is initially set by the game when you place an icon on the map. You can alter it in the appropriate object tab, however.
	Heading indicates which direction the object is facing and is represented by a number from 0-360.
	For all objects, heading describes the object's orientation. 0 means the front of the object is facing due north, 180 means it's facing due south.

Airbases

If you place a flight within 5 miles of an airbase, it lines up on that airfield's runway. Additional flights you place near an airbase start out in one of the airfield's 6 hangars. Use the following chart to find the X-Y coordinates for all airbases in the game. (You can't add or delete airbases — they're permanent objects.)

Terrain	Airbase Name	X	Y	Notes
Las Vegas	Nellis	296780	217510	—
	Nellis Red	493650	236960	Red base (US missions only)
Iraq	Balad	370690	344910	—
	Baghdad Muthenna	381224	272523	—
	Saddam Intl.	359040	268520	—
	Tikrit	318880	419210	—
Vietnam	Gia-Lam	309090	720490	—
	Hoa-Lac	265770	718300	—
	Kep	345560	760270	—
	Phuc-Yen	301000	740780	—
Germany	Erding	317510	518410	—
	Landsberg	274050	487310	—
	Salzburg	402810	457790	Enemy base

Add a Fighter Flight

In this case, "fighters" include all aircraft with a primary mission of killing other objects. None of the fighter flights are controllable – all are controlled by computer AI pilots.

 Add a friendly, computer-controlled fighter (or attack aircraft) flight to the mission.

 Add an enemy, computer-controlled fighter (or attack aircraft) flight to the mission.

○　You add waypoints for fighter flights just as you do for controllable flights. See **Add Waypoints**, p. 258, for details.

Fighter Flight Pop-Up Window Options

Formation Name　Select a flight name from the drop-down menu – ENEMY FIGHTER 1-8 / FRIENDLY FIGHTER 1-8 / FORD / OLDS / PRIMARY TARGET 1-4 / STINGRAY / T-BIRD. (Actual options and order differ between friendly and enemy fighter flights.)

Formation Type　Select an aircraft type from the drop-down menu – A-10A / A-1E / F-1 / F-105 / F-111 / F-117 / F-15C / F-15E / F-16C / F-22 / F-4E / F-4G / MiG-21 (IRAQ) / MiG-21 (VIETNAM) / MiG-23 / MiG-25 / MiG-29 (RUSSIA) / SU-22 / SU-24 / SU-35.

Number of Members　Select the number of aircraft to include in the flight – 1 / 2 / 3 / 4.

Add a Heavy (Support) Flight

Heavy aircraft include all aircraft with a primary mission of supporting other mission elements. You can add up to 10 each of friendly or enemy heavy flights in a mission.

 Add a friendly, computer-controlled heavy flight to the mission.

 Add an enemy, computer-controlled heavy flight to the mission.

✪ You add waypoints for heavy flights just as you do for controllable flights. See **Add Waypoints**, p. 258, for details.

Heavy Flight Pop-Up Window Options

Name
Select a flight name from the drop-down menu – ENEMY HEAVY 1-10 (for enemy flights) / FRIENDLY HEAVY 1-10 (for friendly flights).

Type
Select an aircraft type from the drop-down menu – B-2 / B-52 / BOEING 707 / C-130 / C-17 / E-3 SENTRY / IL-76 / KC-135 / TU-22.

Number of Members
Select the number of aircraft to include in the flight – 1 / 2 / 3 / 4.

Add a Helicopter Flight

You can add up to 10 friendly and 10 enemy helicopter flights to a mission. Each flight can contain up to six helicopters.

 Add a friendly helicopter flight to the mission.

 Add an enemy helicopter flight to the mission.

○ You can add waypoints (see p. 258) for helicopters. Just right-click on the icon, and choose **Create New Path** to add the first waypoint, then move, delete and add waypoints as usual.

Helicopter Flight Pop-Up Window Options

Name

Select a flight name from the drop-down menu – Enemy Helicopter 1-10 / Friendly Helicopter 1-10.

Type

Select an aircraft type from the drop-down menu – AH-1 / AH-64 / COMANCHE / MI-24 (Iraq) / MI-24 (Russia) / MI-8 / UH-1 / UH-60.

Number of Members

Select the number of helicopters to include in the flight – 1 / 2 / 3 / 4 / 5 / 6.

○ You add waypoints for other flights just as you do for controllable flights. See **Add Waypoints** (p. 258) for details.

Add an AAA Site

You can add up to 10 each of friendly or enemy AAA sites in a mission. (Each site can contain up to six AAA units.)

 Add a friendly AAA site to the mission.

 Add an enemy AAA site to the mission.

AAA Pop-Up Window Options

Name
Select a group name from the drop-down menu – ENEMY AAA 1-10 / FRIENDLY AAA 1 -10.

Type
Select a gun type from the drop-down menu – 85MM / ZSU-23x4 / ZSU-57x2.

Number of Members
Select the number of guns to include in the group – 1 / 2 / 3 / 4 / 5 / 6.

Add a SAM Site

You can add up to 10 friendly and 10 enemy SAM sites in a mission. The first two elements in each site are always a radar and/or command center. In addition, each site contains up to four SAM launchers.

 Add a friendly SAM site to the mission.

 Add an enemy SAM to the mission.

SAM Pop-Up Window Options

Name
Select a group name from the drop-down menu – ENEMY SAM 1-10 / FRIENDLY SAM 1-10.

Type
Select a gun type from the drop-down menu – HAWK / PATRIOT / ROLAND / SA-10 / SA-13 / SA-2 (IRAQ) / SA-2 (VIETNAM) / SA-3 (IRAQ) / SA-3 (VIETNAM) / SA-5 / SA-6.

Number of Members
Select the number of guns to include in the group – 3 / 4 / 5 / 6.

Add a Boat Group

You can add up to 10 friendly and 10 enemy boat formations to a mission. Each formation can contain up to six boats.

 Add a friendly boat formation to the mission.

 Add an enemy boat formation to the mission.

You can add and manipulate waypoints for mobile ground objects. Left-click then right-click on the icon, and choose **Create New Path** to add the first waypoint. You can then move, delete and add waypoints as described in **Add Waypoints**, p. 258.

Boat Pop-Up Window Options

Name	Select a group name from the drop-down menu – ENEMY BOAT 1-10 / FRIENDLY BOAT 1-10.
Type	Select a gun type from the drop-down menu – MISSILE BOAT / MERCHANT VESSEL / TERRORIST BOAT.
Number of Members	Select the number of guns to include in the group – 1 / 2 / 3 / 4 / 5 / 6.

Add a Convoy

You can add up to 10 friendly and 10 enemy convoys to a mission. Each convoy can contain up to six ground vehicles.

 Add a friendly convoy to the mission.

 Add an enemy convoy to the mission.

○ Left-click then right-click on the icon, and choose **Create New Path** to add the first waypoint. You can then move, delete and add waypoints as described in **Add Waypoints**, p. 258.

Convoy Pop-Up Window Options

Name

Select a convoy name from the drop-down menu – ENEMY CONVOY 1–10 / FRIENDLY CONVOY 1–10.

Type

Select a convoy type from the drop-down menu – BMP-1 (IRAQ) / BMP-1 (RUSSIA) / BTR-60 / FUEL TRUCK / HUMMER / JEEP / M-1 ABRAMS / M-109 / M-113 / M-1974 / M-2 BRADLEY / M-60 (IRAQ) / M-60(RUSSIA) / MIXED M-1 / MIXED M-2 / MIXED / MIXED T-72 / PT-76 / ROLAND / SA-13 / SA-8 / SCUD / T-55 / T-62 / T-72 (RUSSIA) / ZIL-157 / ZSU-23X4 / ZSU-57X2.

Number of Members

Select a number of convoy vehicles from the drop-down menu – 1 / 2 / 3 / 4 / 5 / 6.

Add a Structure

Structures cannot have waypoints. Airbases are pre-existing structures. For X-Y coordinates of all airbases, see p. 260.

Structure		
Name:	EnemyStruct_1	▼
Type:	AntennaShape1	▼
Heading:	8	
Appear on Tactical Display:	☑	

 Add a friendly structure to the mission.

 Add an enemy structure to the mission.

Structure Pop-Up Window Options

Structure Name   Displays the name for the structure. (You can't change this.)

Structure Type   See list below.

Structure	Description
Aircraft Shelter (1-2)	Aircraft bomb shelter
Antenna (1-4)	Radar and comm antennae
Big Bridge (1-2)	Bridges
Bridge (1-3)	Bridges
Bunker Gulf	Desert Storm bunker
Bunker Weapon	Weapons bunker
Castle	Castle
City (01-19)	City blocks
ComCenter	Communications center
ComCenter (1-4)	Communications center buildings
Cottage House	Cottage
Electric Pole	Single utility pole, electric wires
Factory (1-4)	Factory buildings
Factory Generator	Power generator for factory
Factory Main	Main factory building
Factory Office	Office building
Family Quarters (1-2)	Houses
Farm House	Rural farm house
Fuel Dump	Fuel Tank
Fuel Reserve (1-2)	Fuel Tank
Fuel Tank (1-2)	Fuel Tank
Hangar	Aircraft Hangar
Hut Straw	Straw hut
Hut VC	Hut
Nuke Chimney (1-2)	Nuclear power plant, towers
Nuke Core	Nuclear power plant, reactor

Structure	Description
Nuke Plant (1-8)	Nuclear power plant, buildings
Office (1-2)	Office buildings
Oil pump	Oil pump
Oil well	Oil well
P-14 / P-35 / P-40	Radar
Palace	Palace
Palace Dom	Palace building
Palace Main	Main palace building
Palace Pasade	Palace building
Palace Pool	Palace building
Power Plant (1-5)	Power plant buildings, various
Power Plant Chimney	Power plant smokestack
Power Plant Col (1-2)	Power plant column
Power Plan MSOA	Power plant building
Power Plan Shvl	Power plant building
Priscot	Mobile home
Radome (1-2)	Radar domess
Shack	Light aircraft cover
Sky Scraper (1-3)	Skyscraper
Soldier Quarters (1-2)	Soldier housing
Squad (A1-A2, B1-B2)	Soldier housing
Stardust	City block
Tent	Tent
Watchtower	Watchtower
Watertower	Watertower

Using Mission/Object Tabs

Each type of object in the game has a specific tab. You can select a particular tab by clicking on it, or by clicking on an object of that type on the map.

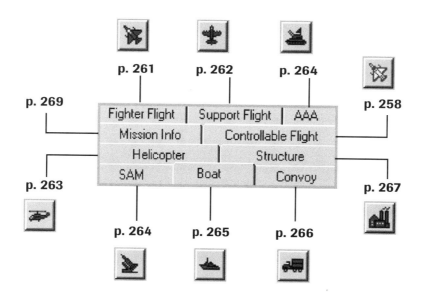

p. 261   p. 262   p. 264

p. 269   p. 258

p. 263   p. 267

p. 264   p. 265   p. 266

Use the *Mission Info* tab to change general mission settings (weather, start time, etc.). Use the other tabs to set parameters for the currently selected object group (type, number of elements, etc.). Since many tabs have nearly identical fields, the tabs are grouped here into three categories:

Mission Info Tab	Describes general parameters you can set for the current mission.
Group Object Tabs	Covers all tabs associated with mobile objects – Friendly Controllable Flight, Fighter Flight, Heavy Flight, AAA, SAM, Boat, Convoy and Helicopter Flight..
Structure Tab	Covers non-mobile structures (buildings, bridges, power lines, etc.).

Mission Info Tab

Use this tab to set general parameters for your mission, create mission events, write a mission briefing, and set pass/fail conditions and messages. The mission briefing is visible in the game from the *Tactical Display Screen* – see **Interface: Briefing Window**, p. 1.16 in the printed manual, for more information.

Fields

Mission name

Displays the name you gave to this mission when you first created it. You can edit the name by clicking in this field and typing. The mission name displays in the *Tactical Display* screen, in the game menus, and in the mission briefing when you play the game.

The mission name also serves as the filename when you save the mission.

Mission description

Type in a description of the mission. By default, this reads "Mission for UME" until you click in the field and type in a new description. This information only appears in the UME. You don't see it when selecting or flying the mission in the game.

Mission start time

Select the starting time for mission. The time is displayed in hours:minutes:seconds AM or PM (military time). Click the up and down arrows to increase or decrease this time in one-hour increments.

The mission start time appears in the mission briefing.

Wind speed

Click the up/down arrows to increase/decrease wind speed, in knots (between 0 and 50).

Wind direction

Click the up/down arrows to set wind direction. Wind direction is given as a compass direction: 360 means wind is coming from the north, 90 from the east, 180 from the south and 270 from the west.

Weather

Choose a weather condition for the mission – CLEAR / CLOUDY / LIGHT CLOUDS / PARTLY CLOUDY / STORM.

Weather conditions can affect visibility, and poor visibility conditions make it more difficult for aircrews to find and hit targets, and maneuver and land safely. The weather conditions you choose appear in the mission briefing.

Buttons

Mission Briefing

| Mission Brief |

(Optional) Click this button to create a custom mission briefing screen. You'll recognize this information since it's the same thing you see in a typical briefing for missions in the game.

To edit a field, click in its white box. If your description is lengthy, use the arrows to scroll through the text.

You can edit the *Mission Description, Intel, Tasking,* and *Mission Objectives* fields. You can't however, change the *Weather, Mission Name,* or *Time* - these options must be set on the *Mission Info* tab.

Pass/Fail Conditions

(Optional) Pass conditions are the conditions a player must meet in order to successfully complete a mission. They include objects that must be destroyed or must survive, and events that must happen or must not happen. If the pass conditions are not met, the player fails the mission.

Click this button to pop up a new window where you specify which objects must be destroyed or must survive for mission success.

You must set pass/fail conditions in order for the mission to end. Otherwise, the mission ends only if no controllable planes exist, or the player manually ends the mission.

This window displays two groups of fields – *Object* fields *(Must Survive / Must Be Destroyed)* and *Event* fields *(Must Occur / Must Not Occur)*.

In the *Object* field, you can Add or Remove any object you've placed on the map.

In the *Event* field, you can Add or Remove any events you've created in the Mission Events window.

Logically, an object (or event) can't appear in both of *Object* fields (or *Events* fields). Items that don't appear on either list, however, don't affect the mission outcome.

Click the X button at the top of the window to close it.

Pass/Fail Messages

(Optional) Click this button to type in custom *Pass* and *Fail Messages*. Another window appears.

To create a message, click in the appropriate field and start typing (up to 150 characters).

These messages display in the *Debrief* screen in the game when the player passes or fails the mission.

Mission Events

Mission Events

(Optional) Click this button to set up special "if ... then" events for the mission. By setting conditions, you can cause certain actions trigger events. This is an advanced feature described fully in **Creating Mission Events**, p. 283.

If these conditions are met ...

... then these events occur.

Group Object Tabs

Group object tabs include the *Controllable Flight, Fighter Flight, Support Flight, AAA, SAM, Boat, Convoy* and *Helicopter* tabs. They allow you to set parameters for an object you've placed on the map and then clicked on.

Not all of the fields below are available for all objects. The order in which they appear may also be different for each object type.

Fields

Name

Click on an object tab (Controllable flight, AAA, SAM, etc.). Then, select a particular group from the drop-down menu.

If you click directly on an object in the map, the correct tab displays. You must, however, choose a particular group name from the drop-down menu.

All groups of a single object type (for instance, all friendly and enemy SAM sites) are listed in this menu.

Type

Alter the object type for the selected group by clicking on a name in the pull-down menu. This menu lists all types available for the selected object (for instance, all fighter types appear if you select the *Fighter Flight* tab).

For lists of the types of objects available in each category, see **Using the Object Toolbar**, p. 253.

Altitude

Set starting altitude, in feet (only available for fighters and helicopters).

Controllable, Fighter Flight Options
0 / 300 / 1000 / 2000 / 3000 / 4000 / 5000 / 10,000 / 15,000 / 25,000 / 30,000

Helicopter Options
100 / 300 / 1000 / 1500 / 2000 / 3000 / 4000 / 5000

If you place an aircraft 5 miles or closer to an airfield and choose a starting altitude of 0, the plane takes off from that airbase.

The first flight you place near an airfield is lines up at the start of the runway. Additional flights are placed in one of the the airfield's 6 hangars.

For the X-Y coordinates of each airbase in the game, see **Airbases**, p. 260

Number of members	Choose number of members in the selected group from the drop-down menu. Maximum number varies according to the type of object.
Formation	Set the default formation the group travels in by default. (Not available on *Controllable Flight, Fighter Flight, Boat, AAA, SAM,* and *Structure* tabs.)

Helicopter Options
WEDGE / LINE / TRAIL

Convoy, Boat Options
SPEARHEAD / TRAIL

SAM, AAA Options
ARC / CIRCLE / SCATTERED

Heading	This field is initially set by the game when you place an aircraft icon on the map, but here, you can alter it by clicking the up and down arrows.

Heading indicates which direction the object is facing and is represented by a number from 0-360.

For all objects, heading describes the object's orientation. 0 means the front of the structure is facing due north, 180 means it's facing due south.

Task	Choose task for the formation from pull down menu; the available tasks vary according to the type of object in the formation. (Only available on *Controllable* and *Fighter* tabs.)

Controllable, Fighter Flight Options
CAS / CAP / NAVIGATE / STRIKE

For player-controllable aircraft, these tasks dictate what the aircraft does when it's not controlled by a human pilot.

For a definition of each task, see **Interface: Tasking Section**, p. 1.18 in the printed manual.

Primary Targets	Choose primary targets using the pull-down menus. (The number you can select varies for each object type.) These menus list all members of groups you have placed in the mission.

Note that you can select individual entities within a formation as the primary target — for instance, you can select Austin 4 as the primary target for an enemy flight.

SAM and AAA sites automatically attack enemy aircraft that enter their range.

A/I controlled aircraft attack primary targets as follows:

(1) A/I controlled aircraft attack their primary target first by default.

(2) A/I controlled aircraft can only attack primary targets that fit into their mission profile. You can only task Strike and CAS flights with ground targets, and CAP flights with air targets.

(3) If you've allowed the flight to carry JDAM (GPS guided) bombs, each flight member's bomb is automatically programmed to hit its primary target. When the aircraft reaches the target waypoint, the weapon is released.

Appear on Tactical Display

When this box is checked, the player can see these objects on the *Tactical Display* screen.

If you don't select this checkbox, the player can only detect the object once it's visible on radar.

Buttons

Add Waypoint

Click this button to add more waypoints to a selected moveable object (not available on *SAM, AAA, Structure* or *Mission Info* tabs).

Loadout

Loadout

Open the *Loadout* screen to set the default loadout for aircraft flights. (Only available for *Controllable, Fighter* and *Support Flight* tabs.)

	1
Weapon	AIM9M ▼
Amount	2
Max	2
Weight	380

You can edit the weapon type and number carried on each of the flyable aircraft's hardpoints. Select a type from the drop-down menu in the *Weapon* field. To adjust the number, click the up and down arrows in the *Amount* field.

You can't edit any grayed-out fields (*Max, Weight, Total Payload, Internal Fuel, Base Operating Weight, Takeoff Weight, Max Takeoff Weight,* or *Gun Bullets*).

Structure Tab

This tab lets you set parameters for the currently selected structure. All structures are immobile, and types range from standard bunkers to castles to power lines.

Structure	
Name:	EnemyStruct_1
Type:	AntennaShape1
Heading:	8
Appear on Tactical Display:	☑

Fields

Name
Displays the name of the structure. (You can't customize the name.)

Type
Choose a type of structure from the pull-down menu.

Heading
This field is initially set by the game, but here, you can alter it by clicking the up and down arrows.

Heading indicates which direction the object is facing and is represented by a number from 0-360.

For all objects, heading describes the object's orientation. 0 means the front of the structure is facing due north, 180 means it's facing due south.

Appear on Tactical Display
When this box is checked, the player can see this structure on the *Tactical Display* screen.

USING THE MISSION WIZARD

Jane's USAF has a mission wizard to make creating missions a simple task. Screens and options presented in the Mission Wizard differ, depending on what options you select along the way

To start the wizard:

1. Open the User Mission Editor if you haven't already (from the *Windows 95/98* desktop, click **Start > Programs > Jane's Combat Simulations > USAF > UME Mission Editor**).

2. On the pop-up menu that appears, choose **Mission Wizard**.

 The Mission Wizard leads you through a series of pop-up windows. Each window has several data fields in which you enter information about mission elements. (These data fields are explained in the following sections.)

The following buttons appear (although not all at once) in the Mission Wizard windows:

Next > Move on to the next step.

< Back Move back to the previous step.

Cancel Close the Mission Wizard without saving any information.

Finish Stop the Mission Wizard, keeping the information you've entered so far. You can then edit and save the mission manually.

You enter information in the pop-up windows of the Mission Wizard using drop-down menus and text fields. The steps involved in creating a mission through the Mission Wizard differ, depending on what options you select.

Drop-down menus

 Left-click on menu and select an option.

Text fields

 Type in information using the keyboard. For any text field, you can type in spaces, letters, and numbers. You cannot, however, use special characters – ?, /, \, <, >, or |.

Mission Wizard Tutorial

This section contains a walkthrough tutorial of how to develop an example mission type with the Mission Wizard. The purpose of the tutorial is to give you an idea of what tasks are involved in creating a new mission. *Keep in mind that the actual steps vary, depending on what elements you select during the wizard process.*

Task 1 – Set Mission Name/Region

1. Type in a name for the mission (up to 64 characters long). You can use spaces, letters, and numbers. You cannot, however, use special characters – ?, /, \, <, >, or |.

2. From the drop-down menu, select a region for your new mission (GERMANY / IRAQ / GRAND CANYON / VIETNAM). This determines what background terrain map displays in the Mission Editor screen.

○ For this example, type in any mission name and choose Germany .

3. Left-click **OK**.

Task 2 – Set Mission Type

1. Select a mission type (BARCAP / CAP / CAS / STRIKE). A description appears in the box..

○ This determines the mission type the player flies and what targets you can place.

○ For now, choose **CAS**.

2. Click **Next** to proceed.

Task 3 – Set Mission Information

1. The *Mission Info* tab displays on the left side of the screen. (Later, you can click its tab to display it.) Note that the mission name field contains the name you typed in earlier

○ See **Mission Info Tab**, p. 269, to find out what each field means.

2. Type in a short description for this mission.

3. Select a **start time**. To change the time, click the arrows next to the time.

4. Select wind speed, direction, and weather condition.

○ Leave wind speed and direction as 0 and CLEAR as the weather condition.

5. Click **Next** to proceed.

Task 4 – Add Ground Object (Friendly Convoy)

1. Add a friendly convoy to the map. To do this, left-click the blue Convoy icon on the Object toolbar, then left-click on the desired location on the map. (Notice that the currently selected object has a yellow box around it. You can select an icon by clicking on it.)

○ The types of objects you can place are different, depending on what mission category you select when you start the Mission Wizard. Here, we can add only friendly ground objects — helicopters, boats and convoys. Available objects types have colored icons; unavailable ones are grayed out.

○ When you place the convoy cursor over the map and click, a popup window appears. You can select the type of convoy from the drop-down list.

2. Once you click **OK**, the *Convoy* tab automatically displays on the left side of the screen.

○ You set the primary target for an object from the drop-down menu after you place it on the map. However, you can't assign targets until you place enemy objects on the map.

3. Since a convoy is a moveable ground object, you can set up waypoints, or routes for it to follow during the mission. This process (explained below) works identically for aircraft, convoys, helicopters and boats.

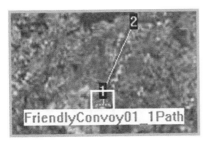

4. To add a waypoint path, right-click on the **FriendlyConvoy01** icon and select **Add New Path**. A numbered waypoint appears next to the icon.

5. Next, move the waypoint to the desired spot and add other waypoints.

○ **Left-click-and-drag** a waypoint to move it around.

○ **Left-click, then right-click** on a waypoint to add a waypoint before it, add a waypoint after it, or delete the waypoint. (Choose from the menu.)

○ **Left-click, then right-click** on a waypoint and choose **Properties** to assign waypoint parameters. (See **Change Waypoint Parameters**, p.259.)

Task 5 – Add Attacking Ground Object

1. Add an attacking enemy ground force to the map. To do this, left-click the red Convoy icon on the Object toolbar, then left-click on the desired location on the map.

2. Add waypoints for the enemy convoy just as you did for the friendly convoy. In this example, we've made the friendly and enemy convoy intersect near waypoint 2.

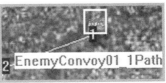

Task 6 – Create Controllable (Player) Flights

1. Add a controllable (player-flyable) flight (click the light blue, leftmost icon on the Object toolbar).

❍ Make sure you place the aircraft icon at the desired starting point for the mission.

❍ We assigned Austin a low recommended altitude so that the flight could fly underneath nearby SAM radars.

❍ Note that for aircraft, waypoint 1 always appears. (For ground-based moving objects, you must manually add the path.)

2. Set waypoints for the flight as you did earlier for the convoy. Continue adding and moving waypoints until the flight path is as you want it.

❍ In our example, we've added a pair of A-10s in a single flight and deleted the other objects for clarity. Place your second and third waypoints near the point where the convoys intersect.

3. Left-click on the *Controllable Flight* tab and change the flight information if you want to. You can change the number and type of aircraft, formation, altitude, heading, and air tasking order. See **Group Object Tabs**, p. 273, for more information on the tab.

❍ All of the flights you create in this step are assigned to attack some of the enemy objects you added already. You'll designate which target(s) in particular later.

5. Click **Next**.

Task 7 – Add Other Enemy Ground Objects (Enemy SAMs/AAA/Structures)

1. Add three other enemy objects to the map — SAMs, AAA, and a structure. Use the same method described for adding other objects.

❍ You can select specific object types within a class (different structures, for instance) from the popup windows that appear.

❍ For this example, we chose an SA-3 site (with 4 elements) for SAMs, and and a ZSU-23-4 site (also with 4 elements) for AAA. Just for target practice we also added a Communications Center structure.

Task 8 – Set Player's Primary Targets

1. With the *Controllable Flight* tab active, let's give the player something to hit. From the Primary Target drop-down menu, select the items shown here.

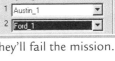

⊘ Player aircraft must destroy objects assigned to them as primary targets, or they'll fail the mission.

2. If you want to, you can set primary targets for other objects as well. Left-click on the appropriate tab for each primary target and experiment with setting different options for each target.

AAA tab (p. 264)	Anti-aircraft artillery
SAM tab (p. 264)	Surface-to-air missile site
Boat tab (p. 265)	Ships
Convoy tab (p. 266)	Jeeps, trucks, and tanks
Helicopter tab (p. 263)	Rotary aircraft
Structure tab (p. 267)	Various buildings and stationary objects

⊘ You assign primary targets to an object by selecting items from the Primary Target drop-down menus on that object type's tab.

3. Click **Next** to proceed.

Task 9 – Create Other Friendly Flights

1. Add a non-flyable, friendly Ford flight. (Click the dark blue aircraft icon.)

⊘ We added an F-15C for this example.

2. Set waypoints for the flight.

3. The *Fighter Flight* tab displays when you place this icon on the map. You can set flight information and primary targets here just as you did for the player's flight.

⊘ We tasked Ford with attacking the SAM site first, then over the convoy. Note the high starting altitude — this allows this flight to evade initial AAA fire. SAMs, however, can fire missiles to this height.

⊘ See **Group Object Tabs**, p. 273, to find out what each field means.

4. Click **Next**.

Task 10 – Create an Enemy Flight

1. Add an enemy flight. (Click the red aircraft icon.)

○ We chose to add a MiG-21.

2. Set waypoints for the flight.

○ We've removed other objects here for clarity. The enemy fighter's goal is to attack the friendly convoy and the player's flight.

3. Left-click on the *Fighter Flight* tab and set the flight information.

○ Assign the enemy fighter two targets — the player flight and the enemy convoy.

○ See **Group Object Tabs**, p. 273, for details.

4. Click **Next**.

Task 11 – Write Mission Briefing

1. You can write a mission briefing for the player, complete with intelligence and tasking information. This information displays in the *Mission Briefing* window in the game. Click inside white text fields to type in information. (Grayed-out fields are unavailable.)

○ You can also write customized Pass/Fail messages for the player in the **Mission Info tab** (p. 269).

Task 12 – Save Your Mission

1. Left-click the Save icon or left-click **File > Save** to save the file — at this point, you're finished with the basic mission parameters.

○ You can tweak any of the information you've entered so far at any time by opening the file, selecting the appropriate tab and editing the information displayed.

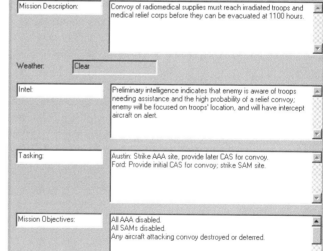

○ If you want to fly your mission and test it, left-click the Run icon. The game automatically opens and launches your mission.

○ All missions you create and save are then available from the Single Mission screen from within the game.

ADVANCED UME FEATURES

The backbone of any mission is the flight path you create for player flights, and the friendly and enemy objects you create along that flight path. By default, the mission ends only if no controllable aircraft remain, or if the player manually ends the mission. The player WINS the mission only if he/she satisfies all of the Pass/Fail conditions you set.

You can make missions interesting by adding special events triggered by certain conditions. Although this is by no means necessary, this advanced feature gives you added creativity when creating missions.

Creating Mission Events

To access the Edit Events window, click the **Mission Events** button on the **Mission Info Tab**. You can use mission events to create more complex missions, in which certain conditions can trigger certain actions. For example, you might have a mission time of 00:30:00 (thirty minutes) before enemy fighters attack friendly units on the ground. This allows you to penalize a player for taking too long too complete ground objectives. For each event you create, you set a *condition* triggering the event, and an *action* that is the event.

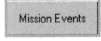

The mission events window lists all of the events you have created, along with a brief description of each.

New	Click to create a new event (opens the **Edit Events** pop-up window, p. 284).
Modify	Click on an event in the list, then click this button to modify the event (also opens the **Edit Events** pop-up window, p. 284).
Delete	Click on an event in the list, then click this button to delete the event.
Close	Close the Mission Event window.

Edit Events Window

The *Edit Events* windows appears when you click **New** or **Modify** on the *Mission Events* window. Click **OK** to close this window, accepting all changes you made. (The following picture only shows the top portion of this window — the remaining options are shown in the "If" and "Then" tab screen shots.)

Event Name   Type in the name for the event (or edit the existing name).

Occur Parameter   Click in the circle next to OCCUR ONLY ONCE allow the event to only happen once during a mission. If you don't check this, the event can reoccur whenever conditions are right.

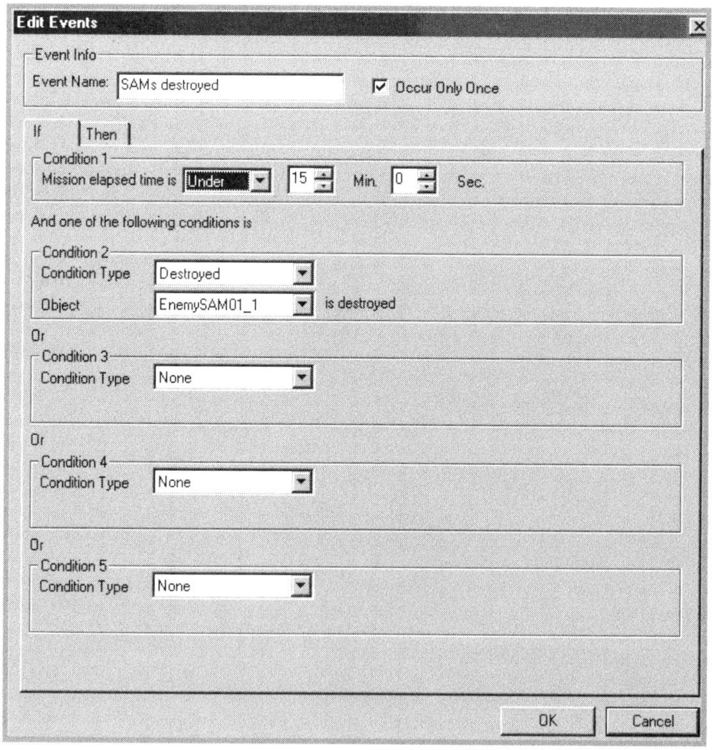

Setting If...Then Conditions

An event occurs when the conditions you have defined for it are met. Mission conditions are things that happen in the overall mission – the mission clock reaches a certain time, for instance. Object conditions are dependent on the behavior or status of a specified object – it's reaching another object, for example.

"If..." Tab   Click the *If Tab* and set up 1-5 "if" mission conditions. *The time limit and at least one mission condition must be met before the event is triggered*.

"Then..." Tab   Click the *Then Tab* and set up 1-5 "then" mission actions.

If Tab

Use this tab to set conditions that must be met before a specific event can happen. Once Condition 1 plus any other condition has been met, actions specified in the *Then Tab* take place.

Use the drop-down menus to select options. For objects, you can only select objects that you've already placed on the map. Other fields require you to type in information, or adjust settings using the up and down arrow buttons.

○   You can set different conditions for a flight leader and his wingman.

○   You can't set the same event trigger twice for the same object in a single mission. This means, for instance, that you can only set the "Destroyed" condition once for a particular entity.

Condition 1

Set a time limit for additional conditions you set on this tab.

```
┌─ Condition 1 ──────────────────────────────────────────┐
│ Mission elapsed time is │Under  ▼│  │15 ▲▼│  Min.  │0 ▲▼│  Sec. │
└─────────────────────────────────────────────────────────┘
```

Select OVER to set a minimum time elapsed condition, or UNDER to set a maximum time elapsed.

If you aren't concerned with time, leave the time set to 0 minutes and 0 seconds and choose Over. This ensures the time condition is met as soon as the mission starts.

   Example: Mission elapsed time is [Over] [10] minutes [30] seconds.

   Result: If 10 minutes and 30 seconds have passed since the start of the mission, the game checks to see that conditions 2-5 have been satisfied.

Condition 2-5

Set a condition type and parameters.

```
┌─ Condition 2 ──────────────────────┐
│ Condition Type  │Destroyed      ▼│ │
└─────────────────────────────────────┘
```

These will be checked only after Condition 1 is satisfied. You can select 5 different conditions from the drop-down menu – NONE / REACH / LEFT / HIT / DESTROYED / SURVIVED.

Reach   Set a horizontal "move within" distance – once the object moves closer than this distance, actions will occur. If a player approaches a target area, for example, you might want to play an audio file that warns the pilot about a nearby SAM.

Example: Distance (m) from [FriendlyFlight01_01] to [EnemySAM02_01] goes under [10,000].

Result: If the distance between element 1 of friendly flight #1 and element 2 of enemy SAM group #1 drops below 10,000 meters, the condition is satisfied, and the *Then Tab* actions occur.

Left   Set a horizontal "away from" distance – once the object moves further away than this distance, actions occur. You might use this to specify how far a player can fly away from an enemy aircraft before he/she fails the mission.

Example: Distance (m) from [FriendlyFlight01_03] to [EnemyFlight01_01] goes over [15,000].

Result: When the distance between element 3 of Friendly Flight #1 and element 1 of Enemy Flight #1 goes over 15,000 meters, the condition is satisfied, and the *Then Tab* actions occur.

Hit   Designate an object that, when hit, will evoke an action. You can use this to make certain objects a vital part of mission success or failure – for instance, a friendly plane may issue a plea for assistance after being hit by an enemy aircraft.

Example: Object [Ford 1] is hit.

Result: If Ford 1 is hit by an enemy object, some action will occur.

Destroyed   Designate an object that, when destroyed, will cause an action to occur. For instance, you might cause the mission to immediately fail if a friendly fleet under protection gets destroyed by the enemy.

Example: Object [FriendlyBoat1_04] is hit.

Result: If element 4 of Friendly Boat group #1 is hit by an enemy object, some action will occur.

Survived   Designate an object that, if it still survives, causes a specific message in the *Debrief* screen after the mission ends.

This condition does not trigger an event.

Example: Object [Bridge1] survived the mission.

Result: If Bridge #1 is not destroyed (either by the end of the mission or by the time set in Condition 1), a message relating this information appears in the *Debrief* screen.

Then Tab

Here, you define actions that occur once Conditions 1 and any other Condition (2-5) have been met. You can set four specific types of actions. Before you can edit fields or select options from drop-down menus, you must select the checkbox for that action. Until you do so, the options remain grayed-out.

Action 1: Play Audio Message

Click the PLAY AUDIO MESSAGE checkbox to cause an audio file to play. (This also makes the Action 1 options usable.)

Select Sound   Click the menu and highlight a sound. To listen to it, click PLAY SOUND.

Action 2: Execute Commands

Click the EXECUTE COMMANDS checkbox to enable the Command drop-down menus. You use these menus to give instructions to up to 4 computer-controlled objects. To pick a command recipient, click on the left-hand drop-down menu and select an object you've placed on the map.

To issue a command, click on the right-hand drop-down menu and select a command. (Commands are listed on the following page.)

Command	Result
ATTACK PLAYER COMMAND	Object attacks player.
DO CAP COMMAND	(Fighters only) Object flies combat air patrol and scouts out opposing aircraft.
DO CAS COMMAND	(Fighters only) Object flies combat air support and covers same-side ground forces.
EXPLODE COMMAND	(All except fighters) Object self-destructs.
GO HOME COMMAND	(Fighters only) Object heads for home base.
NAVIGATE COMMAND	(Fighters only) Object travels toward next waypoint.
ORBIT COMMAND	(Fighters only) Object circles current waypoint.
RESUME MISSION COMMAND	Object resumes its normal mission. (Use to exit a condition/action that has occurred.)
STOP COMMAND	(Convoys, Boats, Helicopters only) Object stops following its current command and waits for a new command.
STRIKE COMMAND	(Fighters only) Object strikes its designated target.
Takeoff Command	(Grounded fighters only) Object takes off.
Weapon Free Command	(All except fighters) Object receives permission to use its weapons.
Weapon Safe Command	(All except fighters) Object ceases using its weapons.

Action 3: End Mission

This action ends the mission. You can trigger this using the Pass/Fail conditions, or automatically pass or fail the mission based on this event.

Click the END MISSION checkbox to activate mission pass/fail conditions. Then, click inside the circle next to one of three radio buttons.

Check Pass Fail Conditions This instructs the game to check the Pass/Fail Conditions you set in the **Mission Info Tab** (p. 269). If any mission-critical object has been destroyed (or survives), or a specific event has occurred (or not occurred), then the mission ends.

Automatic Pass/Fail The player automatically wins/loses the mission, regardless of Pass/Fail Conditions.

Action 4: Display a Debrief Text Message

Check the DISPLAY A DEBRIEF TEXT MESSAGE checkbox to enable the text field. You can type a short, one-line message into this field that displays in the *Debrief* field after the mission ends.